SELL IT
BY MAIL

SELL IT BY MAIL
Making Your Product the One They Buy

JAMES E. A. LUMLEY

JOHN WILEY & SONS

New York · Chichester · Brisbane · Toronto · Singapore

To

SUSAN EVANS BUCHMAN

For her loyalty and help in bringing this book together

Library of Congress Cataloging in Publication Data:
Lumley, James E. A.
    Sell it by mail.

    Includes index.
    1. Mail-order business.   2. Direct marketing.
I. Title.

HF5466.L85   1986   658.8'4   85-16362
ISBN 0-471-87908-8

Printed in the United States of America

10 9 8 7 6 5 4 3

PREFACE

We all want to get better at what we do, and many of us turn to books to tell us how to do so. Books on self-improvement give us the know-how, technologies, tools, and skills we need to get better.

This book is for those of you who want to improve your use of direct mail to gain new customers for products and services and to hold them. Whether you are selling wares, gaining sales leads, or raising funds, this book offers you a tool for marketing success.

If you are a newcomer to direct mail, you will find a complete set of rules to guide you. If you are experienced, you will learn how to use direct mail better.

Much has been written about the concept of "direct marketing," which includes television, magazine, and telephone advertising as well as use of direct mail. But of all the direct-response techniques available, direct mail is the overwhelming winner in selling products and services directly to consumers and businesses.

Direct mail is changing. At one time it was used as a "shotgun approach," in which large mailings were sent out in the hope of gaining some unpredictable number of responses. Today computers permit us to narrow down our lists of potential customers so we can be much more selective in targeting prospects.

And because experience and technology have made us wiser about why and how mail sells, we can double or triple the results we used to gain from the same size mailing.

This book will help you understand the basic truths about using direct mail with today's prospects. First you will learn the fundamental approach of the one-on-one selling-in-print message. You will learn what motivates prospects to act on your offer. Next you will learn how to write and design letters, brochures, response devices, self-mailers, card decks, and catalogs to send to your prospective customers. You will also learn strategies for selecting the most profitable mailing lists and how to plan effective test mailings. Finally you will learn how to gain maximum profit on your mailings by converting one-time buyers into long-term customers.

I believe the best way to attract today's hard-bitten prospect is not with "teaser" gimmicks but with a combination of a straightforward message and a proven format.

This book is not a puff piece on how to make millions in the mail-order business. To be sure, you may end up making a fortune—but only if you pay attention to who your prospect is, what you are offering, how to make your approach, how you encourage action, and how you convert prospects into long-term customers.

You will want to pay special attention to the many "Key Points" and "Caution Notes" throughout this book. Key Points are fundamental truths—the *do's*—of direct mail. They offer positive solutions.

Caution Notes are the other side of the coin. They are the *don't's*; they point out obvious, and sometimes not so obvious, procedures to avoid.

Pay attention to both the problems and the solutions. Good luck in becoming the best at what you do.

JAMES E. A. LUMLEY

Amherst, Massachusetts
December 1985

CONTENTS

3.   STRUCTURING THE OFFER   31

4.   COORDINATING COPY AND DESIGN
      TO GAIN READERSHIP   47

5. USING BENEFITS WHEN WRITING DIRECT MAIL COPY   57

6. BASIC COPYWRITING STRATEGIES   79

7. POWERFUL COPYWRITING TECHNIQUES FOR DIRECT MAIL LETTERS   101

10. DESIGNING AND LAYING OUT THE DIRECT MAIL BROCHURE   189

13. COPY STRATEGY FOR CATALOGS   265

16. BASIC TESTING: PREDICTING PROFITS   317

17. TESTING SHOWS HOW MUCH TO SPEND TO GET BUYERS   331

20. EXTRACTING MAXIMUM PROFIT FROM MAILINGS

PERSUASIVE DIRECT MAIL CAMPAIGNS 1

Everybody is fascinated with direct mail. The volume of mail in America's mailboxes seems to grow each week. The choice of goods and services offered through the mail has been increasing dramatically. No one goes to the insurance agency anymore; it's easier to mail the check. And banking—who wants to stand in line? Parking is hard to find even at the shopping mall, so why not shop by mail?

Business educational institutions, charitable groups, political candidates, and many others are using the mail to promote their policies and sell their merchandise. Now it is your turn. Starting in this chapter you will learn how you too can use the mail to sell your products and services, to get sales leads, and to raise funds.

My definition of direct mail admittedly shows a bias:

Direct mail takes personal selling and translates it into a mailing format to reach more people at lower cost—without losing the benefit of live selling.

This definition highlights the fact that direct mail is a personal communication from one person to another. The bias lies in the implication that mail can simulate a live salesperson talking face to face with a prospect. Not exactly—not in terms of effectiveness, anyway. But in numbers, in terms of sales results? Yes. What you will find in this book is the latest in direct mail technology. Not a rehash of outdated "mail-order" concepts, but everything you need to know to make your direct mail the closest thing to a live salesperson, but in print.

DIRECT MAIL IS BECOMING THE PREFERRED WAY TO SELL

Only a few years ago, $500 was about the maximum value of a product that could be sold by direct mail. Now much more expensive products and services—investment fund offerings, condominiums, even boats—are being offered and sold by mail.

This trend has several major reasons. First, the high cost of gasoline has made it more expensive for people to go out and shop. Consumers are thus more open to using direct mail for purchases.

■ *KEY POINT: People are learning that direct mail saves time, energy, and gas, and that it can be trusted for bigger purchases.*

Second, companies have taken salespeople off the road, because the cost involved in the sale of inexpensive products, such as supplies, is too great. Such salespeople now deal only with larger items, such as computer systems or industrial machines. The result is that low-cost products, which are still thought of as important business and consumer goods, must be sold by other means. This is where direct mail can be used. The mail has become a cost-efficient way for buyers to purchase goods and services and for sellers to sell them.

■ *KEY POINT: Direct mail is becoming the way to sell low-cost products.*

Third, never before in our history has the atmosphere among businesses been as competitive as it is today. Good for business and consumer alike, competition spurs an ever-increasing need to find more effective ways to sell products and services. Consequently there is a strong movement away from the traditional selling method of "space," or "awareness," advertising found in newspapers and magazines to the more direct approach of mail. Whether a company's effort is toward selling a product, offering an opportunity for the public to give to a worthy cause, or obtaining a sales lead, direct mail is becoming the chosen marketing tool.

■ *KEY POINT: Competition drives companies to use the direct approach of mail.*

GENERAL ADVERTISING GAINS ATTENTION RATHER THAN SELLS

Are you aware of the difference between general, or "awareness," advertising and direct mail?

General advertising aims at gaining attention. With it the advertiser wants to make prospects aware of a product or service in the hope that they will go to a store and buy.

■ *CAUTION NOTE: General advertising only makes people aware of products.*

Now this does not mean general advertising is ineffective. Take IBM's awareness advertising campaign for its personal computers as an example. Why have these computers sold well? Primarily because of good advertising. There's nothing special about the computers themselves; many other companies are offering machines with more features at a lower price. But it was IBM's immense and expensive advertising campaign, which featured a Chaplinesque clown, that attracted the public's eye to an admirable if not spectacular product.

You should realize, however, that IBM doesn't even sell its computers directly. Most are sold by independent retail outlets. IBM's expensive advertising campaign did nothing more than bring people in the dealer's door, but this is the key strength of awareness advertising. When backed by a huge budget, it can generate a great deal of attention.

■ *CAUTION NOTE: Awareness advertising is costly.*

Awareness advertising can also be like a snowball that grows larger and larger as it rolls down the hill. Sales of IBM's personal computer snowballed when other companies began writing software programs for it. But if you're IBM, you just snag as many customers as you can produce products for. That's what big bucks awareness advertising does. What do you do if you don't have IBM's millions to spend on such advertising?

RESPONSE ADVERTISING ALREADY HAS SOMEONE'S ATTENTION

Direct mail lets you reach prospects who read your advertisement and have the money and need for your product. Unlike awareness advertising, direct mail does not need to get someone's attention. It already has it. The direct mail piece, whether a letter, reply card, self-mailer, or catalog, is already in the prospect's hands. What you must do now is keep his or her attention.

■ *KEY POINT: Your job in direct mail is to hold your prospect's attention.*

To hold attention, the exterior and interior of your mailing piece must be designed so that the eyes go where you want them to. Controlling the eye path is essential, because the longer you hold your readers' attention, the better your chance of convincing them that they want what you are offering.

■ *KEY POINT: You gain selling time by holding your reader's attention.*

HOW IS THE SALES MESSAGE REPEATED IN DIRECT MAIL?

Direct mail differs from general advertising in its avoidance of exact repetition. Repetition is used in general advertising because the advertiser wants only to leave an impression, not to make a sale. At least not at the moment. All the advertiser wants is to have potential buyers remember the product and maybe the company's name.

In direct mail, however, exact repetition kills prospects' attention. Prospects who realize that a brochure is just repeating what was said in the letter accompanying it stop reading. In fact, repeat mailings to the same customers must be so varied that the customers don't realize they are being sent the same offer.

■ *CAUTION NOTE: Repetition kills your reader's attention.*

But how do we reconcile not repeating ourselves with the fact that we *must* repeat our offer at least twice in every sales piece? How do we get the benefits of repetition without the hazards?

We do it by using wording that has the same or nearly the same meaning as the earlier wording: We use synonyms. We say the same thing, but in slightly different words. Prospects can read the sales letter and move on to the brochure and still not think they are reading the same offer.

■ *KEY POINT:*   **Repeat your offer by using synonyms.**

DIRECT MAIL SELLS A RESPONSE

Direct mail is used to get a *response.* You are selling a response, not a product. There's a major difference. Customers don't buy cameras, grapefruit squeezers, or insurance policies, they buy what those products or that service can do for them, how it can provide a solution to their problem.

Too often direct mail is developed to sell a product or service in total disregard of the fact that people don't buy products, but they do buy the solutions they think meet their needs.

■ *CAUTION NOTE:*   **People buy solutions, not products.**

Pretend you own an insurance agency. You have a new sales associate who will be selling life insurance. You thus develop a piece of mail that will tell your present customers who this new person is and what she can do for them.

You send out the letter with the hope that it will make a lasting impression on your customers and will do the salesperson and your agency some good. But look what happens when the letter arrives. It has to compete with perhaps a half dozen other sales brochures, letters, and demands. If your letter is not personally addressed, it probably won't even get opened. And even if your customers open it, most will probably not read enough of it to learn your new salesperson's name, let alone what she will be doing. You have not given readers anything to do, so they have no interest.

■ *CAUTION NOTE:* *Competition is fierce in the mailbox.*

How do you keep your letter from being tossed into the "circular file" unread, or even unopened? Give your customers something they will see as benefiting them, so they will be willing to take action. For example, you enclose a brochure that describes your services. It includes a photo of your new sales associate with a caption describing the types of policies she will be selling. You give her telephone number and ask them to call her.

With this brochure you are making it easy for your customers to take action. You are showing them who they will be talking to and giving them information on just what life insurance is about. Most important, you are showing them you care about them. You are not just telling them "who's new in the firm," ho, hum. Rather you are satisfying your need to introduce and set up your new salesperson by offering your customers a service. This is what you want: a relationship of dignity in which you are ready to help them.

■ *KEY POINT:* *Make it easy for customers to take action.*

Direct mail should never be used to just deliver information or create awareness. It is too costly to be wasted as awareness or display advertising. But this is what you do if you use the mail to introduce someone without inviting the customer to take action. Direct mail must always sell a response.

PROSPECTS MUST BE INTERESTED IN WHAT WE HAVE TO OFFER

To find customers, we mail to potential customer audiences or prospect *"universes."* Prospects are individuals within a particular universe of people with potential interest who can be reached at their homes or businesses. The best prospects are those who have the same demographic characteristics as our present customers, because they are the most likely to be interested in what we have to offer.

■ *CAUTION NOTE:* **Prospects are always individuals, never companies.**

Several factors affect our success when we contact prospect universes. The first factor is interest. We cannot succeed in direct mail unless prospects already want what we have to offer. The reason is simple: People don't read mail that doesn't offer something that interests them. They must have some underlying psychological need for what the product offers. Direct mail is not a proper advertising medium to create interest in something the prospect has never heard of before and which does not satisfy an existing need. We care that they need what we have to offer, that our product may be the solution to their problem. Interest makes our selling job easier. But it's more important that people have a need for our product or service.

■ *KEY POINT:* **Prospects must have prior interest.**

■ *CAUTION NOTE:* **You cannot force an uninterested prospect to read your mailing piece.**

Let's look at how direct mail differs from in-person selling. Salespeople on sales calls can use many techniques to develop interest. They can use body language, hold eye contact, and ask questions to hold prospects' attention long enough to interest them. Telephone sales calls are similar, although the contact is less personal.

With the mail, however, your recipients or prospects will not even open the letter, let alone read the contents, unless they are already interested or have a need! People must also be able to pay for the product. We must be on guard to seek only those who can afford what we are offering.

■ *CAUTION NOTE:* **Solicit only prospects who need the product and can afford it.**

TIME IS LIMITED TO GAIN
PROSPECTS' INTEREST

Studies show you have only 3 to 8 seconds to gain prospects' attention and get them to open your piece and start reading. During these seconds, they will scan your material quickly to see if it interests them.

This is the first question prospects ask: "Am I interested?" If they have never been interested in politics, detest the idea of supporting any candidate, and get a mail solicitation for money when they don't even plan to vote—it's into the wastebasket! No matter how good your message, how fancy your brochure, or how thrilling your photography, prospects are not going to read your piece.

According to industry experts, only 20% to 25% of any prospect universe (those who have not been contacted before) have a preexisting interest in what you offer. No matter how closely your prospect universe profile matches that of your present customers, no more than 25% of the persons in it will be interested in opening what you send them.

■ *KEY POINT: Sell to those with a preexisting interest.*

WHO READS DIRECT MAIL?

A second factor is that not everybody reads direct mail. This may seem obvious, but think about that 20% to 25% who ought to be interested in what you offer. If even these people don't read your solicitation, the situation looks hopeless.

However, prospects can be divided into four groups (Figure 1.1). The first is *hot responders*, who read and respond to direct mail eight or more times a year. They tend to buy from many forms of direct mail, such as letters, catalogs, brochures, and flyers. These are the people we want most.

■ *CAUTION NOTE: Not everybody reads direct mail.*

Second is the *warm responders*, who reply up to six times a year. Al-

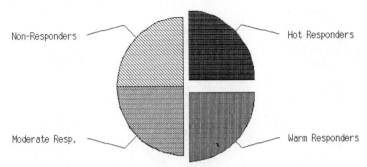

Figure 1.1   Direct mail responders.

though they are more cautious than the hot responders, they also tend to respond to a variety of different solicitations.

The third group is the *moderate responders,* who respond two or three times a year. They are more narrow in their interests and may respond only to solicitations in one format, such as a letter, or to specific types of offers, such as for books or household utensils.

The fourth group is *nonresponders,* who respond not at all or at most once a year. They avoid direct mail and consider it junk. Since they usually throw direct mail pieces away without opening them, they will never know what your offer is, even if it might interest them. They are not people we can reach by direct mail.

What we learn from this is that only two of these groups of prospects—the hots and the warms—will read what we send them. We thus need not only to identify prospects with a preexisting interest but those who will read what we send.

DIRECT MAIL IS A PREY TO MAIL SABOTAGE

A third factor that affects our success is *sabotage,* or whether our prospects even get the mail we send them (Figure 1.2). The problem here starts with the U.S. Postal Service failing to deliver our mail. Most mail, of course, is delivered. But we in direct mail often mail "third-class bulk rate" with no return requested. Unless we specifically request an ad-

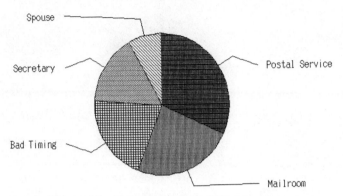

Figure 1.2   Sources of direct mail sabotage.

dress correction and are willing to pay for this, we never know whether the mailing piece was delivered. Unfortunately, many postal workers are aware of this and often dispose of their bulk mail improperly on particularly busy days. About 25% of the time, third-class mail will be returned marked "undeliverable" or "moved, no forwarding address." Too often, however, postal workers use these rubber stamps so they won't have to deliver the mail.

■ *CAUTION NOTE: About 25% of direct mail is never delivered to prospects.*

Mailings are often sabotaged when there are volume deliveries of mail to single locations within a large organization, such as a major business or university. Once the Postal Service's responsibilities end, the mailroom takes over. If mail is not properly addressed, it will often go undelivered. Mailroom workers do not waste time on identifications they don't recognize. Mailings addressed to job titles rather than individuals are particularly vulnerable, and even the use of first-class mail does not help here.

Mail is often sabotaged by secretaries who deem it part of their job to keep unwanted solicitations away from the boss. In a sense they take over the mail as if it were their own. Consequently, much of it gets tossed. What isn't tossed gets stacked in a pile with the rest of the advertising mail and is turned into part of an instant magazine. Now your piece must compete with other direct mail, and the possibility of it gaining single-focused attention disappears.

Mail can also be sabotaged by bad timing. Your mail will never get to your prospects if they are rushing off to a conference or a trip out of town. By the time they return, your mailing piece is just one of many.

Spouses can also sabotage mail. They open the mail, decide on their own that the other won't be interested, and toss it out.

HOLDING CUSTOMER RELATIONSHIPS IS CRITICAL

Direct mail has two basic functions: finding customers and keeping them. You want to find prospects and convert them into customers who have an economic relationship with you as buyers of your goods or as donors, policy holders, or members.

But you also want to keep your customer relationships going over a period of time. It is by maintaining relationships with customers that you make the most money. Keeping customers is much less expensive than finding them, because when we mail to people who have already done business with us, we usually get a better response than when we mail "blind."

It is almost impossible to fail when you mail to your own customers. They have proven their interest in you by their earlier willingness to do business. So don't make the mistake too many sellers make, ignoring old customers and concentrating almost wholly on obtaining new ones.

These sellers fail to look at the expense involved in the acquisition process. Response rates for gaining new customers are often between 1% and 6%, but rates of repeat business with old customers can run from 10% to 90%! After spending so much to get customers, why throw away the relationships in an attempt to entice more new customers, who in turn will be discarded? In short, why spend thousands of dollars finding people who are willing to form a relationship with us and who give us money as their proof of interest, and then tell them we're not really interested in them after all?

■ *CAUTION NOTE:* **Don't forget to maintain relationships with old customers.**

Let's look at an example. Bertha and her husband George own a retail store in which they sell stuffed animal dolls in kit form. All the customer has to do is to sew the doll together and stuff it. George and Bertha decide to expand their sales beyond their own area by using direct mail.

Their first mailing, to customers who have a preexisting interest in stuffed animal dolls, gets an excellent response. George and Bertha are thrilled. They are fulfilling demand. They hire two people to cut more patterns. They mail again, and back come orders. They know they're on to a good thing, so they really start mailing.

But then they find that each new mailing is bringing in fewer and fewer orders. They don't understand why, so they start using more expensive mailings. They create a four-color brochure that shows them sewing the dolls together in their store. As orders keep declining, they start offering a second doll as a free gift. As costs of their mailings rise, they turn to third-class bulk-rate stamps. They start mailing to companies and loading up their mailing package with more and more copy for prospects to read. They are spending more and more money in the search for new customers, but sales still drop.

After a while, their old customers disappear. Now the more old customers they lose, the more important it becomes to find new ones. Bertha and George spend more and more trying to gain new customers to make up for lost revenue.

What has happened to Bertha and George is not uncommon. Many businesses using direct mail for the first time mail to initial demand, that is, to preexisting interest, and are astounded at the results. They then start heavy mailing, but with fewer results because they are exhausting the demand. What they do next—producing more expensive mailings; adding color, bribes, and premiums; and mailing to people with marginal interest—fails to address the basic problem: relationship. In their panic, they focus on the most difficult and expensive part of direct mail: establishing new customer relationships. And they ignore the obvious solution: their old customers.

Maintaining a relationship with an existing customer costs far less than acquiring a new customer, or even converting an inquirer into a customer. The secret of maintaining the relationship is simple: frequent contact.

Therein lies the problem, however, because few mailers make the effort of sending regular mailings. They use money, time, and energy looking for new relationships, and let the old ones suffer. Mailers sometimes learn too late that keeping a relationship with an old customer is cheaper and brings in more money in the long run.

■ *KEY POINT:* **Relationships are maintained by contact, frequent contact.**

The importance of maintenance becomes clearer if we realize that direct mail is the effort to create a relationship with another person. People receive hundreds of pieces of mail every year, but they respond to only a few. When they do respond to your mailing, they feel they are connecting with you in some way or associating with you on a direct, personal, one-to-one basis. Of course, direct mail does not really create a personal relationship, but people feel that it is when they respond to your solicitation.

■ *KEY POINT:* **Direct mail creates a relationship with another person.**

What is the glue that binds a personal relationship together? Frequency of contact. If we never contact our prospects, never call them, write them, or see them, our relationship with them dissolves. However, if we put in the effort to write them, call them, even see them, the relationship has a chance to grow. We refer to the effort as *contact frequency.*

HOW OFTEN SHOULD WE CONTACT CUSTOMERS?

To make a relationship grow, we must relate the number of our contacts to the job we are trying to do, and we should also vary the formats we use to contact customers. If we sell consumer goods—clothes, camping supplies, utensils—through a catalog, we might send out the full catalog quarterly. But we could also send special flyers, such as "sales to mail-order customers only" or even announcements of new products and gift-certificate offerings. Our catalog customers should receive a minimum of 12 direct mail pieces a year.

If we are fund raising, we will need even greater frequency of contact, perhaps 15 to 20 times a year. Not all of these will be direct solicitations for money. We will also send out announcements of fund-raising efforts, newsletters reporting on the fund's progress, and special "letters from the chairperson" thanking donors.

■ *KEY POINT: Maintain contact with customers and donators at least 12 to 15 times a year.*

These mailings need not be expensive. A newsletter costs far less than a letter or a brochure. The point is to maintain contact, not always to sell.

Maintaining customers is a much better use of resources than is pursuit of new customers. This does not mean we will not seek new customers. But as we saw from the example, if we maintain contact with our old customers we will be under less pressure to acquire new ones.

TO WHOM DO WE SEND OUR MAIL?

We mail to three different types of people. The first group consists of *prospects*, people with the same economic, social, and need characteristics as our present customers. Most important, they also have a history of responding to direct mail. Prospects have not expressed any interest in our product or service yet. They are merely prospective buyers.

■ *KEY POINT: The best prospects are those with a history of responding to direct mail.*

The second group consists of *inquirers*, people who have expressed interest in what we are offering. They may be prospects who have indicated interest but not yet bought. Inquirers are expensive and hard to locate, and it is important to follow up on them because they are more likely to become customers than are prospects.

■ *KEY POINT: Inquirers are easier to turn into customers than are prospects.*

Strangely, companies often do not follow up on inquiries as they generate as much as they should. Facts show that fewer than two thirds of all business inquiries are followed up. The minimum period for following up inquiries should be two years.

■ *CAUTION NOTE:* **One third of all inquiries are never followed up.**

The most important group for us, however, is *customers,* people to whom we make maintenance mailings. They are already in a relationship with us and have a preexisting interest in our product or service. Customers are the best readers of our mailing piece and will usually read whatever we send. But we must remember one important fact: We must keep varying how we present our product and what we say about it, because customers must perceive we are sending them something different. If we don't do this, even our customers won't bother to read what we send. The piece will probably be thrown away unopened.

■ *KEY POINT:* **Vary the maintenance mailings you make to customers.**

Many seminar companies send out mailings of marketing and management courses. But the only way their customers can distinguish the different type of courses is by the color of the mailing. For example, a typical mailing would be a self-mailing brochure 8½ inches by 11 inches when folded and 11 inches by 17 inches when open. Each course is as different in appearance and truth as each is a different color. The customer then does not feel he or she is being inundated with mail offering the same seminar even though this mail is from the same source.

What is important here is that contact is maintained with high-frequency mailings, and that because the mailings are perceived as different they keep the bond alive.

THE THREE WAYS OF MARKETING BY MAIL

There are three ways of marketing by mail. Each can be thought of as an overall strategy, with its own philosophy. Here the three are presented in the order of their ability to take successful advantage of the mail.

Relationship Marketing

In *relationship marketing,* customer relationships are found and held for the longest possible time. Relationship marketers are not one-time users of direct mail. They compare what they spend to acquire customers against what they earn during the time they hold them.

■ *KEY POINT:*   *Relationship marketers maintain customer contact.*

Relationship marketers may not make money every time they use direct mail. They may even lose money on the first one or two mailings, when they are turning prospects into customers. But relationship marketers are looking for consistent long-term returns and profits from their customers. Thus they maintain the strongest possible relationship with their customers, who are their sources of income. They know it is easier to sell to current customers than to new prospects. Relationship marketers spend 60% to 70% of their time and money maintaining their existing customer base and the remainder in soliciting new prospects.

■ *KEY POINT:*   *In direct mail we are selling relationships.*

If you want to succeed in selling by mail, you must see your customers as opportunities for profit and become a relationship marketer. Why? Think about why *you* buy from the people you buy from. Isn't it because you've bought from them before, and trust them? You have a relationship with them. Why do you buy your groceries from the store on this corner rather than the other one? Because you have a relationship with the people. You feel guilty if you go to another store or down to the mall. You wish you were shopping at "your regular market, because at least there you know some of the clerks, and the meat department workers know what kind of cuts you like."

■ *KEY POINT:*   *Your goal is to become a relationship marketer.*

The point is: We buy out of relationships. Therefore to take full advantage of direct mail, you must work at forming relationships with your customers.

Semirelationship Marketing

In *semirelationship marketing*, marketers do not maintain contact as frequently as full-relationship marketers do. They look for their profit in the first or second transaction with customers. They often sell more than one product but offer only a limited line that does not encourage repeat sales. Some could easily sell again, but they don't plan on it, and much of their mailing effort is an attempt to obtain new customers.

One example of a semirelationship marketer is a camping tent manufacturer. The company may offer several different tent models, but once a customer has bought a tent, he or she is unlikely to buy another one in the near future. Direct mail can be used to correct this problem, however. Suppose the company offers a line of items a buyer of tents might like. The company could offer knapsacks, outdoor cooking supplies, raingear, and so on. If these are offered in a catalog, the tent company can go back to its hard-earned customers for repeat sales. The company then becomes a relationship marketer.

Here is a key to success in direct mail: If you are a semirelationship marketer, expand into allied product items that fit with your main line, so you don't get trapped into selling only to that tiny group of single product buyers. Move to full relationship marketing.

But the tent company manufactures only tents, you say. True. The other products come from other manufacturers. Do you think L. L. Bean makes everything in its catalog? Of course not. But do its customers care? Most probably don't know, but they wouldn't care if they did. They want that Bean label because of all the good things associated with it.

Nonrelationship Marketers

Nonrelationship marketers sell only one thing at any one time and almost never go back to previous buyers, because once buyers have the product they will not need another. All marketing efforts are thus directed to making a first and last sale to a single prospect. All profits come from this one-time transaction.

Nonrelationship marketers are almost exclusively one-product companies. Sellers of time-share condominiums and correspondence schools are examples. Nonrelationship marketers can spend a lot of money quickly to meet the demand for any single product, but they lack a base of customers to whom they can make repeat sales of the same or allied products.

■ *CAUTION NOTE: You need a customer base to make money in direct mail.*

If you are a nonrelationship marketer, think about how you might move into the semirelationship or full relationship position.

UNDERSTANDING 2
RESPONSE PSYCHOLOGY
OF DIRECT MAIL
RECIPIENTS

In this chapter we will look at factors that motivate prospects to buy.

SELLING MEANS HELPING PEOPLE DO WHAT WE WANT THEM TO DO

The *psychology of selling* means helping people decide to do what we want them to do. To be successful at all, we must offer things people perceive as valuable. We must help them to see that the benefits of buying outweigh the negative aspect of having to spend money. For example, we are selling a grapefruit squeezer. Prospects who decide to buy must feel that what they will be able to do with that grapefruit squeezer —to make new and exotic drinks, to make healthy fresh-squeezed juice—is more important than the money they will have to spend for the squeezer.

■ *KEY POINT:* *Selling means helping people do what you want them to do.*

PEOPLE ARE NOT RATIONAL BUYERS

Businesses and oganizations that use direct mail often have difficulty grasping the fact that people are not rational buyers. People don't buy for exactly what an object will do. They buy for emotional reasons. They

19

buy for the intangible rewards—feeling better, feeling healthier, looking better—the object they buy will give them.

■ *CAUTION NOTE:* *People don't buy for rational reasons.*

■ *KEY POINT:* *People buy for emotional, intangible rewards.*

To put it another way, people don't buy tangibles. Take the toaster oven. People don't buy this item for the utilitarian fact that it toasts bread. They buy it because it saves them time. Also using it is less trouble than roasting bread over an open fire.

■ *KEY POINT:* *Stress the benefits of your product or service, not its features.*

People buy because they believe a product or service will save them time, offer them riches, make their life easier, make them feel and look better, or for other emotional reasons that don't at first seem to make sense. Sellers must act on these reasons. Direct mailers who do not understand this will be eaten up by competitors who do.

The same holds true for business-to-business mail. Too often we assume that businesspeople, from vice presidents to purchasing agents, are interested only in facts. Nothing could be further from the truth. Everyone in a company is afraid of someone, especially of someone above. All fear being crushed by someone else's manipulating, and they all scrap among themselves to take credit for things that benefit the company. Our mail must help them do this.

We must make them believe that buying what we offer will enhance their position and make them more respected. We must make it a personal, an emotional investment. They want their boss to come up and say, "That was a smart choice," not, "That was a dumb purchase you recommended."

HOW DO WE GET PEOPLE TO BUY?

Before we can get people to take action and buy our product or service, we must realize that they base their decision on emotions that may not seem rational at first, but which do make sense when examined.

People want to know what the product or service will do for them. So tell them that your million dollar insurance policy will enhance their status with others, that their donation to charity will improve their feeling of self-worth.

This is the *WIIFM*—what's-in-it-for-me?—formula of selling. People will read our mailing if they perceive that it offers something of value specifically for them. The key here is "specifically for them." They must see that we are offering them increased personal prestige, worth, or self-esteem.

■ *KEY POINT: Tell people what's in it for them.*

■ *KEY POINT: People buy products that give them personal value.*

This is why direct mail should never stress features, or the obvious characteristics, of a product. Instead the sales message should stress the *benefits* of the features. We must translate features into emotional benefits for our readers. This is how we get our buyers to perceive that what we are offering them is of more value than what they have to pay to get it.

■ *KEY POINT: Translate features into benefits—the emotional aspects of your product or service.*

In selling by direct mail, we are asking people to do something they are not used to doing. To succeed, we must show prospects how they will benefit from what we offer. We must balance the "what's-in-it-for me" with the money they must pay to buy it. In fact, we have to over-compensate, because otherwise they won't buy. It won't be worth it to them. If we are to make sales by direct mail, we must load up our side with more perceived benefits for buyers than what they must give up.

■ *KEY POINT: Overcompensate with benefits.*

In direct mail, we start with the benefit and lead to the feature. This is the nonmanipulative way of helping prospects to buy.

■ *KEY POINT: Start with benefits and lead to features.*

BENEFITS GIVE PEOPLE THE EMOTIONAL REASON THEY NEED TO BUY

Have you ever bought insurance from a salesperson who described what was in the policy? Probably not, because that isn't what insurance salespeople do. Rather, they describe what a policy will do for you: how it will protect you, how much money is in it for you, and what you will get back when you retire. In other words, they tell you the benefits.

Another example: Suppose you get two pieces of mail. Both envelopes have messages on them. The first says, "Inside! Details on a brand new life insurance policy from Colonial Penn." The second says, "Inside! Details on how you can receive $875 per month after age 59!" Which one do you open? The second one. Why? Because the envelope offers you a concrete benefit to which you can relate.

■ *KEY POINT:* **Benefits make people act.**

THE JOB OF DESCRIPTION IS TO SHOW HOW BENEFITS FIT INTO PEOPLE'S LIVES

Benefits by themselves are not sufficient motivators. They need the support of *description*, which gives people a concept of what we are offering and lets them see how the product or service fits into their lives. We have to make prospects visualize themselves using or enjoying our product. They must see themselves enjoying the electric wok in their home or feeling good about that $50 charity donation.

■ *KEY POINT:* **Descriptions reinforce benefits.**

DESCRIPTION MUST BE VIVID

We must use the most vivid language possible to make people feel, see, and experience our product. We must show them exactly how it will work in their lives by giving them the mental experience of the object. This is how we make benefits come alive, by using tangibles to sell the intangibles of something tangible.

■ *KEY POINT:* **Keep description vivid.**

The copy part of description is supported with photographs. These photographs should show people like the ones we are soliciting enjoying the benefits that we have described.

■ *KEY POINT:* **Use photographs to show people enjoying benefits.**

DESCRIPTION HELPS RELIEVE RISK

Risk is a major problem in direct mail selling. Prospects are often afraid to buy something from someone they cannot see or talk to. This is a reasonable fear, and can prevent them from doing what we want them to.

We must address the problem of risk directly, by answering all the possible questions: "How does it work?" "What do I do if I don't like it?" "Can I return it?" "What if it's damaged in the mail?" "Are you going to call me? Or high pressure me?" "Will a salesperson show up at my door?"

We must assume that prospects have these questions, and we must use description to eliminate the sense of risk that may keep prospects from deciding to act.

■ *KEY POINT:* **Use description to reduce risk.**

Description tells people what to do. It tells them what will happen when they send in their check, who will talk with them if they call, or how long it will take to receive their order. All this information helps reduce prospects' sense of risk.

PROOF OF WHAT WE SAY
ENCOURAGES BELIEF

Another fear prospects have is that you are lying to them. This is another form of risk. We counter by giving proof of what we are offering and describing. We must build belief into our offer.

■ *KEY POINT:* **Proof enhances belief.**

We can use charts, graphs, surveys, test results, and other techniques to prove that our claims are believable. One of the best forms of proof is legitimate *testimonials* from satisfied users, customers who have bought from us and are active users of our product. Testimonials help reduce the feeling of risk.

RESPONDING TO DIRECT MAIL IS NOT A
NATURAL ACT

Another psychological problem is that people don't like to respond to direct mail. It may be that the telephone has allowed us to communicate so directly and immediately that we have lost the old skill of communicating by letters. People don't feel comfortable writing letters anymore.

■ *CAUTION NOTE:* **Responding to direct mail is not a natural act.**

We might say that direct mail tries to retrain people to perform an almost-forgotten skill, responding by mail. This may be one reason it is easier to sell to customers the second time. If they have bought from us once, the chance is good that they will do so again. When seeking new prospects, the most important thing we can find out is whether they have responded to direct mail in the past.

■ *KEY POINT:* **Knowing which prospects are likely to respond is important.**

How many people out of 100 chosen at random are likely to perform the "unnatural act" of responding to direct mail? If we're lucky, 1% or

2%. What do we do? We make the act as natural as possible by presenting our sales message in a way that makes it easy for prospects to reply.

■ *KEY POINT: Teach people to respond by making it easy for them.*

For example, display your toll-free telephone number prominently, near the main part of your message. Or offer a prepaid postcard or envelope for the reply. Later chapters on copy and design show how to use these tools efficiently.

SENDING OUT INFORMATION IS NOT SELLING

Many people, whether out of boredom or out of sincere interest, like to collect advertising literature. Maybe they just like to keep up on what is for sale, maybe they feel they can learn from the information sent them. But they never buy anything. Can they afford what we offer? Maybe or maybe not. Do they have a need for what we are offering? Not at this time. Steer clear of these collectors—they only cost you money.

■ *CAUTION NOTE: Avoid soliciting "information collectors."*

Studies have shown that most of us are so deluged with information that only a small portion gets through to us. Of the 1500 or more advertising messages that bombard a typical American each day, from radio, television, signs, and direct mail, only perhaps a dozen get through.

■ *CAUTION NOTE: Most people are overloaded with information.*

SPEAK DIRECTLY TO PROSPECTS WITH DECISIONS TO MAKE

How do we make sure we are among that dozen? Fancier brochures? Longer sales messages? More color? No.

The only way we can make an impression is by taking our product and positioning it in the minds of people who have a need and must do something about it. Only prospects who have decisions to make will care about the information we have to offer. These are the people to whom we want to appeal.

■ *KEY POINT:*   *Seek prospects who must do something about a need.*

We reach these prospects by speaking directly to them and telling them what's in it for them if they respond to what we send them. They will not respond otherwise. They get so much mail that they will not bother with our piece unless we give them the ultimate bribe, an irresistible something that will benefit them immensely.

This is the winning strategy in direct mail: having prospects perceive that they will derive immense benefit from what is offered. If prospects are even to read our mail, they must perceive at the outset that it truly offers something they need.

■ *KEY POINT:*   *Bribe prospects with irresistible benefits.*

The envelope is the first thing prospects see. One envelope reads, "Free gift for business owners only . . . $29.95 for anyone else." Who's going to open that envelope? People who are interested? No. People who are not business owners? No. But business owners would be likely to open that envelope, and they are the ones you want to open it.

Do you care if anyone else opens the envelope? No. Nor do you care if everyone else throws it out. You only want qualified prospects to open that envelope, people who have a need and must make a decision about this need and can pay for it. It's strange but true that success in direct mail means getting rid of those who are not prospects just as much as it means selling to those who are.

■ *KEY POINT:*   *Get rid of those who are not qualified prospects.*

PEOPLE BUY FOR THE DARNEDEST REASONS—FIND OUT WHY

One of the best ways to find out what prospects want is to look at your present customers. Find out why they bought from you in the first place. Ask them what they like about the product now that they have it. Even ask them what they like about you. The answers may surprise you. You may find that their reasons are not the ones you would have expected.

■ *CAUTION NOTE: **Prospects don't buy for obvious reasons.***

Maybe they didn't buy your kitchen knife set to cut meat. Maybe they didn't buy the insurance policy because of its death benefit. Maybe they didn't give to public television because they like to watch *Masterpiece Theater.*

Rather the polished wooden handles of the cutlery set are the showpiece of their glass-fronted hutch. The insurance gives the woman a feeling of equality with her husband. The public television donors' names are announced over the air and they feel that their neighbors will respect them more because they watched *Masterpiece Theater.*

If you survey your present customers about your product or service, they will tell you about benefits you never knew existed. Often they're not buying because of what you say in your literature. They're buying for other reasons. And you should be offering those reasons to other prospects in your literature.

SELLING BY MANIPULATION DOESN'T WORK

The world of marketing is full of books and formulas on just how to sell. I say, however, that there is no exact formula. There are different ways to present what we have to offer to different prospects. I believe we must look into the deep emotional reasons why people buy any particular product or service. Each case must be looked at on its own.

Trying to manipulate a prospect, to twist a sale out of someone, won't work. Snake-oil pitches will do only one thing. They will get our sales literature thrown in the garbage can.

■ *CAUTION NOTE: **Never manipulate prospects.***

Instead of manipulating prospects, our aim is to control how prospects read our sales message. We must do everything we can to get readers to read only what we want them to. Because people seldom read our whole message, we must get them to read the right part first, so the major points of what we are saying are not lost.

■ *KEY POINT:*   *Control what the prospect reads.*

GET PROSPECTS IN THE RIGHT FRAME OF MIND TO READ

We must also get prospects in the right frame of mind to read our mail. Prospects don't like to feel that they are being "sold," just as they don't like to feel manipulated. Pitches don't work in direct mail. If prospects feel a sales pitch coming on, they will rebel.

This does not mean you cannot be a salesperson. But selling means helping people buy, guiding them in their purchase. In this sense, good salespersons, like good direct mail pieces, don't sell. They get out of the way. They help prospects buy.

■ *KEY POINT:*   *Good salesmanship is not pitching, but helping people buy.*

Good salespeople know two things: (1) how to *nurture,* and (2) how to *listen.* Selling by direct mail is no different from selling in person. It is a *negotiation.* Manipulation or trying to squeeze prospects will often kill an almost sure sale because today's buyers have too many options. Face to face, prospects will tell us to get lost. In direct mail, they just throw our piece away.

■ *KEY POINT:*   *Selling is negotiating.*

So what do we do? We start by finding out what problems our prospects have and then we position our product in their minds so they perceive that what we are offering will solve those problems. Sound complicated? It isn't, but we do have to be creative; our product must be sold in a different way to every prospect. The same motivators will not work with everyone, but we begin by showing that our product is different and can solve your prospect's problem better than any other product. Forget the standard old-fashioned sales pitches—prospects do not want to be sold. They do, however, want what you can give them: help in buying.

■ *KEY POINT:* **Help prospects perceive your product as different.**

■ *KEY POINT:* **Selling means solving people's problems.**

If you still believe people buy for purely practical reasons, consider the last time you bought something to wear. Did you do an exhaustive survey on quality of fabric and how well something was made in many different stores? No. You probably just tried something on and knew it was "you" or "not you." Now if you were selling that same piece of clothing by direct mail, would you emphasize benefits like the close stitching and the durability of the fabric? No, because while these are important to buyers, more important is the way they think they will look wearing the clothes. This might best be done with a photograph showing a man or woman handsomely admired in new clothes by his or her peers. The written copy could also emphasize the heightened interest of those around the person. This mental picture is the major benefit. The others are secondary.

Take cars as another example. Did you buy the one you now have because it would be reliable or because it had low gas mileage? Perhaps both of these were factors. But the car also had to be "you." You had to like sitting behind the wheel, and the design had to please you. The car probably didn't have to be a Ferrari, but it had to fit your notions of what you want in a car.

If you don't think this is true, here's a test. Would you rather buy a gas-efficient car that looks as if it had been in a demolition derby, or an attractively styled car that gets low gas mileage? You would probably opt for style, because it is worse for your friends and fellow workers to see you driving a junker than paying more for gas. You probably wouldn't buy a car that would not enhance your self-image in some way. Irrational? Perhaps not, if you realize what your priorities really are. It's the same with your customers. You must find the real issues that motivate people. Scrap the nonsense too many people have offered about what makes people buy and appeal to the real reasons.

PEOPLE BUY HAPPINESS

People are all looking for the same thing: happiness. Happiness can come from convenience, comfort, status, respect, attractiveness—a long list of tangible and intangible things. If Bill achieves more leisure time, he will be happy. If Charlotte looks good, she will be happy. People don't buy to be healthier, to gain wisdom, or to gain wealth. They want this because they think it will make them happy. That's the key. So sellers must give people what they want, something that will make them feel outstanding about themselves. This message of happiness dominates what we say to our prospects. Happiness is the most important single factor we must deal with in crafting our direct mail.

■ *KEY POINT: Sell happiness.*

If we are not giving people the perception that our product or service will make their lives happier, we cannot really be said to be selling at all. This may sound as if we are all trying to sell the same thing. This is true. Then how do we personalize what we tell prospects? We do it by saying something different.

SUMMARY

Because people are not rational buyers, we must appeal to them on an emotional level by giving them benefits as emotional reasons to buy. Descriptions reinforce benefits and reduce prospects' fears of risk. We also offer proof, such as testimonials and surveys, to encourage belief in what we are saying and reduce anxiety.

Responding to mail has become an "unnatural act," so we must make responding as easy as possible. To get our mail to the best possible prospects, we eliminate those who like to collect information for its own sake.

To get prospects to make decisions, we speak directly and nonmanipulatively to them in our sales literature. We show them that what we have to offer is different and can make them happier by improving their comfort, convenience, status, or other parts of their lives.

STRUCTURING 3
THE OFFER

In this chapter we will discuss how to build an offer and use it to communicate with people.

AN OFFER COMMUNICATES THE BENEFITS OF THE PRODUCT TO OUR PROSPECTS

An offer can be thought of as a talk with our prospects and customers. It is the means we use to communicate information on what we have for sale and how we want them to respond.

■ *KEY POINT: Offers communicate the benefits of the product and how the prospect should respond.*

In Chapter 1, we learned that direct mail is live, personal selling translated into the print medium. This is the basis of successful selling by direct mail. Some of the best copywriters of direct mail are salespeople, because they know how to sell. We are not advertising, as in "awareness" advertising. We are selling. We are asking for an immediate response.

■ *CAUTION NOTE: Direct mail is selling, not advertising.*

We will now start using much of what we learned in the last chapter on the use of selling to build an offer. We saw that people must be given emotional reasons to buy, that they are not used to responding to mail and need to be shown how easy it is to respond, that in order to sell we must speak directly and not manipulate, and that we must load up our

31

offer with benefits that prospects will perceive as giving them convenience, comfort, or security—the happiness all people seek. All these elements must be considered when we build our offer.

As we saw in the last chapter, the success of direct mail depends on the difference between the benefits people perceive themselves getting from what we offer and what they must give up to get them. In a sense, this defines what an offer is: It describes what people can get and what they must do to get it. The psychology of selling also says that to succeed, you must emphasize the benefits so that they seem to outweigh the negative aspects.

■ *KEY POINT: The offer tells what people will get and what they have to give up to get it.*

PEOPLE MAKE A SERIES OF DECISIONS WHEN BUYING

When we make an offer, we are selling a series of decisions. People make decisions in stages, one step at a time, and the elements of an offer are devices that buy time in the decision-making process.

If the first impression of our mail works, we will retain our readers' attention for a few more seconds and they will read on. If we continue to give them what they perceive they want, they will stay with us long enough to understand fully what we are offering and what they must give up to get it. Then, if we have done our job right, they will make a favorable decision.

■ *KEY POINT: People buy by making a series of decisions.*

Our job as creators of direct-mail offers is to conceive of and present the offer to prospects. We apply the right kind of tool, with the right amount of power, to each step in the decision-making process. We start by asking ourselves what it is we really are selling. As we saw in the last chapter, we are not selling a product. We are selling what the product will do for someone in an intangible, psychological sense. That's how we gain a favorable decision. And we do it by selling steps in the decision-making process.

■ *KEY POINT:* **Sell steps in the decision-making process.**

It is easier to get people to take steps than to take leaps, so we give people a series of little decisions they find it easy to say yes to. This is the key to creating a successful offer.

BUILDING AN OFFER STARTS WITH GETTING PROSPECTS TO READ THE MAILING PIECE

Let's look at what we want our direct mail to do. First, we want prospects to read our offer. Even the most interested prospects must read the terms we are offering before they make a final decision. If prospects fail to read what we have to say, all is lost.

■ *KEY POINT:* **We must get prospects to read our offer.**

Companies often believe people are dying to get their product. Therefore they mistakenly think people are anxious to read their direct mail literature. They don't know how much of themselves they must apply to the intricate task of bringing about a sale. They think that the demand for what they offer is such that they do not need to position their product in the prospect's mind. But the first thing to do is to get the mail read.

■ *CAUTION NOTE:* **People are not dying to get your product.**

There are many design and copy techniques we can use to get people to read what we send them. For one thing, we can simply ask them to read it. We can increase by up to 25% the number of people who open and read our mailing by simply telling them to open the envelope: "Read inside to learn about. . . ," "Open to find out how you can. . . ." We must sell reading to them because they won't do it by themselves. They have too much inertia.

■ *KEY POINT:*   *Ask prospects to read.*

To get prospects to read, we give them a benefit for reading. We give them the impression that if they do nothing except read this offer they will be better off. We must make them perceive they will know something they didn't know before. This is not done just on the envelope. It is done throughout the sales literature by use of language such as "Read below to learn. . . ," "Turn the page to find out. . . ," "Look at the chart to learn. . . ."

■ *KEY POINT:*   *Give prospect a benefit for reading.*

OUR GOAL IS AN IMMEDIATE RESPONSE

After we get prospects to read, our next goal is to get them to make decisions. As we saw in the last chapter, we don't use direct mail just to give information. We want a result, an immediate response.

■ *KEY POINT:*   *Direct mail is sent to get an immediate response.*

It is true that some high-frequency mailings, particularly announcements, bulletins, and newsletters for information and are not expected to generate responses. But these make up only a small percentage of all direct mail, and are usually used only as adjuncts or supplemental material to a larger mail campaign. Direct mail usually generates an action, and to get this action, we need people to make decisions.

■ *KEY POINT:*   *Successful direct mail generates action.*

There are three basic strategies to get prospects to make a decision.

Tell Prospects What You Want Them to Do

Prospects should know what we want them to do within 20 seconds of picking up our mailing piece. They should know what they are going to get, how much it will cost, and what they must do to get it. We have just 20 seconds to achieve that.

■ *CAUTION NOTE:* *Prospects have to understand the offer within 20 seconds.*

Some companies make the mistake of hiding what they want prospects to do. They try to hide the decision by sneaking it in somewhere on the bottom corner. They believe prospects are encouraged to read on if they don't know just what is being offered and at what price. This is a mistake. People will not read an entire offer if they do not realize what it is about. First they will scan to get a general sense of what it is about and does it interest them. They will not read it at all unless they first know what they're going to get and what they have to give up to get it.

■ *CAUTION NOTE:* *Don't hide the decision the prospect should make.*

If people do not grasp what we are offering within 5 to 8 seconds, they will not even open the envelope—which is why many sales messages start on the envelope. We must make a favorable first impression within that time. If we don't, our mailing will be thrown away, even if the prospects might have been interested when they opened it. Remember, they are not dying to read our mail. They resist it.

■ *CAUTION NOTE:* *We must make a favorable impression within the first 5 to 8 seconds.*

Companies make the mistake of writing as if everyone who receives their mailing will actually read it. This is false. As we will see later, many people who buy never read everything they receive. Only 10% to 15% of people who receive direct mail ever read the copy contained in the letters at all. Companies put too much emphasis on what is being said and too little on their offer and how it is presented.

■ *CAUTION NOTE:* *Most people don't read sales copy.*

Essentially, we must buy readership. We do this by presenting in a flash what's unique and exciting about our offer. The key is "in a flash." What we do to interest prospects must be done quickly so they can react immediately. Remember, we have only those few 5 to 8 seconds to begin enchanting our prospects.

Make clear right away what the offer is and what decision you want your readers to make. Put the whole deal on the envelope: "Pick up the phone now and call 800-833-8000 to find out how you can save up to 75% on your next order of copy paper," or, "This manual describes 231 of the smartest ways to use your small business to save thousands of dollars a year in tax-free income." Both are specific messages that explain everything. Both will buy readership.

■ *KEY POINT: Buy readership by impressing quickly on the prospect what's unique and exciting about your offer.*

By contrast, here are two messages that are *not* likely to encourage prospects to read: "How can you keep on the cutting edge of strategic management?" Ho, hum. Do we really care? The language is hackneyed, too. Or: "I've reserved a new and useful free gift for you. The details are inside." These overused words will put prospects to sleep.

Here is an interesting point. If we've done our job—made our message clear and stimulating and offered a capsule of the whole deal—do we care if the mailing gets tossed into the wastebasket? Not at all. As long as the tosser is not someone with a need for our product and the ability to pay for it. In fact, next to an order, it's the best thing that could happen, because these people have given us a "no" decision. They have at least been decisive about it. They have told us they are not our prospects after all.

■ *KEY POINT: You don't care if an unqualified prospect rejects your offer.*

Create a Sense of Urgency

The second way to encourage prospects to make a decision is to create pressure. Not pressure in a manipulative way (we don't box someone into a corner) but a sense of urgency. One way is to put a time limit on your offer: "Offer good for 30 days." This is excellent for decisions no one likes to make, such as for insurance. Again we want prospects to make their decisions promptly. We want action now. Even if the decision is no, a prompt result is better than postponing the decision, which usually becomes "no" by default.

■ *KEY POINT:* *Create pressure to get prospects to make a decision.*

Another way to create pressure for a decision is to use discounts: "Forty percent off on all orders received before April Fool's Day." Here we combine a discount with a time limit. We are rewarding buyers for acting quickly by saving them money.

We can also create a sense of urgency by putting limits on any special options we offer. "Once and only once will the ginsu knife be offered at this price . . . act now, you'll never have another chance." The key to this approach is that if people think they won't ever be offered something again, they're more likely to want it now. This works, and is an excellent strategy for product sales.

■ *KEY POINT:* *Time limits, discounts, and limits on special options help to create pressure.*

Limits on special options are not appropriate for gaining sales leads or for fund raising. Obviously, once someone has given money to a cause, we want to approach them again and again.

■ *CAUTION NOTE:* *Don't use limits on special options for fund raising.*

Ask People to Respond

The third way we get people to make a decision is to simply ask them to act. Ask them to call on the telephone, fill out the coupon, or mail the return envelope today. This is called the *action step*. We ask them to act, to take the action step immediately.

■ *KEY POINT:* *Ask prospects to act immediately.*

To encourage action now, we must not only ask (meaning urgently request) prospects to act but also make it easy for them to do so. We give them toll-free numbers, easy-to-fill-in response cards, prestamped and addressed envelopes, prominent order forms. If we make it hard for people to respond, we lessen the chance of response.

■ *KEY POINT:*   *Make it easy to respond.*

"SWEETENERS" ARE THE EXTRAS PEOPLE GET

To further encourage people to read, make a decision, and act, we use marketing techniques called *sweeteners*. Sweeteners are additional amenities that are not the product or service itself; they are the free gifts, accessories, and bonus items that get prospects to take action and do what we want them to do. They are the bribes, if you like, that we use when prospects resist what we have to offer.

■ *KEY POINT:*   *Sweeteners are bribes designed to influence a prospect's judgment.*

Sweeteners work well in some cases but can be disastrous in others. For example, book clubs often give away a number of books free or for a small amount just to get people to join. They have found that this is a successful strategy, but it's actually a strategy they must follow, because there are not hoards of Americans anxious to join book clubs. Book clubs have found that the United States is not a nation of avid readers, and that the public must be encouraged by bribes. The clubs make the bribes so attractive that these alone get people to join.

In fund raising, the problem can be more acute. A local public television station gives away a chrome-plated director's chair for every $100 donation. On the surface this sounds reasonable, as long as the chair doesn't cost too much. This strategy can backfire, however, because the television station has gained a donor who may not give again unless another sweetener or bribe is offered. This can become a losing financial strategy for the station.

■ *CAUTION NOTE:*   *Often a bribe gains support from a less committed supporter.*

Thus one problem with sweeteners is that once we start offering them, we can't stop. We're trapped. People will expect to receive some sort of gift. This can be very difficult to reverse, and it's the result of trying to get uncommitted people to begin with.

■ *CAUTION NOTE:* **Once you start with bribes, it's hard to stop.**

How do companies get started offering sweeteners in the first place? The story usually unfolds like this: A company sells a product for which there is a reasonable demand. After a while, when about the top third of the market has been combed, interest wanes. The most avid buyers have bought. The wrong-headed marketing genius thinks "a little something" needs to be added to the pot. The downward spiral begins. Instead of opening up new marketing territory with committed and strong campaigns, the old company offers bribes to traditional types of buyers.

■ *KEY POINT:* **Bribes often begin after firm support drops off.**

Sweeteners can be used in proportion to the amount of profit you get out of the relationship. You cannot spend more than your margin of profit, in that way lies bankruptcy. But even offering a bribe is an indication that your demand has flattened out.

■ *CAUTION NOTE:* **Don't spend more on a bribe than your profit margin.**

Sweeteners do work well in single-product sales. Some products, like grapefruit squeezers and complicated 21-blade pocketknives, are often sold by offering bribes alone: "Included with this knife are the secrets of the universe . . . ," "a silver-studded thong belt . . . ," "a fine leather holster . . . ." Because demand may have peaked for the knife, the company must up the ante.

But in the sale of most products and services, when the seller is a relationship marketer and wants repeat sales, the use of sweeteners, particularly if they are too glamorous and unconnected to the product, can be a bad marketing strategy. If you see a product offered with a substantial sweetener, you know the product is in trouble, or will be soon. Beware of using bribes: They mean you are buying less interested people.

Sweeteners must never be given away or thrown in just to make an offer look better They must be used only as a technique to get your prospect to read, make a decision, and act on your mailing.

"FACILITATORS" HELP BY RELIEVING RISK

We also use *facilitators* to further relieve risk and anxiety on the part of prospects, to get easier and quicker responses, and to encourage payment.

Risk Relievers

Risk relievers are designed to reduce the risk of taking action. These are statements like "money-back guarantee," "complete 30-day refund," "no-risk offer," "100% satisfaction guaranteed," "free trial issue," "use on approval for 30 days, no charge," and "no-risk membership."

The use of risk-relievers is essential in direct mail. As we said before, prospects don't know us personally. We must give them the psychological reassurance that if anything goes wrong, they can get their money back or otherwise gain satisfaction.

■ *KEY POINT: Facilitators help remove risk.*

Federal law states that buyers have up to 30 days to return, for any reason, anything they have bought in the mail and to get their money back. Most risk-reducing facilitators thus do nothing more than guarantee what the buyer is already entitled to. At the same time they increase the number of sales.

■ *KEY POINT: Often risk-relieving facilitators promise buyers what they're entitled to.*

Response Boosters

The second group of facilitators are the *response boosters*. They make it easy for people to reply. The name of the game is to get responses. Make response easy by using a stamped, self-addressed envelope, a business reply card, a fold-up envelope form in the catalog, tear-out coupons, or a toll-free telephone number on every page of your brochure or catalog. These are all techniques that help gain responses. They broaden the range of possible buyers by helping to interest those with marginal need.

■ *KEY POINT:* *Response-boosting facilitators make it easy for the prospect to reply.*

People with only marginal need who respond, however, bring up another problem. The easier you make it for people to respond, the more unqualified inquiries you will get. You can't afford to spend money on generating unqualified inquiries. When the value of what you are offering exceeds a certain level, perhaps $100 in today's market, you have more money to deal with inquiries.

■ *CAUTION NOTE:* *Ease of response leads to many unqualified inquiries.*

In catalog sales, however, in which case a response is usually a definite order, anything you can do to make ordering easier for your prospect will boost sales. A toll-free telephone number on every page of the catalog is an example of a good strategy.

Payment Increasers

Another kind of facilitator is the *payment increaser*. Payment increasers allow us to get more money faster by using a simple principle: The easier we make it for prospects to pay, the more we will get paid. The use of credit cards is one obvious payment increaser that is appropriate for almost any product and for many services. The credit card is even being used in fund raising. All we need for a mail order is the card name, the number, the expiration date, and the customer's signature. If the order is taken over the telephone, we eliminate the signature.

■ *KEY POINT:* *The easier we make it to pay, the more we will get paid.*

Some buyers want to pay by check. Many firms wait 10 to 15 days for the check to clear before sending out the product. This is unfortunate, because as we will see later, part of keeping customers is making sure they are happy with your product. And part of their satisfaction is getting the product quickly. Since prospects probably responded quickly, their orders should be processed in the same manner. Customers should not be penalized for paying by check. However, the validity of a check may depend on the type of market you're mailing to. A check sent by a doctor may (or may not) be less apt to bounce than one sent by a freelance writer.

■ *CAUTION NOTE: Do not delay a shipment while waiting for the check to clear.*

We must remember that prospects do not make well-thought-out decisions. They make largely impulsive "now" decisions. The easier you make it for them to pay, the more positive impulsive decisions you will gain. Easy ways to pay like use of a credit card let prospects decide to buy even when they don't have any money in their checking account.

■ *KEY POINT: Allowing payment by credit card increases sales and solves the payment problem.*

When businesspeople order by direct mail for the company, payment is usually by company check. But not always. Extended billing privileges are the way to go to increase sales when doing business-to-business direct mail. "No bill for 60 days," keeps slow company channels open.

■ *KEY POINT: Stronger sales for companies when billed.*

Do you insist on payment up front, or extend a billing privilege? The answer depends on what is being bought and who is buying it. As in the case of checks, you may assume that high-paid professional people are likely to be better payers than other groups. But the evidence is not in.

We should follow the principle that any reasonable offer is likely to work if it's clearly spelled out. In other words, suppose someone who orders a magazine subscription is told, "no payment for 30 days," but we send the bill with the first issue and without any special instructions. We may not only destroy our credibility but also delay payment, because the buyer gets confused. The point is: We can increase the rate of payment by making it easy for buyers to pay, either when they order or in the near future.

■ *KEY POINT: Most offers are successful if clearly spelled out.*

Discounts

The last kind of facilitator is the *discount*. A discount can bring in a sale that would not have been made without it, but the sale may also mean that a marginal buyer has been added to your customer list.

Discounts are strange, however. Some people never buy anything unless it's discounted, because the perception that something is a bargain is a major consideration. They can tell their friends, "I bought this at half price," and feel smug about it. These people will often buy whatever comes along, even something for which they don't have a need, as long as it is discounted.

■ *CAUTION NOTE: Discounts often bring in marginal customers.*

■ *CAUTION NOTE: Some buyers only buy when a product is on sale.*

Buying by mail is an impulsive decision. If prospects can get the gadget they were thinking about five years ago, they may just go ahead and get it now. "After all, it's on sale, and we don't know when it will be again."

The danger of discounting is that it is like bribing prospects: Once we start, it's hard to stop. People will expect discounts on everything we sell. Some catalog retailers make the big mistake of offering twice-a-year sale flyers. This leads some customers to wait for the sale, to decide they won't buy at any other time. Beware of doing things like liquidating inventory and overstocks with your customer base. This can work against you, as can adding cheap products to your expensive product line. If you have many sale customers you will eventually turn, however unintentionally, into a discounter.

■ *CAUTION NOTE: Discounting makes some prospects expect to buy everything on sale.*

SIX STEPS IN BUILDING AN OFFER

Determine Your Objective

When you build an offer, the first thing you should do is determine your *objective*. You must know what you're trying to accomplish with your mailing. If you don't, everything that follows will likely fail. Your objective is what you want to have happen—new customers, sales leads, new donors. What do you want? Do you want prospects to write or call you? How will you follow up on leads when you get them? These are all objectives that define just what your mailing is about.

Be specific. Write your objective down. Don't put down "making more money" or "increasing sales"; this is too general. Everybody wants to make money. The point is, what are you going to do to make it?

Once you determine your objective, you'll be able to see exactly what you are selling and to define the most important thing you want from your mailing. Once you know that, sell it. Devote your offer to it.

Identify Benefits

Next identify the benefits of your offer. Begin by identifying the most important ones, what most people would find valuable about having your product or service, or about giving money to your organization. Not the features of the product, but those intangible qualities that prospects can perceive as enhancing their self-image or self-esteem. If you don't know what the benefits are, refer back to Chapter 2 and survey your present customers to see why they bought from or gave to you. Ask them what they got out of their purchase or donation. The things most frequently mentioned are the major benefits.

Other benefits are less important and will be given minor billing in your sales literature. They are the things only a few prospects may consider special. When we write copy and design mailing pieces, the major benefits come first and the others are given secondary importance.

Describe Delivery of Benefits

Next describe exactly how your prospects get these benefits. What do they have to do to get them? Sell prospects on taking the next step.

Identify and explain what they will get for responding in some way—requesting a demonstration, seeing a sales representative, asking for more literature.

Offer Proof

Offer proof to support what you are saying. Prove to prospects that they are going to get what you say they will get. Use testimonials, charts, graphs, independent surveys, any evidence you can to prove that what you say is true. Tell them what is going to happen to them, how it is going to happen, and give them the proof. Some sort of verification is critical to direct mail success.

Establish Sweeteners and Facilitators

Decide on your sweeteners and facilitators. What extra features will you offer? What sweeteners might help prospects make decisions? Make sure they are things that will stimulate prospective buyers, not things of unique interest to you. Choose the facilitators you will use to get people to respond. A toll-free number? Combined order form and envelope? Stamped self-addressed card? Put in the facilitators that will make it easy for prospects to do business with you. Ease will help them respond.

Indicate How to Respond

Finally, tell your prospects exactly what to do to respond, step by step. Tell them exactly how to fill out the form, tear it off, enclose their check, seal the envelope, call this number. Unfortunately, you must never underestimate the inability of people to do some of the simplest tasks. Now that they have decided they want what you offer, don't make it complicated for them to get it. Give them exact instructions.

COORDINATING COPY 4
AND DESIGN
TO GAIN READERSHIP

In this chapter we will see how to coordinate copy and design to gain readers for our offer. Further, we will explore the readability of different direct mail formats. This material lays the groundwork for specific copy and design techniques that are detailed in the chapters that follow.

COPY AND DESIGN HAVE AN INTIMATE RELATIONSHIP

In direct mail there is an intimate relationship between copy and design. *Copy* refers to the words we use to persuade prospects of the value of what we offer. *Design,* in a general sense, refers to what we do to present visually what we say in the most favorable terms. In a specific sense, design guides the reader's eye where we want it to go. Control of the reader's eye path is a critical part of design. The best designs in direct mail are those that hold the eye, because attention must be gained before a sale can be made.

■ *KEY POINT:* **Design guides the reader's eye.**

This element is the difference between design in direct mail and design in general advertising. General advertisers are interested only in making readers aware of their product. Readers will do little more than glimpse a few words, so the design has the responsibility of carrying what must be a simple message.

Since in direct mail the message is crucial in getting responses, design supports the copy in this method of selling, not the reverse. This is the most difficult concept for advertisers to grasp when they must switch back and forth from general advertising media to a response medium like direct mail. It is almost impossible for advertising agencies to understand unless they have separate staffs for and extensive experience in direct mail.

■ *CAUTION NOTE: The only function of design in direct mail is to support copy.*

Copy and design, however, are almost impossible to separate. They are linked together more in direct mail than in any other advertising medium. The difference between the two and how each is used is critical.

COPY, NOT DESIGN, PERSUADES IN DIRECT MAIL

In direct mail it is copy that sells, not design. The only function of design should be to draw attention to the right sections of the copy. Design must draw readers to the parts of the copy that will motivate them to act.

■ *CAUTION NOTE: In direct mail, copy sells, not design.*

As an example, let's consider an age-old question in direct mail advertising: Do pictures help to sell? Well, yes and no. Yes, when they show people happily using a product we wish to sell. Also people usually look at pictures before copy. The dilemma is that pictures do not help people make decisions. They don't have persuasion power. What they do is draw the eye to a particular spot. Once there, the prospect will read the copy that captions the picture.

■ *CAUTION NOTE: Pictures are useful only for getting prospects to read copy.*

We thus use pictures as bait to get readers to read the caption copy. If the pictures are interesting—and it's easy to make them so, particularly when people similar to the prospect are shown enjoying the benefits of the product—people are even more likely to read the captions under them. The reason, then, for use of pictures is to get readership for the captions. This is true of other aspects of design. All aspects have one function: to get copy read. It is copy that sells, not design.

PLAIN DESIGN WORKS BEST IN SUPPORTING THE SALES MESSAGE

There is another unique truth about design and copy in direct mail that can upset many an advertising person: "Homely" performs! Design that is not much to look at can work spectacularly well in its intended purpose of seducing the reader to focus in on the copy. Homely works! White space, balance, and symmetry don't matter when it comes to direct mail. They're only in the way when it comes to getting copy read.

■ *KEY POINT:*   *"Homely" designs, without white space or balance, work in direct mail!*

Notes in the margin, no space around the picture, and uneven alignment of paragraphs all work better than does fancy type separated by lots of white space on embossed stationery.

Direct mail is not the place to build an image. That is the role of awareness advertising. Direct mail is not the place for "pretty" or "elegant." Leave that, too, for its slicker cousin, awareness advertising.

■ *CAUTION NOTE:*   *Don't use direct mail to build image.*

One of the mistakes some direct mailers make is to wait until they can afford to send their present customers an elaborate mailing. In the meantime, they don't send them anything. This is the worst possible strategy. Our overriding consideration with customers is to maintain contact. Send them anything—even photocopies, if you have to. Send an inexpensive black-and-white newsletter if you have to wait a month before your four-color catalog is back from the printer.

It's not your image you want to impress them with, it's your concern. You want to show them you care about the growing relationship between you and them. Mail is the personal medium. You must keep the contact personal and frequent for it to be effective. This is how you treat people you care for.

■ *CAUTION NOTE:*   *Copy, not design, proves you care for your customers.*

Don't use design to carry a fancy image. Design can never express the emotions and feelings you can express in personalized copy. So to keep design from intruding on copy, keep it homely.

COPY AND DESIGN TEAM UP TO GAIN READERS

Most of us stumble along reading an average of only 250 words a minute. Those who read faster have spent time learning and experiencing what reading is all about. With advertising copy, the problem of the readership is even more acute. We're trying to sell something, but our prospects don't want to read our advertising. We have to entice them to read with dynamic copy backed up by a design that draws them to read it. We must recognize these problems when we write our copy and design our mailing pieces.

■ *KEY POINT:*   *The job of direct mail is to get people to read.*
■ *KEY POINT:*   *Work copy and design together to draw in readers.*

Let's look at the problem of readership more closely. When average people open our mailing piece, they are not going to start at the beginning and read right through. They will skip around a lot. In a sense, they will read snatches while skipping around looking for a good reason to STOP! People read advertising literature to reinforce their natural instinct that the offer is not for them.

■ *CAUTION NOTE:*   *People read for a reason to say no.*

Our task seems insurmountable. That is why half our battle in direct mail is to get our sales message into the hands of prospects who have a preexisting interest in our product. If they do, and if our message manages to stay out of the wastebasket, we have a chance to increase our prospects' interest—if they are willing to read further.

READERSHIP OCCURS IN THREE STAGES

As we have seen, people will read advertising when they perceive that it offers them something. Although we may have excellent potential prospects for our offer, at best only 15% to 20% of them will even consider reading what we send them. Those who do tend to read and make decisions in three stages.

■ *KEY POINT: People read direct mail in three stages.*

People Scan for Relevancy

The first stage of reading is called *scanning*: Prospects take a few seconds to scan a mailing piece to see if the offer is relevant to them. If the mailing piece is an envelope with letter, brochure, and reply card inside, they may spend 15 to 20 seconds scanning the various parts. If it is a self-mailing brochure, they will spend only four to six seconds on the average.

■ *KEY POINT: People start reading by scanning for relevancy.*

Here's where design is so important. In those few seconds, we must make sure our prospects see messages they feel are relevant to them. We have to lead their eye to areas where we know they will look. These areas are *headlines, subheads, picture captions,* the *postscript* on the letter, and the *acceptance statement* on the response device. They are the key areas, because people know from experience that they can get a quick idea of the offer by looking at them. Our job is to load these locations with the information about benefits and about what we want prospects to do.

People Read for a Reason to Say NO

The second stage of reading is the *decision* stage. At this point prospects have already decided an unconscious "yes" that the product offers them a what's-in-it-for-me benefit. Now, at least, they're moving forward. At this stage they must decide if anything about the offer indicates that it's wrong for them. Now they are reading to find out if they should stop reading. They're looking for some way to get out of moving closer to a sale. If we're not careful, we can unsell them.

■ *KEY POINT: In the second stage of reading, people have said yes but seek reasons to change their mind.*

How do we keep from unselling them? We again use design to give them a visual "roadmap" that guides them to what we want them to look at and read next. We use arrows, underlining, marginal notes, highlighting, and so on, to draw the eye to copy and graphics that are our statements of further benefits and that offer them ways to follow through and make a decision. We also point them to other charts, graphs, tables, and diagrams that prove the substance of what we are telling them. All these graphics, like our pictures, have captions that explain what we offer and how to respond.

People Read to Confirm a YES Decision

The final stage of readership is the *confirmation* stage, when people read the remaining *body* copy. By now they are favoring a "yes" response but are not convinced they should buy. So they read to confirm their favorable decision. They take more time to read in this stage than in the others, because they want to be sure they are making the right decision. Only 4% to 6% of those who receive our mailing piece will reach this stage.

■ *KEY POINT: In the last stage of readership, people read to confirm a favorable decision.*

Designers often wonder why, if only 5% of readers read body copy, they can't use more pictures, on the assumption that more pictures would buy more readers. It doesn't work that way. Pictures buy readership, but they don't sell. At least not by themselves. We still need a written message to convince prospects to act.

Readers who get to the third stage know just what we are offering and how it will benefit them. They have done their homework. They have done the work of qualifying themselves. We hope most of them will become buyers.

■ *KEY POINT:*   *Those who read through copy qualify themselves.*

WE SEEK PROSPECTS WHO WILL CLIMB TO THE TOP OF THE READERSHIP PYRAMID

The whole process of bringing someone through these stages of readership can be thought of as a hike to the top of a high pyramid. The climb is hard work, and only the hardy make it. Many grope up the sides only to be pushed aside by others, as room farther up becomes more and more scarce. Many drop out, allowing other climbers to go on. Many quit, while a few reach the top (Figure 4.1).

Many who begin scanning may already have a preexisting interest, especially if we have done our homework and selected the right prospects for our message. Readers who reach the decision stage are half convinced and will spend a little more time reading, especially our graphs and charts. Finally, readers who remain favorable will enter the confirmation stage. They verify this is right for them and they respond.

The point is: The longer you hold your readers through these stages of readership, the more likely you are to get them to do what you want.

■ *KEY POINT:*   *The longer readers are held, the more likely they are to buy.*

DIRECT MAIL FORMATS DIFFER IN READABILITY

Let's look at some of the more popular direct mail formats and how well they gain readership. The *envelope,* or *letter-mailing,* usually contains a *letter,* a *brochure,* and some sort of *response device.* This is the most common type of mailing piece and comes closest to approximating the traditional, personal letter.

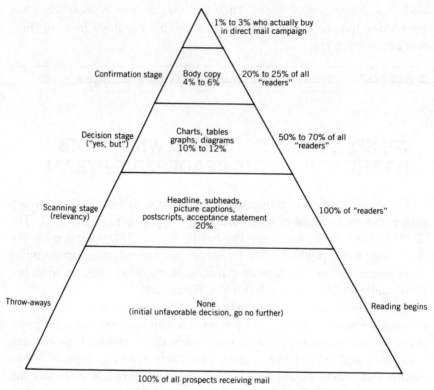

Figure 4.1 Stages of readership.

The *self-mailer* resembles a brochure but combines letter, brochure, and response device all in one mailing piece. Although obviously an advertising piece, it is economical to produce and send and therefore is less costly to distribute to large numbers of potential buyers.

The *catalog* is the third most popular way of selling products by direct mail. Its main advantage is that it can contain descriptions of many products. The catalog is the primary way for relationship marketers to reach customers, because it lets them offer an expanded line of products.

Cards are used several ways in direct mail. One is the "card deck," in which all necessary sales copy and the response device are on one card and the card is just one of many in a deck. The product thus must compete with other similar products but the cards will be distributed to many prospects with specially targeted interests. Cards can also be bound in magazines as reply devices to accompany a full sales story.

Each direct mail format has varying degrees of readership, and each will be discussed in detail later. The chart that follows compares readability of the different formats.

■ *CAUTION NOTE:* *Readership varies for different direct mail formats.*

Readability Chart

Stage of Reading	Letter	Self-Mailer	Catalog	Card Deck
Scanning	Fair	Excellent	Good	Fair
Decision	Good	Good	Excellent	Good
Confirmation	Excellent	Fair	Good	Fair

Several observations can be made from this chart. Initial readership is highest for self-mailers, perhaps because they are open. The lack of an envelope gives the advertiser every opportunity to use both copy and graphics to interest readers.

Letter mailings must be opened first if their contents are to be considered. *Teaser* copy—enticements tied to the offer like "open for free magazine offer" on the envelope—can help, but the piece must not look like junk mail. Cards come with many others in a deck, so singling them out for initial readership is difficult.

■ *KEY POINT:* *Self-mailers get highest initial readership.*

Readership in the decision stage is excellent for catalogs, especially if they contain enticing descriptions that explain how products can be used. The other mailing formats also hold up well for strong visual identification.

■ *KEY POINT:* *Catalogs hold readership best during the decision stage.*

In the confirmation stage, reading is highest in the letter mailing. This may account for its popularity—it works. Again we must note, however, that the letter mailing must be opened. Someone who goes to the effort of opening the letter is a more committed reader. Catalogs do well in the confirmation stage, too, especially when they editorialize on how products can be used. Complete readership falls off for self-mailers and card decks because of the increased amount of design necessary for these formats.

■ *KEY POINT:*   *Letter mailings rank highest in overall readability.*

USING BENEFITS WHEN 5
WRITING DIRECT MAIL
COPY

In this chapter we will see how to use benefits when we write copy to get prospects to read, make a decision, and act on their decision.

THE COPYWRITER'S FIRST JOB IS TO GAIN READERSHIP

The job of gaining readership falls on the shoulders of the copywriter. He or she is the salesperson who must get the decision. This may seem like an immense task, but basic tools make the job easier.

■ *KEY POINT:* *The copywriter does the work of the salesperson.*

The copywriter's writing style does not matter. The main thing is to say as much as possible about benefits, so that prospects can identify elements that are of personal value. We must say these things straight out, as fast as possible, to give readers lots of reasons for following through with what we want them to do.

■ *CAUTION NOTE:* *Copywriting style is of minor importance.*
■ *KEY POINT:* *Give readers lots of reasons to make decisions.*

As we've learned, readers skip around a lot. They start off reading defensively, to say "no." Readers know you want them to decide something, but they don't like to make decisions, because that means cutting off alternatives. Nobody likes to make decisions. Once we buy one kind of lawnmower, or car, or boat, we won't be able to buy another kind for several years. We're stuck with our decision.

■ *CAUTION NOTE:*   *Nobody likes to make decisions because then they're stuck with them.*

IDENTIFY UNIQUE PRODUCT BENEFITS AND ALSO UNIVERSAL APPEAL OF THE BENEFITS

In writing about the benefits of a particular product, we must also identify the universal emotional appeals that make people buy. This sounds as if we're talking out of both sides of our mouth—universal emotional appeals versus the benefits of a particular product—but both are necessary. The benefits of a particular product will give some prospects emotional satisfaction that other prospects would gain from other products. In that sense, the need for emotional satisfaction is universal.

It's a twofold problem: highlight benefits that are unique to our product but universal, and target these benefits to prospects who will feel emotionally satisfied by what those benefits offer.

Thus when we write copy, we make sure we highlight the unique benefits of our product while also appealing as universally as we can to prospects who may already be interested in what the product will do for them.

STIMULATING COPY REDUCES THE PROSPECTS' FEAR OF RISK

One of the biggest tasks copywriters have is to reduce the prospects' sense of risk in making a decision. If risk is not removed from the prospect's mind, nothing will be sold.

■ *KEY POINT:*   *Gain readership by removing risk.*

Often people don't make decisions because doing so appears to be too difficult. People just say to themselves "Oh, I'd rather not do that right now." They feel the risk, they feel scared. We can counter this feeling by offering something easy and interesting to read.

But we must never overwhelm readers. We must never tell them how great our company is, or how many things the gadget we are selling can do. If we inundate them with features, they won't bother to read our copy.

■ *CAUTION NOTE: Don't overwhelm readers with uninteresting information.*

Prospects must be seduced. Start by stimulating them. Appeal to their dreams. Enchant them. Don't be afraid to touch on fantasies; this is fair if it ties into what you are offering. Stimulating copy helps get more copy read. And reading in turn leads to a decision.

■ *KEY POINT: Getting the prospect to read with stimulating copy is the first step in getting a decision.*

THE COPYWRITER'S GOAL IS TO GET A DECISION

The copywriter's ultimate objective is to get the prospect to make a decision. The decision may be a reply through the mail with an order for a specific product, or a donation, depending on the solicitation.

■ *KEY POINT: The objective of the copywriter is to get a decision.*

Often prospects may not be deciding on a product but only on one step toward buying it. The response could be a telephone call or even a request that a salesperson call. Your objective is a decision of some kind, and everything must revolve around getting it, whatever format you use.

■ *KEY POINT: All copy revolves around getting a decision.*

The basic tool copywriters use to get decisions from prospects is the

benefit statement. We talked earlier about benefits and how they motivate people. Now we will see how they are used in copy, first to buy
readership and then to gain a decision and response.

BENEFITS MUST BE TARGETED, UNDERSTANDABLE, AND CONVINCING

Benefits must first be targeted to the right prospect. We can have the
most exciting copy, describing the best benefits of our product, in the
fanciest full-color mailing package, but the mailing piece will die if it's
opened by people who are not prospects for our product or service. Our
prospects must have a preexisting interest in the benefits our product
provides.

■ *KEY POINT:* *Target benefits to prospects who already have an interest.*

A brochure for a seminar that says "You will gain the technical background necessary for understanding energy conservation by this review
of peak heating and air conditioning loss using bin method load curves"
will appeal only to an energy conservation engineer, not to home owners trying to save on fuel costs.

The chapter on selecting prospect lists examines targeting in more
detail. For now we must realize that our copy has to be written for that
hypothetical prospect who is already interested in what we offer. The
copywriter's task is to tie the benefits of a particular product to the individual needs of already interested prospects.

Benefits must also be understandable. Copy must be written so that
what the benefits do is absolutely clear. Our sales message must be targeted to readers who will understand its meaning. In the energy conservation example mentioned, home owners are not likely to understand or
care what heat loss curves are. Keep copy clear and direct it to the right
reader.

■ *KEY POINT:* *Copy on benefits must be written so that prospects can
understand it.*

For example, copy from *National Geographic* used to sell children's
books to parents reads, "BOOKS FOR YOUNG EXPLORERS are thrill-

ing true-life adventures specially created for 4- through 8-year-olds. . . .
Your children will have a ringside view as a sea otter anchors itself for
the night in a floating bed of kelp."

Understandable? Yes, at least for parents who want to broaden their
children's intellectual horizons. Complicated? Not at all. No academic
wrote those words. They were written by a copywriter who knows how
to sell!

Benefits must also be promised. It is not good enough to mention
them. They must be guaranteed. There can be no question in our prospects' minds that if they buy the product or service they will get those
benefits.

■ *KEY POINT:* **Benefits must be promised.**

"Your satisfaction is guaranteed. Send no money now. You will be
billed. . . ." "You have our guarantee that should *Consumer Reports* ever
fail to meet your needs, you may cancel and receive a complete refund
for all undelivered issues." Such statements promise buyers that they
will be satisfied.

POSITION BENEFITS WITH A SELLING STRATEGY

Even if benefits, targeted to the right prospects, are understandable
and guaranteed, they must also be communicated by a strategy that
positions them in the minds of our prospects. In other words, we must
have a logical way to present benefits to our prospects so they will accept them.

■ *KEY POINT:* **Benefits must be positioned to convince the prospect of their
value.**

Our strategy has four aims: (1) to get our prospects' attention, (2) to
develop their interest, (3) to get them to make a decision, and (4) to get
them to follow up with a response.

■ *KEY POINT:* **Position benefits by (1) getting attention, (2) developing
interest, (3) getting a decision, and (4) getting a follow-up.**

The basic strategy for getting attention is to focus on strong benefits that will appeal to prospects on an intangible, emotional level. Benefits must make a mundane product seem spectacular and make prospects believe the product can add magic and style to their lives.

■ *KEY POINT:*   *Get attention with strong benefits.*

The copy should then offer stimulating blocks of information that will enchant prospects, so they will continue reading and become interested. Copy must connect the benefits, even continue the magic started by them.

■ *KEY POINT:*   *Develop interest through stimulating information.*

Finally, you want to get a decision. Prospects are asked to "accept a free premiere issue . . . send no money, and be billed later." It's almost too good to be true, almost risk free, they think. For the right prospects, those with desire and money, it's an appeal that will work.

■ *KEY POINT:*   *Get decisions by making your offer easy and risk free.*

Copy should flow in this way: first, large benefits to gain attention; then, supporting descriptions to develop interest and lead to a decision; and finally, a closing message that asks firmly for the order. Figure 5.1 gives an example.

COPY INTRODUCES PRIMARY, SECONDARY, AND COMPARATIVE BENEFITS

Now that we've discussed general elements that characterize all benefits, let's look at three different types of benefits with which the copywriter works.

Primary Benefits

Primary benefits are the major things our product or service does for a prospect. They are the result of owning or using a particular product

ART & ANTIQUES

89 Fifth Avenue
New York, New York 10003

You are cordially invited
to receive the premiere issue of the
brilliant, new

A R T   &   A N T I Q U E S

the first and only magazine
that blends beauty and brains,
magic and meaning, style and substance,
to help you understand and appreciate
all dimensions of the fine and the decorative arts....

This is your opportunity
to send for your first issue <u>FREE</u>
as a preferred subscriber.

Dear Friend,

If you're passionately fond of art and yearn to better
understand what you see;

If you've tried to read some of those impenetrable academic
art analyses, but were put off by lofty language that confused,
rather than clarified;

If you've had enough of the fads, fashions, hype, and trendiness
that have become so much a part of the art scene these days;

I have good news for you. It's called ART & ANTIQUES, the
magazine that is at once beautiful and bright, a delight for the
eye and the mind, a magnificent showcase of the fine and the
decorative arts, that is at the same time intelligent, articulate,
clearly written, provocative, and stimulating.

If this combination of style and substance
intrigues you, maybe ART & ANTIQUES is the
magazine you've been looking for. And maybe
I've written to the right person.

In a moment, I'll explain how you can get the premiere issue
of ART & ANTIQUES on a complimentary basis and find out at our
risk (not your own) how valuable this elegant magazine can be to
you. But first let me sketch in a little background....

Imagine, if you would, a magazine that is magnificently
designed, beautifully illustrated in vibrant color, produced with

Figure 5.1 See how this copy flows—first getting attention, then developing interest, then stimulating desire, and finally calling for action. (Courtesy *Art & Antiques*)

all of the care and attention you'd expect to find in a fine and rare book.

You're imagining ART & ANTIQUES.

Now, in your mind's eye, picture a magazine that discusses the fine and the decorative arts in clear and lively language. With texts from some of today's leading novelists, poets, historians, scholars, journalists, even other artists — always superbly written and edited, and dazzlingly informative.

That's ART & ANTIQUES, too.

The truth is, ART & ANTIQUES gives you the best of both worlds, so you have something that is beautiful to look at and important to think about. It's like no other magazine you've ever read or seen.

This extraordinary exhibition-in-print, oversized, in a grand-scale format to take a position of prominence in your home, is bound with the care and perfection of a keepsake edition that you will refer to for years to come.

The design and photography are unparalleled in American publishing, with an award-winning staff of art directors and editors taking meticulous pains to be certain every inch of this grand magazine is perfectly phrased and magnificently presented.

Through this powerful combination, you'll take tour after unforgettable tour of the past, present, and future of painting, drawing, graphic arts, photography, book design, sculpture, and more. You'll get fresh insights on objets d'art, folk art, antiques from every period, furniture design, even architecture.

And, in each issue, you'll read fascinating profiles of the artistic powers-that-be, notes on auctions and museum events, market information for collectors, historical news for preservationists, and editorials that strongly call for a reaffirmation of excellence in every aspect of the fine and the decorative arts.

In short, ART & ANTIQUES will become your guide to the highest achievements of civilization...your companion in celebrating all things beautiful and of true quality.

Take a look at this sampling of what you'll be reading in the premiere issue of ART & ANTIQUES:

LOUIS AUCHINCLOSS ON HENRY JAMES AND JOHN SINGER SARGENT

A visit back in time to the day of the drawing room and the salon where the ladies of society were captured in prose by Henry James and on canvas by one of America's most prominent artists, John Singer Sargent.

Figure 5.1 (Continued)

GOODNIGHT,SWEET PRINCE: THE STATE BEDS OF ENGLAND

In the great English country houses a room was always reserved and kept ready, in case the reigning monarch should deign to pay a social call. A symbol of wealth, status, and grandeur, the state bed is rich in history — and gossip!

MIMBRES POTTERY: MESSAGES FROM A LOST WORLD

A lost civilization, high on the cliffs above the scorching deserts of the Southwest, faced with untold adversity, fashioned its everyday utensils and ritual artifacts with consummate artistry. Recently unearthed and examined here for the first time, these clay pieces are haunting reminders of man's quest for the beautiful and the sacred.

FROM FAUVE TO FASHION

An intriguing rediscovery of Raoul Dufy's little-known work in the decorative arts. Beyond his too pretty paintings of harbors and racetracks, his most fascinating work — wild and abstract fashion designs — clothed the most glamorous women of his day.

THE CASE OF THE MISSING ORMOLU

When the Getty Museum bid $1.7 million for the Louis XV ormolu corner cupboard by Jacques Dubois, the art world gasped. Where had it been all these years? Who owned it when? Now the Getty's curator of the decorative arts unravels the mystery surrounding the provenance of this much photographed but seldom seen masterpiece.

THE BALTHUS RIDDLE

The jury is still out on Balthus, the Polish-born aristocrat, whose paintings — many of suggestively posed pubescent girls — have divided even the most informed critics for thirty years. Was he a master of hidden meaning or a shameless charlatan? Now, as the Metropolitan Museum of Art gears up for a major retrospective, one of our leading writers, Peter Schjeldahl, offers his own trenchant assessment.

And this is just a taste of the kind of articles and features you'll be reading in every issue of ART & ANTIQUES....We'll review the rise of Empire furniture; take a look inside the remarkable Florentine villa of the great collector, Sir Harold Acton; marvel at the eccentric family of patrons, the Clarks of Cooperstown (who were instrumental in creating the Museum of Modern Art and the Baseball Hall of Fame!).

Month after month, ART & ANTIQUES will bring you the best of the world of fine and decorative arts — an objet d'art recently discovered, a fresh new insight on a beloved Old Master, exhibitions never seen before on these shores.

Figure 5.1 (Continued)

Doesn't this sound like the magazine you've been
looking for? One that preserves the intrinsic
excitement of fine art and generates some of its
own? That captures the magic and the meaning of
the decorative arts. That challenges your
intellect, stimulates your imagination, and
helps you sharpen your critical abilities.

ART & ANTIQUES will give you the background and
cultivate the sensibilities you need to make
your own judgments and decisions with greater
confidence. Could you possibly ask more — or
get more — from a magazine of fine art?

Yes, one more thing: a rewarding aesthetic experience. You'll
get that from ART & ANTIQUES, too, as you'll see in the enclosed
brochure, a colorful preview of what's to come in this elegant
new magazine.

So why not take a moment, right now, to accept your free premiere
issue of the new ART & ANTIQUES?

SEND NO MONEY TODAY. Just return the enclosed
order card in the postpaid envelope provided.
We'll send your FREE issue, enroll you as a
preferred introductory subscriber, and bill you
for just $19.95 for the year.

You get your free issue plus nine additional
issues. Ten fascinating and beautiful issues
in all. But only if we hear from you right away!

There's absolutely no risk on your part. If you're not delighted
with ART & ANTIQUES, keep your FREE premiere issue and write cancel
on your bill. That will be the end of it. But my guess is that
this is just the beginning. Because I think you're going to love
ART & ANTIQUES and, frankly, I can't wait to send you our premiere
issue.

I look forward to hearing from you.

Sincerely,

Wick Allison

Wick Allison
Publisher

P.S. — This introductory offer for preferred readers can't be
offered indefinitely. Reserve your premiere issue today.

Figure 5.1 (Continued)

with particular features. They appear to be part of the product we are selling.

■ *KEY POINT:* **Primary benefits give the prospect something of value.**

We highlight primary benefits at the beginning of our sales copy to draw attention to important parts of the sales message.

Every product has four or five primary benefits. For example, the benefits of a book on saving business taxes might be "comprehensive listing of hundreds of tax-saving techniques," "all in one volume," "easy-to-understand language," and "scores of shelters, loopholes, little-known tax tips."

These benefits are the major ones because they appeal to prospects who wish to be better off by saving money on taxes, and who want secret information few others know. They are made to seem universal in the minds of prospects who need the features offered by a particular product.

■ *KEY POINT:* **Benefits appear universal to those who need product features.**

Secondary Benefits

Secondary benefits refer to minor features of the product or service and are used in reinforcing the argument. They are usually the main body of the sales message, and can be accentuated by graphics or used as topic sentences in each paragraph. They are also used to draw the eye to important parts of the copy.

Secondary benefits follow primary benefits. Continuing the last example, they might be "58 sources of tax-free income," "how to get your best salary," "how to make $250,000 and avoid. . . ." The secondary benefits can number 8 to 20, depending on the product.

■ *KEY POINT:* **Secondary benefits add weight to the sales message.**

Comparative Benefits

Comparative benefits are a subtype of secondary benefit. They compare the product with other products offered by competing companies. They are important, because in today's competitive world we have to position our products against other similar ones. Even though one advantage of direct mail is that individual mailings do not usually compete with one another, prospects still compare products. We deal with this by using comparative benefits.

■ *KEY POINT: Comparative benefits position our products against the competition's.*

Copy about comparative benefits, however, must never knock competitors, especially not by name. A *Reader's Digest* survey found that the company being slammed is better remembered than the company doing the slamming. One strategy is to build up competitors. This creates an honest, straightforward image. We don't say anything derogatory. Rather we build them up, and then we sit on their shoulders.

■ *CAUTION NOTE: Never knock competitors.*

■ *KEY POINT: Build competitors up, then compare favorably with them.*

For example, "Most food processors are chrome plated with high-speed motors, but our Model 400 is solid stainless steel with a nonwearing ball-bearing motor for lifetime service." This builds up the competition but allows us to compare ourselves favorably with them. This is the best way to position our benefits above those of competitors.

Comparative benefits are also used in charts, graphs, and tables. These devices help prospects visualize what we are saying about our product and how it compares with other products. Charts, graphs, and tables give us a double whammy of salesmanship, because we can also add a caption that repeats our offer and asks for a decision.

■ *KEY POINT: Put captions summarizing the offer under charts of comparative benefits.*

ENGAGE PROSPECTS WITH A HEADLINE OF THE MAJOR BENEFIT

Copywriters should start with a *headline* that gives readers a benefit, a major what's-in-it-for-me up front. Such a headline may open a letter, splash across a brochure, or accentuate a point in a catalog or card deck. Whatever the format, the headline puts in capsule form the most important benefit of the product or service. Headlines are usually 10 to 25 words long: Stay away from the short headline used in awareness advertising.

■ *KEY POINT:*   **Start with a long headline highlighting the major benefit.**

Put the best benefit in your headline, and hit it hard. People won't read very long, but they'll grab that headline, so make sure it tells everything about the best benefit. "Now—you can begin an executive self-development program without spending a lot of time or money." "Take the mystery out of reading financial statements." "Order this book to help you carve a bigger slice of the rich $140 billion direct mail market."

All of these are headlines that get right to the point. They give the benefits and tell your readers what you are offering. They tell them happiness is in it for them, the happiness they will gain from the benefits your product will give them.

■ *KEY POINT:*   **Put happiness in your headline.**

PACK BENEFITS INTO LONG COPY

As mentioned earlier, copywriters will fail to reach prospects if they talk in terms of a product's features. This is like talking about what is in it for us, the sellers. Features do not stimulate people to buy because they offer nothing. Features do not get buyers to make decisions.

■ *CAUTION NOTE:*   **Features don't get decisions.**

Getting decisions is what copywriting is all about. Copywriters succeed by weighing copy down with a lot of benefits to cut through prospects' natural resistance. The more weight, the better. You have only this one time to tell prospects what's good for them.

■ *KEY POINT:*   **Copy must get decisions from prospects.**

Thus the direct mail copywriter constantly tries to squeeze in one more benefit, even if it's on a separate piece of paper: "If you decide not to buy this special offer of Bag Balm, please read this. . . ."

■ *KEY POINT: The heavier the weight of reasons for buying, the better.*

Generally, the longer the copy, the better the product or service sells. People who want your product will read through your copy to confirm their initial thought that your product is right for them, and to find new reasons for buying.

■ *KEY POINT: The longer the copy in direct mail, the better it sells the product.*

As we saw in the readership pyramid in Chapter 4, prospects first scan our material to see if it interests them. If it does, then and only then do they actually begin reading copy. At this point they already want the product. However, you can change their decision if you don't say enough or give enough benefits of the product. So add more copy. You need to give many reasons to buy to outweigh a potential "no" decision.

■ *CAUTION NOTE: Many benefits are needed to outweigh a "no" decision.*

Two exceptions to long copy must be noted. If you are generating leads to be followed up later, don't use a long message. You don't want to put your whole sales story in the copy because then you'll have nothing left to talk about when you finally meet with prospects. Second, in fund raising it is difficult to keep up the essential emotional fervor for any length of time. Concentrating on a single emotional reason works best in fund-raising pieces (Figure 5.2).

■ *CAUTION NOTE: Exceptions to long copy are mailings used for sales leads or for fund raising.*

Massachusetts Easter Seal Society

30 Highland Street, Worcester, MA 01609 (617) 757-2756

Michael S. Robertson
President

Dear Friend:

Oh, what a little love can do!

Take seven-year old David, for example. He's not unlike any youngster living in your neighborhood except that he has a birth defect called spina bifida that affects his mobility.

But, because he has the special love of his parents who provide him with encouragement...

And, the love of his physicians who carefully monitor his development and progress...

As well as the love of Easter Seal therapists who insure that his rehabilitation is attainable...

He's really someone quite special!

As president of your Easter Seal Society, I can tell you that there are thousands of Davids in Massachusetts who must face life differently and with greater difficulty than perhaps you and I do. They succeed in their struggle just because of "what a little love can do."

Make your Easter Seal gift of love now and help back "fighters" like David.

Thank you,

Mike Robertson

P.S. Please use the free Easter Seals and send your gift of $5.00, $10.00 or more to me as soon as you can.

Figure 5.2 A somewhat softer close is used for this familiar worthy cause. (Courtesy Massachusetts Easter Seal Society)

DESCRIPTION MUST MAKE BENEFITS COME ALIVE

Benefits must be supported by description. We talked about benefits and description in a general way in Chapter 2. Here we'll see how description specifically relates to copywriting.

We must use description that makes people feel the product in a physical way. They must be able to see it, visualize its color, and use it in their mind's eye. "The VITA-CRUSH 460 can grind whole-kernel wheat and mix and knead it into dough for bread, so you can have it in the pans for rising and baking all within three to five minutes . . . with its controlled impact you can heat and cook gravy . . . impossible to burn, scorch, lump, or curdle . . . juices in seconds." You can feel the machine grinding and kneading. When good description makes a product come alive, it also makes the tangible intangible and, of course, vice versa (Figure 5.3).

■ *KEY POINT: Description can make benefits animated and dynamic.*

Descriptions must be oriented to benefits. "You can freeze ice cream or make juices in seconds without straining . . . from whole grain to baked bread in less than one hour." Features refer only to a product's color or temperature-control dials or other attributes. But when you say, "This heat-penetration system gives you total control over your plant environment," you present a benefit to the reader, not a function of the product. Talk about the *results* of what your product can do. That's what benefits are all about.

■ *KEY POINT: Make description tell what your product can do for prospects.*

BENEFITS CAN LEAD TO FEATURES

We said earlier that features often follow benefits. Let's say we're selling a typewriter and are targeting the college market. We know students need a large pica type style and correctable printing ribbon. We might start with something like this: "Need a typewriter with easy-to-

MAINE
ANTIQUE
DIGEST

Dear Collector:

I was at the auction where the little box was sold.

It was just 2-7/8" long and painted mustard-yellow. The lid was inscribed "From C.A., Enfield, N.H., March 1835." The bidding started at $1000. Two minutes later, the auctioneer knocked it down to a collector for $8800.

Of all the things the Shakers made, their most perfect design was the bentwood oval box with its lapped fingers held in place with copper rivets. The Shakers made the boxes in various sizes. Collectors often strive to get a full stack of graduated sizes. Painted boxes are rare, and <u>tiny documented painted boxes are the rarest of all.</u>

The collector who won the bidding told me later that he felt he had "concentrated all my Shaker collecting into that one perfect box."

The dealer who lost the bidding said, "That was exciting, let's do it again."

THE PASSION FOR PERFECTION

<u>Maine</u> <u>Antique</u> <u>Digest</u> is about the passion that inspired the maker of that little box...about the passion of the collector for the perfect box...and about the business that brings the two together, a century and a half later.

The collector's passion is more than an admiration for the past. It is the desire to enjoy--in finding, acquiring, and possessing-- the rare and now valuable artifacts with which people of earlier times surrounded themselves in daily life.

WHY <u>MAINE</u> <u>ANTIQUE</u> <u>DIGEST</u>

Sally and I bought our old house in Maine in 1958 and decided to furnish it in period pieces. We sold off some Victorian furniture (I now wish we hadn't!) that came with the house and started looking for early American--knowing nothing about antiques.

We soon found ourselves deeply involved in the antiques business, running an antique shop part-time and learning about collecting. By the time we were able to get into antiques full-time, we'd had a long time to think about the antiques and art marketplace. We realized that there was no good source of reliable news and information about the business. <u>Nobody wanted to talk about the simplest thing--prices-- and yet we found that this was the first question people asked when they came into our shop.</u>

Figure 5.3 This antiques magazine letter is laden with descriptions to interest buffs. (Courtesy *Maine Antique Digest*)

read type and correctable ribbon for typing your thesis? Our SCN 221 model will do all this and more because . . ." Then we describe some features to back up our claim.

■ *KEY POINT: Features reinforce benefits.*

Notice that the copy starts with a benefit-oriented statement and then leads to the feature. This is better than saying: "Here's a neat pica, 10-pitch typewriter that corrects so you can use it for your thesis, and it comes in three colors." At first glance, this doesn't read too badly. In fact, a lot of copy is written like this. But it doesn't hold the reader's attention as well as use of a major benefit would.

■ *CAUTION NOTE: Never start copy with features.*

When readers see the benefits, the what's-in-it-for-me, up front they will stay and read about the features that provide those benefits. But if readers start out reading about features, they may not be able to visualize what the product can do for them, and they will give up reading. Start with benefits, then lead to the features that provide those benefits.

■ *KEY POINT: **Always start copy with benefits.***

TESTIMONY AND MARKET INFORMATION SUPPORT DESCRIPTION WITH PROOF

Another problem in copywriting is that we've got to make prospects believe in our benefits. Prospects need to be reassured that the benefits that entice them are actually there. Our copy must offer proof of benefits, because prospects are afraid to take risks.

■ *KEY POINT: Proof makes benefits stick.*

There are various ways we can build proof into copy. The first, and often the most powerful, is the *testimonial*. Testimony from satisfied users strikes readers as real and convincing. "I love my VITA-CRUSH 460. I bought three for my grandchildren. . . ." "I wish to say I have never been so pleased. . . ." "No longer do I delay a Sunday afternoon project because I am missing a critical bolt. . . . In my opinion, anyone who ever picks up a screwdriver needs this nut and bolt collection." All of these, used in direct mail copy, create a strong sense of legitimacy for the benefits of the products offered.

■ **KEY POINT:**   *Testimony helps make benefits legitimate.*

Testimony should always be specific and related to the product (Figure 5.4). If it is anecdotal or entertaining, it deflects prospects from making a decision and a response. Once people start being entertained, it's hard to get them back on track to a decision. Testimony must not get in the way of decisions.

■ **KEY POINT:**   *Testimony should always be specific to product and benefits.*

■ **CAUTION NOTE:**   *Testimonials should never be entertaining.*

The next most powerful proof is *market samplings*. These resemble testimonials but are not as strong. "Hundreds of people use our software." "Thousands of people have tried the Benzomatic Torch and found out it works for them." These are samples of the many ways you can generalize information from satisfied users. They tell prospects that because the product has worked for others, it can also work for them.

Another kind of proof is the independent *laboratory statement*. "We have tested the Rocky Mountain Oyster Cracker in our laboratory and found out that it works," or "The General Council on Water Safety has decreed that the Concord-brand water purifier filters more impurities than . . ." suggests that an independent, and supposedly objective, testing facility has found proof that the claims for a product are legitimate.

Above all any material designed to reassure prospects that the benefits we offer are real should be objective. It will always appear to be more truthful if it comes from an outside or detached party. Figure 5.5 illustrates this.

The last type of proof is in-house *research data* to support our product. "Our company has found through diligent research that this can opener surpasses all . . ." gives prospects a comparative estimate of how the product performs. But since the information comes from us, it will be viewed with suspicion. Thus this is the weakest type of support.

Here's what
people are saying about

BOOKS FOR YOUNG EXPLORERS!

Every day, parents, relatives, educators, and children write National Geographic to praise Books for Young Explorers. Read just a few of their comments:

"I can't tell you how much our entire family enjoys sharing Books for Young Explorers. They're always my children's first choice when it's time to read."

Mother—Ohio

"Thank you, National Geographic, for the very important part you are playing in the lives of our grandchildren. Their bright, receptive minds have taken full advantage of these wonderful books."

Grandparents—Missouri

"You will be pleased to know that I hardly have time to process and re-shelve Books for Young Explorers without eager little hands reaching for each volume. The children love them."

Librarian—California

"We like those books you write. Kids bring them from home and our teacher reads them to us. We especially like the pictures."

First Grade Class—Ohio

"Several years ago, I ordered Books for Young Explorers for the children in my classes. Their interest in reading soared!"

Teacher—New York

"Thank you, National Geographic! You are nice to take the time to make such great books for kids."

Youngster—Maryland

"The children are always excited when there is one Book for Young Explorers left on the shelf."

Librarian—Mississippi

"Congratulations on this excellent set of books. I'd also like to thank you for the More About . . . booklet that comes with each set. It's very useful."

Parent—Ontario, Canada

PRINTED IN U.S.A.

Figure 5.4 What others say is powerful testimony. National Geographic uses testimonials effectively. (Courtesy National Geographic Society)

Lynda Ehrlich
READING CONSULTANT

Dear Friend,

    As a teacher and reading specialist, I can't stress often enough the important role you play in developing positive attitudes toward reading — early in your child's life.

    Studies have shown that when young children are encouraged to view reading as a natural, enjoyable home activity, they will develop strong reading skills by the time they reach the age of ten.

    And you'll find no better means of instilling an early love of reading in youngsters than BOOKS FOR YOUNG EXPLORERS!

    These high-quality publications generate the kind of excitement necessary to capture the natural interest, curiosity, and enthusiasm of children four through eight. The lively, full-color illustrations and stimulating text of BOOKS FOR YOUNG EXPLORERS are specially designed to attract — and hold — the attention of young readers, to encourage them to ask questions, and to discover more about their world.

    BOOKS FOR YOUNG EXPLORERS make learning fun! That's why I was so pleased when the National Geographic Society asked for my assistance in preparing this new series.

    I saw how subjects were selected for testing and then chosen by youngsters themselves. I worked with researchers, writers, and editors during every stage of the books' production.

    As you and your children look through these four new animal adventures, I know you'll be as impressed as I am with the careful planning, creativity, and hard work that have gone into each book.

    I urge you to share these exceptional books with your favorite youngsters. Take advantage of National Geographic's free-examination privilege. Then sit down with your children...and watch their excitement grow with the turn of every new page.

    You'll be satisfied in knowing that you're giving your children a lifelong advantage — a lasting love of reading.

Sincerely,

Lynda Ehrlich
Reading Consultant

Figure 5.5 Testimonial letters can also be from "objective" observers like this reading specialist. They add credibility. (Courtesy National Geographic Society)

■ *KEY POINT: Laboratory, market, and research data are seen as more biased than testimonials.*

Any kind of proof—testimonials, laboratory reports, market information—must be specific to the product. All proofs are often viewed by prospects as being biased in favor of the seller, or even deceptive. To help dispel these notions, they must reinforce what you're saying about the product.

BASIC COPYWRITING STRATEGIES 6

In the last chapter we saw how benefits increase readership. This chapter explores the do's and don'ts of basic copywriting for all direct mail formats. In the following chapter we will apply what we have learned to the writing of the direct mail letter.

DO WRITE TO A READER WITH NEED

In the last chapter we saw how important it is to target our sales message to the right prospects—those who need what we offer and have money to pay for it. This point cannot be emphasized too much. Our job as copywriters is to write to the right prospects. All our copy must be directed at them.

The readership chart (Figure 4.1 in Chapter 4) showed that only 20% of any group to whom we send our mail will actually take the first step to reading it: Only 20% will scan what we have to offer, even if 100% have a preexisting interest!

The point is: Why write to the 80% who won't read our mail anyway? If we write to try to win a large readership, our sales message tends to get argumentative, because we are trying to overcome the resistance of readers who are not all that interested in what we have to offer.

■ *CAUTION NOTE: Don't write copy for the 80% who don't read direct mail anyway.*

Too often direct mail copy tries to appeal to everybody. Argumentative and feature-oriented copy is the wrong strategy for direct mail. It's a holdover from general advertising, in which advertisers want only to make people aware, not sell them.

■ *CAUTION NOTE: Never argue with readers.*

Write to readers as if they have a definite need for what you are offering. Tell the 20% why they should buy your product or service; give them reasons. That's what copywriting is all about.

■ *KEY POINT: Write copy for the 20% who have a need and will read your copy.*

Writing for the 20% keeps your copy on the positive side, because you don't have to berate the reader. You can give reasons for people to buy, and these are what they look for.

■ *KEY POINT: Those who open direct mail look for reasons to buy.*

DON'T WASTE VALUABLE COPY SPACE ANSWERING OBJECTIONS

Another mistaken strategy too often used in direct mail is use of copy to answer objections. In personal face-to-face selling, a salesperson must always be ready to answer objections. In fact, in live selling objections often indicate that prospects are interested in the product but need reassurance. After all, prospects who have strong objections don't give salespersons the time of day.

The same holds for direct mail: Recipients with serious objections don't even bother to open the mail, let alone read it. They're part of the 80%.

■ *CAUTION NOTE: Prospects who object don't read direct mail.*

Thus if you are writing copy for the 20%, you don't need to counter objections. Because copywriters make it their business to know the product or service they're selling, they are often aware of the common objections raised by purchasers, and they think they must try to counter these in their copy. This is the worst possible strategy. Since only the interested 20% begin to read, thus qualifying themselves out of the whole group who have received the mailing piece, the mention of objections only draws the attention of our best potential buyers to problems they may not even have considered.

■ *CAUTION NOTE:* *Mentioning objections only brings them to the prospect's attention.*

And though live salespeople can deal with objections face to face, we don't have this ability in direct mail.

DO COORDINATE "TEASER" COPY WITH OFFER AND BENEFITS

Direct mail experts often disagree about how to handle *teaser* copy, the short messages that try to tease or entice the reader into opening and reading the direct mail piece. Teaser copy is often used effectively on the outside of an envelope to encourage readers to open the envelope. It can also be the introductory paragraph of a letter or a headline on a brochure or self-mailer. Teaser copy can be a message printed on a letter or brochure that can be read through a "window" in the envelope. Like the other techniques discussed here, teaser copy has been borrowed by general advertising, where it is used to gain attention.

■ *KEY POINT:* *Teaser copy is used to gain attention.*

Occasionally copywriters attempt to tell a story in teaser copy, in the belief that having prospects read a narrative increases their emotional interest. The problem is that a long story can pull attention away from the product.

■ *CAUTION NOTE:* *Beware of telling a story to gain attention.*

Our goal is to get our mail opened and read, but we already have our prospects' attention once our mailing is in their hands. Our job is to keep the attention we've gained.

We do this best by highlighting a major benefit in the headline of our mailing piece. This doesn't mean we can't use teaser copy in this headline. It does mean that if we want to sell rather than just attract attention, we must focus on something that gives emotional value to our prospect—a benefit.

■ *KEY POINT:*   *Teaser copy must focus on a benefit, a product, or an offer.*

Teaser copy works in direct mail when it introduces a benefit. It is often used effectively on the outside of an envelope to encourage readers to open the envelope.

Here are some examples of teaser copy to be avoided:

THE ONE MISTAKE NO GROWING COMPANY CAN AFFORD TO MAKE.

IF YOU USE ONLY ONE SALES TRAINING PROGRAM THIS YEAR, IT
SHOULD BE THIS ONE.

THE ONE MANAGEMENT TOOL YOU NEED MORE THAN ANY OTHER!

NEW WAYS TO BUILD YOUR COMPANY'S WEALTH.

Here are some that work:

NAME ONE PRODUCT YOU'D PAY $200 OR MORE FOR WITHOUT EVEN
SEEING WHAT IT DOES FIRST.

This works only if the offer includes free demonstrations, which it does—the product is a magazine that offers computer software demonstrations in print.

SUPPOSE YOU WERE WALKING DOWN A STREET AND SPOTTED A CRISP
$1,000 BILL LYING ON THE SIDEWALK. WOULD YOU STOP TO PICK IT UP?
OF COURSE. WHO IN HIS RIGHT MIND WOULDN'T? YET EVERY DAY,
THOUSANDS OF BUSINESS OWNERS PASS UP $1,000 TAX SHELTER
OPPORTUNITIES. . . .

This is an analogy that works. The copy is tied to the offer, a proposal for sheltering taxes.

> MAKE THE TRADITIONAL CHOICE IN HORSE FEED . . . PURINA OMOLENE.
> BUY ONE, GET ONE FREE!

This works well only if readers are in the market for horse feed. But it's specific, and there's no question about what is being offered.

> IT WAS THE SOUND OF HIS VOICE THAT FIRST CAUGHT HER ATTENTION,
> TUGGED AT HER AWARENESS. A DEEP, DARK-TIMBERED VOICE THAT
> ELICITED A CURIOUS DESIRE TO FOLLOW IT AND DISCOVER THE MAN TO
> WHOM IT BELONGED. . . .

A story, yes, but one that works because the offer is for a "romance novel." Again, the reader must be in the market.

> YOU MAY ALREADY OWN THIS HUNTING AND FISHING LODGE . . . BUT
> THE ONLY WAY TO CLAIM IT IS TO OPEN THIS LETTER.

Obviously, a sweepstakes-style offer, but one that works.

> ENCLOSED ARE YOUR *SIX ENTRY NUMBERS,* AND EACH HAS AN EQUAL
> CHANCE OF WINNING A PRIZE IN THIS BIG NEW $100,000 GIVEAWAY.

Again, sweepstakes. It does get these envelopes opened. Rumor has it, however, that the public is tiring of extravagant sweepstakes offers.

> FREE HAVANA CIGAR OFFER INSIDE.

Of course, only cigar smokers or people who know cigar smokers will look inside, but both groups will want to see what is said about the offer.

> READ ABOUT A "NECESSITY" OF LIFE MANY PEOPLE FORGET. AND HOW
> THOUSANDS OF MATURE MEN AND WOMEN TAKE ADEQUATE CARE OF
> THEIR LIFE INSURANCE NEEDS FOR $6.95 A MONTH.

Explicit, stating the full offer.

> YOU ARE OVERPAYING BY 30% TO 70% ALMOST EVERY TIME YOU FLY.
> READ MY PROOF BELOW AND DISCOVER HOW THE ENCLOSED FREE
> CERTIFICATE CAN SAVE YOU UP TO 70% ON MOST BUSINESS FLIGHTS
> WITH FEW OR NO RESTRICTIONS.

Again, gives the essence of the offer. Only details follow.

DON'T USE COPY THAT SEEKS TO VALIDATE ITS SPONSORS

Stay away from copy that tells readers how great your company is or employees are unless you are fund raising and have a famous name that will attract readers' attention. Actor Glenn Ford let his name be used on an emotion-filled six-page letter soliciting funds for the Simon Wiesenthal Center (Figure 6.1). Though we may all agree on the issues raised in the letter, Ford's name lends credibility to the actual organization. Most of the time, however, the 20% who read our offer don't care how large or reliable we are, or who is on our board of directors.

■ *CAUTION NOTE: Avoid copy that seeks to legitimate your copy and staff.*

The only prospects interested in copy about who you are are necessarily those with motivation enough to buy your product. With self-oriented copy, you will weaken your basic message. Furthermore, like the mistake of answering objections, it can raise the question of legitimacy with readers who wouldn't have questioned it in the first place.

■ *CAUTION NOTE: Never raise the question of your company's or product's legitimacy.*

DON'T USE COPY THAT TELLS HOW THE PRODUCT WAS DEVELOPED

It is also a mistake to write copy explaining how the product was developed. Rarely is this information related to the offer or to any benefits.

Background information does nothing to support the selling effort and does little to maintain prospects' interest. History is like features: Neither does much good unless it provides benefits.

■ *CAUTION NOTE: Avoid explanations of how a product was developed.*

Recounting the history of a product can be appropriate when you

Glenn Ford

* THE NAZIS DID NOT SYSTEMATICALLY EXTERMINATE SIX MILLION JEWS AND MILLIONS OF NON-JEWS.

* THE OVENS IN NAZI CONCENTRATION CAMPS WERE USED ONLY TO BAKE BREAD, NOT TO CREMATE PEOPLE.

* THE POISON GAS IN THE CAMPS WAS USED ONLY TO KILL LICE, NOT PEOPLE.

* THE THOUSANDS OF BOOKS ABOUT THE HOLOCAUST ARE BASED ON FALSIFIED INFORMATION AND PHOTOS.

* ANNE FRANK'S DIARY WAS A FRAUD.

* TESTIMONIES AT THE HISTORIC NUREMBERG WAR-CRIMES TRIALS WERE COERCED AND UNTRUE.

* ADOLF EICHMANN'S TRIAL WAS A FRAME-UP BY THE JEWISH PEOPLE.

* THE HOLOCAUST IS A HOAX PERPETRATED ON THE WORLD BY JEWISH PROPAGANDISTS.

Dear Friend,

As one of the first Americans to enter Dachau after World War II, I can personally attest to the fact that the above statements are blatant lies. The scenes of horror I witnessed at that concentration camp will haunt me forever. So when I hear such preposterous claims whitewashing Nazi brutality, I am enraged. And I find it frightening to believe that anyone could believe these outrageous lies. But the fact remains that these lies are beginning to be believed.

The seeds of doubt about the existence of the Holocaust have been planted and are already taking root in the minds of many, especially that 60% of the world's population born after

(over, please)

Simon Wiesenthal Center
9760 West Pico Boulevard Los Angeles, California 90035

Figure 6.1 A famous name lends credence to this strong emotional appeal. (Courtesy Simon Wiesenthal Fund)

need to legitimate its value. For example, the Bradford Exchange sells commemorative plates designed by Norman Rockwell. It is entirely appropriate for the Exchange to talk about the history of the ceramic firm and the moulding and firing techniques it uses, because these add credibility to the plate offer.

Another exception is when we need to give readers a particular understanding of a product's creator. If we see this person as an alive, warm human being like ourselves the benefits of the offer tend to be enhanced. For example, "One of the secrets of the magazine is our editor, a pleasant chap with some gray in his hair, a twinkle in his eye, and his tongue in his cheek. Perhaps we should also mention the world of experience under his belt. He's the kind of fellow you love to have a chat with," gives the reader an excellent word-picture of who the editor is.

DO PUNCTUATE YOUR COPY WITH DETAIL

Detail is what gives our sales message credibility. It shows our readers that what we say is backed by knowledge and understanding of our product. Detail heightens story content (Figure 6.2).

■ *KEY POINT:*   *Use detail to enhance credibility in copy.*

For example, here's the beginning of a letter offering an outdoor magazine.

Dear Friend,

Some might regard his behavior as strange, dismiss him as a daredevil, perhaps, But you, I think, would understand.

His name is Neal Watson, a man who has demonstrated, time and time again, Hemingway's definition of courage: grace under pressure.

On October 14, 1968, near Freeport, off the island of Grand Bahama, he dived to a record depth of 437 feet, using scuba gear. Since then, at least twelve others have attempted to break that record. All have perished.

Diving below 200 feet requires a diver to take into account narcosis—Cousteau's rapture of the deep. At 200 feet, the nitrogen in compressed air goes into the brain and becomes a powerful hallucinogen. At 300 feet, the oxygen component of compressed air, too, becomes toxic—depriving a diver of the simplest skills, sometimes bringing unconsciousness, convulsions, and death.

Defying these dangers, Watson succeeded in setting a new world diving record. And what he experienced, at 437 feet down, may explain . . .

HORIZON

P.O. Drawer 30, Tuscaloosa, Alabama 35402

```
*   *   *   *   *   *   *   *   *   *   *   *   *   *   *   *   *   *
*    If you will accept my invitation to preview    *
*    a free, introductory issue of HORIZON....I      *
*    will reserve a special discount subscription
*    in your name that is a substantial savings     *
*    from the regular price should you decide to     *
*    become a regular reader.
*                                                    *
*                                                    *
*                              Gray D. Boone          *
*                                                    *
*   *   *   *   *   *   *   *   *   *   *   *   *   *   *   *   *   *
```

Dear Reader:

You're aware of a wonderful new trend, just as I am because...

> ...when 3,000 people buy $75 tickets to
> attend a performance by Mikhail
> Baryshnikov in Jackson, Mississippi

> ...when SRO crowds jam New York's
> Lincoln Center for a chamber music
> concert

> ...when more people attend dance performances
> in one year than NFL football games

...it's undeniable that we are witnessing a veritable explosion
of interest and participation in the arts across America.

Only <u>one</u> publication captures the essence of this dramatic movement. Its talented editors continue to draw forth relationships in
the world of drama, music, painting, architecture, literature, film,
television, photography, sculpture and more. Each page is filled with
absorbing features on every aspect of contemporary and historical
artistic achievement.

<u>That one magazine is HORIZON</u>.

To open your home to the same delights experienced by our present
readers, I would like to send you, with my compliments,

> <u>a free preview issue of HORIZON...and reserve</u>
> <u>a special discount subscription in your name-</u>
> <u>at a substantial savings over the regular</u>
> <u>ten issue cover price of $20.</u>

Figure 6.2　Gobs of interesting detail flood these two pages of a four-page letter.
(Courtesy *Horizon* magazine)

Then, if you are pleased with the preview issue when your subscription reservation invoice arrives, you can choose to receive
the additional 9 issues due.

In that case, simply submit your payment and mail it in the
postage-paid reply envelope we'll provide with your invoice.

You also have the option of deciding not to subscribe but just
to keep the free preview issue. If so, mark "cancel" on the invoice
when you return it and that will end the matter.

With your wide ranging interest in the arts you are sure to
enjoy features like these from recent issues....

- The Forbidden Paintings of D.H. Lawrence
- Genesis of Radio's Immortal Lone Ranger
- Twenty Museums You've Never Heard Of
- The Luminous Literary Ghosts of Bloomsbury
- Repertory Theater Follies in New York
- John Cage: Music's Grand Old Radical
- Innovative Choreographer Laura Dean
- Art & Politics: Armand Hammer vs. Bill Buckley
- Pulitzer Winner Lanford Wilson captivates Broadway

HORIZON explores the minds of the world's most fascinating per-
sonalities in the visual and performing arts like....

.....Pavlova...fifty years gone yet her legend lives on...more
than any other person spreading dance to the corners of
the world.

....."She eats light," says her producer in the television
series "East of Eden." And she's bruised all over from
playing Mozart's wife in Amadeus. Jane Seymour, talented,
beautiful, and indefatigable, has arrived in America.

.....intense Michael Cimino, whose original concept and
direction resulted in the film The Deer Hunter, the Oscar-
winning film which many have designated as the "final
statement" on an unpopular Asian war.

.....buoyant Angela Lansbury who, in contrast to her high-
kicking character Mame, describes her new Broadway
success in Sweeney Todd as "the hardest piece I've ever
had to play."

Figure 6.2 (Continued)

This is dramatic copy, highlighted with the kind of detail that makes the story come alive. It gives us the quality of writing that we will expect from the magazine.

Here's another example from a mailing piece for a magazine on Americana.

> Dear Reader,
>   Welcome to the friendly world of yesterday. A world where you'll experience the authentic touch of tradition and continuity; a world where you'll—
>
> savor the taste of an elegant Colonial dinner you created with traditional, delicious recipes that might have been used in Monticello's kitchen . . .
>
> re-create an early-19th-century needlepoint sampler with authentic patterns and motifs from old New England . . .
>
> feel the pride of craft and artistry as you apply the final touches to a handsome wall sconce you made from a 200-year-old Dutch-colonial design . . .
>
> admire the marvelously detailed face of a quaint Victorian mantel clock that you discovered among the curios and antiques in a local flea market . . .

Though this letter does not offer as much detail as the first, it gives us the same impression of detail. It goes a long way to truly picturing the world of yesterday. Will it work? Yes, it will do the job as well as any other competently written copy if, and only if, it is targeted to prospects who already have some interest in the subject matter.

DO SHOW READERS, DON'T TELL THEM

Telling people how something works or how it was developed is no way to convince them of the benefits it can bring to their lives. Telling people is not the same as grabbing them emotionally.

You've got to make them see it, experience it. For example, look at how uninspiring this copy is: "There is no single great secret to taking great photographs. But there are dozens of small secrets, dozens of simple, easy-to-learn tricks and techniques that can transform an everyday snapshot into a memorable photograph." Telling prospects they can "transform an everyday snapshot into a memorable picture" doesn't give them a vivid feeling that they can do it. Telling asks for too much faith on the part of readers.

■ *CAUTION NOTE: Don't tell readers, show them.*

Our job as copywriters is to make our readers experience. For example, testimony-oriented copy could say, "I never would have believed that this picture of my grandparents vacationing at the lake that summer could have so much color and resolution. It's as if I were there with them." This copy is not perfect, but it's better than telling.

Here's another sales message that could be improved: "Like the rare and beautiful things it selects, . . . adds grace and dignity to life—for those with eyes to see, for those who are confident that they know the best and are proud of it. I suspect that you are among the discerning few who. . . ."

The word "beautiful" is usually a tip-off that the copywriters didn't know how to define what they were writing about. It's too vague. "Grace" and "dignity" are also too general. These words tell rather than show. They force readers to translate the meanings of the words to achieve understanding.

Mentions of porcelain, silver, fine linens, and crystal work best when the objects are described as specifically as possible. For example, "When opened for the first time in 2,000 years, the casket was flooded with sunlight, which gleamed on the woman's face for a moment before the fresh air ruptured her corpse into instant dust." Readers won't care about artifacts in museum storerooms if they can't feel them. Readers must feel emotional responses, and you can elicit these by being specific and showing as exactly as possible what is happening.

Similarly, fund raising should also be specific. Show that an animal digging in the sand for food in an environment rapidly being destroyed by mankind, show specific actrocities that can be solved with the donor's money. This is the way to write copy.

Make your fund-raising letter show readers by specific description just why funds are needed and what is done with the money. This gives psychological value to the donor.

DO USE STORY NARRATIVES, BUT WISELY

Most of us love stories. Stories tell us about ourselves and give us a way of verifying our humanness. Much of our advertising draws on the importance of stories.

■ *KEY POINT: Story narratives can convey feelings to the reader.*

Story narratives are often used to open a sales message. When used effectively, they help maintain our prospect's interest by showing how other people came to value a product or realized they needed it. When done well, stories provide emotional value prospects can feel.

■ *KEY POINT: Story narratives provide emotional value.*

Story narratives are not easy to write. They require more facility with words than does most copywriting, because they must give readers a feel for what the product or service offers.

Stories must never be used to tease or trick readers, nor should they detract from the main objective of copy: to maintain and build interest in the offer. If a story is too good—if it deflects interest from the offer—it should not be used. Stories must be tied directly to the benefits and the product (Figure 6.3).

■ *CAUTION NOTE: Story narratives must never deflect the prospects' attention from the offer.*

DON'T USE HUMOR

This list of do's and don'ts must include a comment on the use of humor in copy. Like a good story, we all enjoy humor. A well-told joke, a television comedy, a P. G. Wodehouse novel—each gives us pleasure. Some of the best advertising depends on humor; "I can't believe I ate the whole thing" is etched in the memories of a whole generation of television watchers.

But that is just the point: Humor is usually aimed at getting prospects' attention. Humor makes them aware of the advertisement, which makes them aware of the product.

However, since we already have the prospect's attention in direct mail, humor does not need to play that part. In fact, clumsy attempts at humor can only detract from our sales message. For example, "Your Fortune phone is loaded with the latest electronic features. . . . And, best of all, it can save you a small fortune by . . ." Doubling up on

THE WALL STREET JOURNAL.

PUBLISHED BY DOW JONES & CO.,INC. 22 CORTLANDT ST. N.Y.,N.Y. 10007

Dear Reader:

On a beautiful late spring afternoon, twenty-five years ago, two young men graduated from the same college. They were very much alike, these two young men. Both had been better than average students, both were personable and both--as young college graduates are--were filled with ambitious dreams for the future.

Recently, these men returned to their college for their 25th reunion.

They were still very much alike. Both were happily married. Both had three children. And both, it turned out, had gone to work for the same Midwestern manufacturing company after graduation, and were still there.

But there was a difference. One of the men was manager of a small department of that company. The other was its president.

What Made The Difference

Have you ever wondered, as I have, what makes this kind of difference in people's lives? It isn't always a native intelligence or talent or dedication. It isn't that one person wants success and the other doesn't.

The difference lies in what each person knows and how he or she makes use of that knowledge.

And that is why I am writing to you and to people like you about The Wall Street Journal. For that is the whole purpose of The Journal: To give its readers knowledge--knowledge that they can use in business.

A Publication Unlike Any Other

You see, The Wall Street Journal is a unique publication. It's the country's only national business daily. Each business day, it is put together by the world's largest staff of business-news experts.

Each business day, The Journal's pages include a broad range of information of interest and significance to business-minded people, no matter where it comes from. Not just stocks and finance, but anything and everything in the whole, fast-moving world of business. The Wall Street Journal gives you all the business news you need--when you need it.

Knowledge Is Power

Right now, I am reading page one of The Journal. It combines all the important news of the day with in-depth feature reporting. Every phase of business news is covered; from articles on inflation, wholesale prices, car prices, tax incentives for industries to major developments in Washington, and elsewhere.

(over, please)

Figure 6.3 See how the story is woven into the letter. "Two young men graduated from college . . ." just like WSJ hopes its readers imagine themselves. (Courtesy *The Wall Street Journal*)

92

And there is page after page inside The Journal, filled with fascinating and significant information. If you have never read The Wall Street Journal, you cannot imagine the breadth and scope of its coverage. Nor can you imagine how useful it can be to you.

Much of the information that appears in The Journal appears nowhere else. The Journal is printed in numerous plants across the United States, so that you get it early each business day.

Your Own Personal Subscription...Save 7% to 14% Off the Cover Price

Will you put our statements to the proof by subscribing for the next six months for just $47? Or you may prefer to take advantage of The Journal's better buy--two years for $174.

Simply fill in the term you wish on the order card and mail it in the postage-paid envelope provided. And here's The Journal's guarantee: Should The Journal not measure up to your expectations, you may cancel this trial arrangement at any point and receive a refund for the undelivered portion of your subscription.

If you feel as we do that this is a fair and reasonable proposition, then you will want to find out without delay if The Wall Street Journal can do for you what it is doing for more than six million readers. So please mail the enclosed order card now, and we will start serving you immediately.

About those two college classmates I mention at the beginning of this letter: They were graduated from college together and together got started in the business world. So what made their lives in business different?

Knowledge. Useful knowledge. And its application.

An Investment In Success

I cannot promise you that success will be instantly yours if you start reading The Wall Street Journal. But I can guarantee that you will find The Journal always interesting, always reliable, and always useful.

Sincerely yours,

Peter R. Kann
Vice President/Associate Publisher

PRK:rg
Encs.

P.S. It's important to note that The Journal's subscription price may be tax-deductible.

Figure 6.3 (Continued)

"fortune" may have seemed funny to the copywriter, but to readers it's an obstacle. They will have to stop reading momentarily and reconsider what was meant. Rarely can we use humor to keep reading momentum going in direct mail.

■ *CAUTION NOTE:*   *Humor often detracts from a sales message.*

DON'T USE TIRED AND HACKNEYED WORDING

As we saw in the last chapter, stimulating copy provokes interest. But if we try to write copy the easy way, by bringing in everyday slang or conversational words, our message often falls flat. Failure can also result if we try to adapt and rewrite the direct mail copy of others so it fits the benefits of our product. Purloined copy seldom, if ever, fits our own purpose.

■ *CAUTION NOTE:*   *Rewriting others' copy often means tired writing.*

Copy that relies on lazy worn-out words in an attempt to convey the emotional impact of benefits doesn't work any better in direct mail than in any other kind of advertising. In fact, hackneyed wording is the curse of copywriting.

■ *CAUTION NOTE:*   *Avoid overused, hackneyed wording.*

How many times have we seen words like "convenient," "opportunity," "valuable," "changes," "information," and others used in copy? It is not that these words are false or inaccurate, they do tell people about benefits. What they don't do is show prospects how the benefits fit into their lives. They don't make benefits come alive so prospects can feel them.

■ *CAUTION NOTE:*   *Worn-out words don't show readers how benefits fit into their lives.*

Here are some examples of tired and overused wording that have appeared in some contemporary direct mail written for large, well-known companies:

> Here's an opportunity to save—and at the same time to guarantee you receive valuable information on U.S. industry as soon as it's off the press. . . . This book is popular because it is well-planned, and conveniently organized. . . . We know you'll be satisfied with the quantity and quality of the information you receive in the . . .

It's not that the message is bad, it's that prospects have read the same expressions in many offers. Find a more stimulating way, see other examples in this book.

> I'd like to tell you about a new book to help you create the office that's just right for you—the kind of office you can design with efficiency and comfort as well as with beauty in mind.

Once you interpret, the product sounds great. But readers shouldn't have to go through that mental leap of interpreting. Explain directly, make it come alive.

> It's a well-known fact. The best . . . the fastest . . . the most effective way to increase sales is to sell to your present customers. They have faith in your salespeople. In your firm. In your products. And, in the service you provide.

Absolutely true, but the copy is telling, not showing.

> With today's high production costs of introducing new products to the marketplace, thorough searching and cross-checking of reference sources becomes even more necessary.

OK, but you're boring us with the overused words that get in the way of understanding the message.

DO KEEP COPY POSITIVE

Now that we realize we are writing only for that 20% of readers who are interested enough to scan our teaser copy and headline to see if our offer is really for them, we have no reason to be scared. We're really writing to friends—those who have selected themselves out of the masses as being interested in what we have to say. So we might as well enjoy ourselves and give them some nice things to read about. We can make our message positive, because we only have to be argumentative with those who don't seem to want to listen. That's not a problem with our "good guy" 20%.

■ *KEY POINT:* *Your copy should read as though written to a friend.*

Now that the pressure's off, relax and enjoy. Show your readers the benefits of your offer. Give them solutions, not problems. *Stay away* from negatives; they only create complications. Don't compromise your prospects so you can ride in artificially on a white horse to solve their problem. Show prospects that your product is trouble free. Avoid comparing yourself with competitors; knocking them can backfire. Rather build them up so you appear taller.

■ *KEY POINT:* *Show prospects that your product offers them a solution.*

Always keep the tone of your copy positive and uplifting. Too often copy tries to use negative situations to show prospects why they should buy a product. At first glance it seems to work; sales are good. But closer inspection may show that the negative copy didn't perform as well as another mailing that used a positive approach.

■ *KEY POINT:* *Keep the tone of copy positive.*

Negative copy may trigger questions prospects had not previously considered. For example, "Our customers are the top real estate professionals in Idaho; they not only survived, but continued to grow." Why bring up the question of "survival" at all? It only impedes the sale.

Another form of negative copywriting occasionally used even by experienced writers is pleading with prospects to read material. "Would you give this letter the next two minutes of your time, if you had reason to believe it could help you do. . . ." Asking makes for a weak start.

Here are some examples of negative and positive writing:

Negative

There's a sad atmosphere in the corporate world these days. The concrete towers in which staff executives used to practice their arcane crafts are teetering on the brink of collapse, if not already lying in ruin. The mounted bones of seat-of-the-pants line executives for whom "long-term" meant tomorrow afternoon are stuffed in dusty museum halls alongside diplodocus and triceratops. But Darwinian forces are at work and to save yourself. . .

Positive

Within the changing business world, a new breed of executive is developing, the executive who understands that solid formulas for short-term success can be coordinated with long-term strategies. An executive who knows that brilliant ideas. . .

The negative copy seems a misguided attempt to be interesting. The rewrite is confident without all the metaphors and wordiness.

Negative

The next few years will see a gigantic leap in inflation. This may be hard for you to accept. But the fact remains that those who have the knowledge will avoid the blunders others will make.

Positive

The next few years will see business climb to the highest level this country has ever known. Those who prepare for this growth will reap big dividends for their foresight.

Better: Accentuate the positive.

USE FRIENDLINESS TO ESTABLISH A BOND WITH PROSPECTS

Nothing can ever be sold without a measure of friendship between the seller and the buyer. This is a bold statement, but it's true. In any sale, unless the product is being given away the buyer must feel good old-fashioned trust and confidence in the seller.

In direct mail copy, we must show trust and friendliness toward our prospects. Then they in turn will reciprocate. Copy like "You and I, we've got something to share . . ." is intimate and conveys a desire for friendship, at least on a psychological level, to readers.

■ *KEY POINT:*   *Use friendliness to establish a bond of trust and confidence.*

Here's a businesswoman's offer of a time-management diary to real estate agents:

> I just finished closing on a brand new home and feel very confident that my real estate agent negotiated the best possible arrangement for me. Throughout the negotiations, I met with him and many times came to realize just how hectic his schedule is. For this reason I introduced him to the unique pocket-sized diary/time management system that I use. . . .

This friendly opening to a sales letter makes a good attempt to establish a bond between writer and reader.

And here's a letter from the White House:

> Dear Friend,
> I am very grateful for all you have done to support me over the past 2½ years as I have worked to rebuild our economy and our defenses.
> Together, *you and I* have brought our nation away from the brink of economic disaster facing us when I took office in 1981.
> In just 30 months our policies have led to a clear economic recovery at home and renewed respect for America abroad.
> But I want to emphasize that the dramatic action we have taken is only . . .

In reality, "you and I" did nothing. But receptive readers will respond to the picture of a friendly relationship.

DON'T EVER "SELL"

The best sales strategy you can use is never to appear as though you're selling. The minute prospects feel you are selling something, their minds fog over and they tune you out. No one likes sales pitches.

■ *KEY POINT:*   *The best way to sell is never to sell.*

It's hard not to come on strong in direct mail. We often have our company's future riding on our results. But when we pitch our product, or try to cram it down our prospects' throats, we must realize people will stop reading immediately, even if it's an offer that interests them. They've heard it all before and they don't want to listen anymore.

The solution is benefits. It doesn't work to talk about why our product is good or about its features. Nobody cares. Prospects don't feel emotional about features, and they must feel emotion to buy. So benefits are what we talk about, because they are what gain the attention, arouse the interest, and motivate prospects to take action.

If you follow the commonsense suggestions in this chapter for writing copy, you should succeed in getting your sales message read and a decision made. The secret is nothing more than addressing your readers as you'd like to be addressed.

POWERFUL 7
COPYWRITING
TECHNIQUES
FOR DIRECT MAIL
LETTERS

In the last chapter we learned about general copywriting techniques that apply to all forms of direct mail. In this chapter we will see how copy should be written for the direct mail letter.

DARE TO BE DIFFERENT IN YOUR LETTERS

Everything we learned in the last chapter pertains to writing a direct mail letter. But if there is one principle that should guide copywriters in creating a successful direct mail letter, it is: "Do not say the same things everybody else says." Don't tell prospects the same old thing they've heard before.

■ *CAUTION NOTE: Don't say what everybody else does.*

Remember, most of your prospects receive an average of 5 to 25 mailing pieces each week. As you know, they may not read them all, but they will probably take at least a quick look at what each offers. Those prospects who have an interest will scan. But the sheer monotony of so much direct mail too often numbs their mind.

If nothing else, we as copywriters should realize that most of our prospects have read more direct mail than we have. It's partly because they've read the same old thing so many times that they've given up

101

reading. They don't want to read anymore. They can be reasonably sure they already know what we're going to say.

This circular argument is only perpetuated by copywriters who tell people exactly what they expect. No wonder it's called junk mail.

■ *CAUTION NOTE: Prospects are inundated with direct mail.*

GAINING BELIEF MUST GOVERN COPYWRITING

People expect us to tell them our product or service is the greatest thing ever. But because everybody is always telling them the same thing, they don't care anymore.

■ *CAUTION NOTE: People expect you to say your product is the greatest.*

How do we avoid this dilemma? This homogenized message typical of Madison Avenue syndrome of direct mail? It may sound too simple, but the answer is, make the product or service believable. People expect us to make exaggerated claims, they don't expect us to use limitations. They're not used to it. Very little direct mail has the courage to use limitations to gain belief.

■ *KEY POINT: Use limitations to gain belief.*

Suppose you tell prospects, "If you wish to use this window-washer fluid in low-temperature conditions, we warn you to add a solution of ammonia so that it won't freeze up," they will tend to believe you. You've told them something no one else has. You've broken the greatest-product-in-the-world mold that governs most copywriting. You've made yourself different. The interesting thing is, now you've bought more credibility for the rest of your copy. Disclosing limitations thus is a double-edged advantage: it gains you credibility and gets more of your copy read.

■ *KEY POINT: Disclosing limitations gains credibility and gets copy read.*

The underlying message in all this, and what must govern your letters, is: Tell people the truth. Tell them what you're up to. They don't want to be led around by the nose. They don't want to be conned. All they want is to know exactly what's in it for them and how your product is going to solve their problems.

■ *KEY POINT:* **Tell prospects truthfully what's in it for them.**

FIRST WRITE A HEADLINE THAT STRESSES A MAJOR BENEFIT

As we saw in Chapter 5, sales messages often start with a headline about a major benefit. This is also true for copy in letters, though starting a letter with a headline may seem strange. After all, traditional letters to friends don't start with headlines, and in copywriting we're supposed to pretend we're writing to friends, right? Yes, but there's another principle to maintain in writing sales letters: We must present our full offer on each piece within our mailing package.

■ *KEY POINT:* **The full offer must be on each piece in the mailing package.**

Many times not every piece gets read. Many prospects will only read the letter and will discard the brochure, or the response device, and vice versa. So the message must be on every piece, but stated differently each time. The repetition drums home the point we are trying to make—how the product or service benefits the prospect. To do all this, we should preface most of our sales letters with a headline trumpeting our offer's greatest benefit.

■ *KEY POINT:* **Start the letter with a headline about a major benefit.**

Headlines are often as long as 40 or 50 words. The goal in these longer messages is the same as in the others. Because the headline draws the eye first, it is the best place to tell readers the major benefit of the product and what we want them to do about it (Figures 7.1 and 7.2).

■ *KEY POINT:* **Long headlines are often needed to convey the full advantage of the benefit.**

SIERRA CLUB 530 Bush Street, San Francisco, California 94108

```
*******************************************************

            In the course of seeking out candidates
         for membership nomination in the Sierra Club,
            we look for people who have demonstrated
                an interest in the outdoors and/or
          a concern for protecting the environment.

                 We send you this invitation
                      in the hope that
                    you are such a person.

                   We therefore invite you
                to join the more than 300,000
                   men, women and young people
                 who have augmented that interest
                  and given voice to that concern
               by becoming members of the Sierra Club.

*******************************************************
```

Dear Friend,

    Come with me to the great outdoors for just a moment.

    Imagine, if you will, that you're standing on a hillside. Below
you sweeps a quiet valley gently carved out by the stream that meanders
along its floor. The slopes around you are covered with a subtly
colored blanket of wildflowers, fern, low brush and thistle. Above
you, a hawk circles patiently, ever so patiently. In the distance, the
setting sun silhouettes the pine-covered hills with a brilliant red and
orange glow. The only sound you can hear is the song of a meadowlark.
You feel at peace and at one with nature. The troubles of the world
are temporarily forgotten.

    It's a magic moment, part of an outdoor experience you don't soon
forget. I describe such an experience to you now because I am inviting
you to become the newest Member of the Sierra Club. And it is just
such outdoor experiences -- to take pleasure in, thrill to, learn
from -- that the Sierra Club offers to its members.

    Whether you particularly enjoy hiking, backpacking, camping,
canoeing, white water rafting, or simply appreciation of nature, I
think you'll find Club membership adds a new dimension to your outdoor
activities and understanding.

(over, please)

Figure 7.1 A long headline, but dignified; it gets to the point. Notice that it's done in the same type style as the body copy. (Courtesy Sierra Club)

Have you ever wished for a book that
would encourage your children's interest
in America's past...

introduce them to men and women of
courage, compassion, and vision...

guide them through historical events
as though they were happening right now...

and leave them with a sense of wanting
to know more?

Dear Member,

Your wish is on its way from National Geographic.

Now, America's past comes alive in an exciting new book from your
Society...complete with so many colorful illustrations, original letters,
diaries, anecdotes, and songs that your children will <u>ask</u> to read it!

THE STORY OF AMERICA

This <u>new historical picture atlas</u> takes you and your youngsters on an
incomparable journey through our nation's past.

Beautiful old photographs, specially commissioned art, period paintings,
and drawings show you an America as rich and abundant as the land itself.

You'll meet the <u>earliest arrivals on the continent</u> -- nomads making
their way across the <u>land bridge from Asia</u>. And, before you're through,
you'll applaud the <u>successful orbit of America's first woman in space</u>!

It's all here! Often in the words of the people who lived it.

Don't miss this opportunity to reserve your copy of the
Society's latest companion volume to our popular children's
atlases. You will be giving your youngsters, 9 years and
over, <u>an understanding of America that is unavailable in</u>
<u>any other single source</u>. It's a book your entire family
will want to have handy for ready reference. And for the
sheer joy of reading it!

What a story it tells.

Readers will see a triumphant John Adams leading the Massachusetts

Figure 7.2 The long headline of over 50 words tells everything but price. It tugs
at the concerned parent's heartstrings. (Courtesy National Geographic Society)

Headlines can also be short and take the place of a masthead (Figure 7.3). Because we already have our prospects' attention, we don't need to startle them to get it. Generally, however, short headlines do not have as much impact as longer ones in direct mail, because short headlines are often attempts to "tease" prospects into reading (Figures 7.4 and 7.5).

■ *CAUTION NOTE:* **Short headlines tend only to tease prospects.**

Headlines can be incorporated into the masthead. For example, a club seeking members may use an "extra," such as life insurance, emblazoned across its masthead to draw attention to one major reason people join the organization.

Headlines can also be combined with graphic symbols that accentuate the message. For example, a simulated note pad, shaded to give a three-dimensional effect, contains the date December 31 and a message, "This is it! Either I buy my computer today or lose my '83 tax break!" (Figure 7.6). This draws attention to the biggest benefit in that direct mail offer.

■ *KEY POINT:* **Headlines are often combined with graphics in visually oriented mailings.**

Headlines can also be personalized (Figure 7.7).

Figure 7.3 This example illustrates the problem of a short headline—it doesn't say anything important—and also a negative approach. (Courtesy Computer Shopper)

Gain new confidence and expertise
. . . with THE JOY OF WATERCOLOR
and your sketchbook!

Dear Artist,

In less time than you ever dreamed possible, you can start filling your world with a whole new array of exciting, original watercolor.

It's easy — and satisfying — with The Joy of Watercolor . . . the new book by David Millard that shows you how to develop — in as little as 15 minutes each day — watercolor techniques that use your sketchbook as both personal workbook and portable laboratory.

Using The Joy of Watercolor's practical, vibrantly illustrated lessons, you'll quickly enhance your artistic understanding as you learn new concepts and different approaches to drawing . . . designing . . . working with colors . . . and creating new ones. It's all here in this delightful book! Plus, you'll be motivated by the record of progress growing in your sketchbook. Proof of your ability . . . proof that you are making it as an artist and gaining intimacy with the material.

Author/artist David Millard not only gives the facts, he offers you practical advice, handy tips, <u>and lots of encouragement!</u>

With his chatty, casual style and undeniable charm, he inspires you to paint better than you've ever imagined. He sparks your enthusiasm . . . motivates you to practice . . . and builds your confidence. You'll experiment, you'll be daring, you'll try new techniques, follow your intuition—and develop your own style.

You'll find page after page of practical pointers on putting your sketches to work now and in the future—readily shifting from pencil to watercolors. You'll discover the value of your sketchbook and see how to use it as a ready reference and source of inspiration. And you'll realize that it's your own private gold mine filled with material for future watercolors!

You'll learn things you probably never thought about before. For instance

· How to design a moving subject . . . and be able to put it in your sketch just as it reaches the right spot!

· How to develop your memory so you can continue working long after your subject has gone or the lighting has changed!

(over, please)

WATSON-GUPTILL PUBLICATIONS
1515 BROADWAY, NEW YORK, N.Y. 10036

Figure 7.4 Nothing new here. The problem is it's hard to be different in a short headline. And with "gift certificate" you've really got to be in the market. (Courtesy Watson-Guptill)

Dear Executive:

Because you are a business traveler, the odds are overwhelming that you're <u>grossly overpaying</u> every time you fly.

If you'll invest just two minutes reading my letter, you'll know why. And you'll also learn how the special free certificate I've enclosed for you will let you save 30%-70% on each flight, <u>without</u> the restrictions normally associated with discount air travel.

Thousands of Unpublicized Discounts You're Missing Out On
Ever since the Civil Aeronautics Board deregulated air travel, airlines have been competing frantically to fill seats. Unpublicized "fare wars" have erupted on most routes. Though most business travelers don't realize it, steeply discounted fares are available from almost anyplace in America to anywhere else. And you can get these discounts <u>without</u> the hassles of group travel, "package" plans, long minimum stays, cancellation penalties or other restrictions normally associated with discounts.

What Travel Agents May Not Tell You
There's only one catch in taking advantage of these discounts. <u>Travel agents may not tell you about them.</u> How can they? They usually don't know about them either! You see, each month there are

Figure 7.5 A better headline: no masthead, it gets right to the point, and it's signed, too. (Courtesy Airfare Discount Bulletin)

IT'S REALLY TRUE! UNTIL DECEMBER 31
OF THIS YEAR YOU CAN BUY AN APPLE® PERSONAL
COMPUTER TO IMPROVE YOUR BUSINESS, SAVE
MONEY AND GET A 1983 TAX BREAK FROM UNCLE
SAM, TOO.

First, if you buy your Apple system before year-end, you can credit
8% of the purchase price as an ITC
(Investment Tax Credit) under the As-
set Cost Recovery System during the
first year (1983).

Second, write off 15% as first
year depreciation (22% the second
year, 21% each following year on
a 5-year write-off) under the same
ACRS provision. Alternatively, you
can expense up to $5,000 in equipment
in 1983.

Your accountant can detail
these new benefits for you.

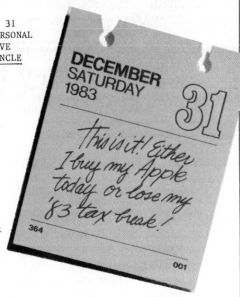

Dear Taxpayer:

Among the provisions of the "Economic Recovery Act of 1981" there are
at least three specific items that give a particular boost to the owner
of a personal computer. In fact, it provides a full write-off for many
personal computers, as well as more advantageous rates for depreciation
and improved investment tax credits.

Those are solid, money-saving reasons to put an Apple computer system
to work for your business now -- before 1984 arrives. But these savings
are just the tip of the iceberg when you consider all the ways an Apple
personal computer can streamline the operations and cost effectiveness of
your business.

Take the Apple IIe as an example. Apple just sold its millionth computer and many of them were bought by the small business community. And
the Apple IIe is perfect for a small business. It simplifies just about
every aspect of your accounting system and can maintain your inventory on

(over, please)

Apple Computer, Inc.
20525 Mariani Avenue
Cupertino, California 95014

Figure 7.6 A long headline combined with graphics. It says exactly what is
needed, gives all benefits. (Courtesy Apple Computer, Inc.)

SMITHSONIAN INSTITUTION
WASHINGTON, D.C. 20560

JAMES LUMLEY

YOU ARE ONE OF A SMALL GROUP OF

AMHERST RESIDENTS

INVITED TO BECOME NATIONAL ASSOCIATES

OF THE SMITHSONIAN INSTITUTION

I know you receive many "personal" (i.e. computer-printed) invitations but this is special.

By accepting this particular invitation you will join a special group of Americans whose importance to our national culture I'll explain later.

Enrollment ends October 31st and we can only hold the enclosed Registration Number in your name until then. Let me review the benefits of membership reserved for you:

Chief among them is SMITHSONIAN Magazine -- perhaps the most talked-about periodical of recent years. A monthly journal of science, history, technology and the arts, it is handsomely printed, lavishly illustrated, compellingly written -- and published especially for Smithsonian Associate members.

SMITHSONIAN glows with color photographs -- of bobcat kittens, miming clowns, renaissance clocks, illuminated manuscripts, jewel-like fish.

SMITHSONIAN also gleams with thought-provoking articles -- about how computers are re-creating reality, how exercises can re-program the mind, how mothers impart diverse social skills to newborn infants.

This splendid magazine is but the first of many pleasures in store for you. Among the others:

Money-saving opportunities to travel and study abroad -- in Alpine villages, Welsh manor houses, Portuguese fortified towns, African game parks, the Himalayas.

Invitations to stimulating events at home. Concerts, lectures, seminars on 18th and 19th century horticulture, Byzantine splendors, Chinese ceramics, World War I aviation. Scenic hiking expeditions,

(over, please)

Figure 7.7 A personalized headline. Both name and hometown are here. Too hokey for most offers, but it works for the Smithsonian. (Courtesy Smithsonian Institution)

Now every letter needs a headline. Headlines are often not used in fund raising because they are considered undignified. Because they do draw attention, headlines may detract from the emotional appeal required of a fund-raising letter. Your own judgment must guide you. But remember, headlines are used in so many lettters because they work.

■ *CAUTION NOTE:* **Headlines may detract from the emotional appeal needed in a fund-raising letter.**

PROSPECTS OFTEN READ THE POSTSCRIPT FIRST

After writing the headline, the next step is to jump to the end of the letter and write the postscript. This may sound backward, but prospects often read the postscript first. The postscript is therefore crucial to a good sales letter.

■ *KEY POINT:* **Prospects often read the postscript first.**

Because the postscript is so important it must be used to the utmost. For excellent results it can contain our offer and what we want prospects to do.

Sometimes prospects only read the postscript before deciding to act; they don't need to read further. Therefore they must have all the information necessary to follow through on their decision.

■ *KEY POINT:* **Have the postscript contain the offer and what the prospect should do.**

A postscript can combine an offer with a sweetener or can offer a sweetener alone, to motivate prospects. For example, you could extend the offer: "If you order before the end of the month, you'll get an extra 15% discount." Since some people only buy when products are discounted, this information may make them act. This technique also has the advantage of making prospects go back to the letter to reinforce what is being offered. You have increased your readership by giving them something they want.

■ *KEY POINT: A sweetener can be combined with the offer or be used by itself in the postscript.*

Here are some examples of postscripts that contain the offer:

P.S. Please take a few minutes to review the enclosed OFFICE PLANNER. Note how it is designed to organize your employees' efforts, simplify work, and build good customer relations. Then, on your no-obligation *FREE*-Trial Certificate, write in how many monthly PLANNERS you wish to try *FREE* for 30 days and mail it. We'll do the rest.

This is more than adequate. It doesn't give the price, but that works with this type of offer. It also points to the response card.

P.S. This seventh edition of the *Software Directory* is the most comprehensive guide available to the world of microcomputer software. And it can be yours for just $29.95 . . . with a 15-day *MONEY-BACK GUARANTEE* that you'll be satisfied. So order now.

Excellent. If prospects read nothing but this postscript, they will know what is offered and what they have to give up to get it.

P.S. Fill in and mail your no-obligation free-offer card today. You will immediately receive *FREE* the 175-page *Portfolio of Sales*. . . . As part of your subscription, you will receive 12 monthly issues of *Sales and* . . . PLUS 5 surveys (they would cost you $145 alone if bought separately). All this for $45, and the *Portfolio* is yours to keep absolutely free even if you decide not to continue your subscription.

This contains the full offer, enhanced by sweeteners. If prospects read only this copy they could follow through and order.

P.S. Subscribe for two years (only $46) and we'll send you a *FREE* copy of *Dynamite Your Taxes Now*—50 ways to blow away your tax burden this year. This exciting report includes an explanation of every item in this letter marked with a blue... Get it now!

This gives information on how much the offer costs, enhances the sweetener, and helps bring the prospect back into the copy.

P.S. *Want to save more?* Take a two-year subscription for just $24.00, and save $32.35. You'll get 11 more regular issues and another annual buying guide issue as well!

That's what *Consumer Reports* really wants to do anyway, sell a longer subscription. So they plug it in the postscript.

P.S. This is by far the most important letter I've ever written. If you've ever thought of contributing to a just and worthy cause—*this is it!*
Don't hesitate! Send President Reagan your personal ballot and your contribution of $33—just $1 for each Senate seat up in 1984—in the enclosed envelope today!

Some of the most dramatic and effective direct mail copy is in sales letters seeking campaign contributions. This letter is no exception. It contains the full offer plus a little emotion.

Here are some examples of use of the postscript solely to enhance the only sweetener:

P.S. Yours *FREE*—a 178-page manual on *How To Supervise* . . . (a $49.50 value). See your enclosed Trial Subscription Card for details.

This emphasizes the value of the sweetener and draws attention to the response card.

P.S. If your gift is $25 or more, we will be pleased to also provide you with a subscription to *Opera News* magazine, your personal companion to all Metropolitan Opera radio and television broadcasts.

Many on the verge of donating will do so because of the magazine added as a sweetener, appropriate for this offer.

P.S. Don't forget to bring in the enclosed certificate for your free book, *Personal Computers in Business.* And when you do go in for your test drive, ask about our Apple IIe and Apple III special business systems promotions.

Here's Apple using a sweetener to generate store business.
Here are some weak examples of use of the postscript:

P.S. If you are already a member, you know how much better we are. Why not pass this along to an artist friend? Thanks.

If you haven't targeted this to the right prospect in the beginning, it's unlikely to get passed along. A last-ditch effort.

P.S. See the card for special bonus offered for payment with trial offer.

Why waste good selling space on directing prospects to another part of the mailing package? Sell here.

P.S. Last year's pages came to 2312—an average of 192.6 pages each month.

So what? Again, wasted space. Put this in the body copy.

P.S. See other side for some revealing comments.

No, no, no! This offers no reason to turn to the other side. If it doesn't buy readership, it's a waste of good selling space.

HOW DO WE ADDRESS OUR PROSPECTS?

How should we begin sales letters? Can we address our prospects by name? In many cases we can. As we will see in a later chapter on mailing lists, computers let us address our customers and many prospects on prospect lists by name. But if individual personalized mail is not cost effective, or if we don't have the names to use, we need another way to address our prospects.

■ *KEY POINT: Use the prospect's name if available and when cost effective.*

If we don't know our prospects' names we can use appropriate titles, such as an occupational or professional title. "Dear Engineer," "Dear Professional," "Dear Accountant," "Dear Doctor," and "Dear Home-maker" will suffice as titles of address.

Another option is to address prospects according to the role that is related to your product or service. For example, if you're selling ski equipment, you could say "Dear Skier." If you don't have the names of your organization's members, you might say "Dear Member." Just use a salutation that would be appropriate.

There are literally hundreds of possible salutations: "Dear Colleague," "Computer User," "Artist," "Insured," "Executive," "Investor," "Realtor," "Service Repair Person." If all else fails, use "Dear Reader."

■ *KEY POINT: If you don't have the prospect's name, use an appropriate working or functional title.*

There are several forms of address to avoid. Don't use "Dear Sir" or "Dear Madam." There is no possible business or professional activity or household sale for which we could use a title for one or the other sex. Also to be avoided is "Dear Friend." It is too anonymous, is too condescending, and misuses the meaning of the word "friend."

■ *CAUTION NOTE: Avoid using sexist or condescending titles.*

START THE BODY COPY BY STATING THE OFFER

We start our first paragraph of copy by stating our offer. We may have already put it in the postscript, the most read part of any sales letter. We will now place it in another highly visible location—the beginning paragraphs. Why? Because if prospects read only the postscript or the first part of the letter, they will know what our offer is. As we saw earlier that's why the postscript is an excellent place to state the offer.

■ *KEY POINT: Start the letter with a statement of the offer.*

Though we are duplicating the intent of the postscript, it is important that we not use the same words to restate our offer. To avoid giving readers a sense of repetition, we use synonyms—words that mean the same thing. Synonyms let us say the same thing in different ways in both places.

■ *KEY POINT: Use synonyms to avoid same wording of offer.*

A restatement of the offer gives prospects a second chance to apply it to their lives. It gives them more time to see how the product or service fits into the image of how they would like to see themselves. It lets them think, "Maybe this will work for me." It's all part of roping them in, intriguing them while letting them apply the offer to their own lives. As we will see in the next several chapters, the offer will also be repeated twice more, on the brochure and on the response device.

■ *KEY POINT: Restating the offer gives prospects time to see how the product or service can work in their lives.*

Here are some examples of the offer placed in the beginning of the letter:

Dear Reader,
　　You will receive FREE the current 500-page issue—not one penny's cost, not one bit of obligation.
　　Hard to believe, maybe. But you just peel off the token, press it on the reservation card, and drop it into the mail. It's easy to get—free—the rewarding current issue.
　　And, if you wish to not continue your subscription for the next 12 months for a modest $21 (that's only $1.75 per issue), just write CANCEL on our invoice. We're sure you won't, once you see this month's issue.

Long, but the message says it all for those prospects who may only read the beginning. Also, enough is given here to not only make a decision but also order.

Dear Handyperson,
　　Ever drive 5 miles to buy one little 10¢ bolt? Dig through a jar of odds and ends trying to find a fastener?
　　If you're like me, that's happened more than once. But never again! For $19.95 you can own the Nut & Bolt Kit . . . a complete size-by-size selection of over 2100 fasteners (that's less than 1¢ apiece)—all organized and labeled in a multibin cabinet.

Excellent. Both offer and cost are right up front so the prospect can see exactly what's being offered.

Dear Mr. Lumley,
　　What would you say to a new way to add useful programs, utilities, games, data files to your software library *every month*? A way to get as many

as 12 ready-to-use pretested programs and files *every month?* A way to have a software collection of almost 50 new programs in just six months?

This doesn't tell us the cost or how to order, but we know what the deal is.

Dear Colleague,
   Now, just initial below, return this letter to me, and I'll show you how to double the effectiveness of customer relations in your entire operation. It's all in our great new volume called . . .

The offer in a nutshell. No price, but we know what is expected.
Here are some ways of wasting the beginning paragraph of a letter:

Dear Computer User:
   You have probably thought how valuable it would be to have software that would sort through thousands of stocks and precisely identify those that meet your personal investment criteria. Now you can do exactly that.

Never mind the features. Tell us what we're getting. The problem here is that this lead will entice only prospects with a strong interest. For better sales, we should open by emphasizing what is being offered.

Dear Executive,
   Even though we have never met, I know you.
   You are experiencing the same problems . . . and frustrations of so many sales and marketing managers I do know.
   And, as if a shaky economy and tougher competition weren't enough, you somehow have to find enough time for your most important job of all: *Keeping your people motivated—and moving.*

This gives only a general allusion to specifics. We certainly don't know what is being offered. Also it is too negative; prospects will be turned off before they read much further.

Dear Collector,
   What do you really want to know about antiques and art? A collector once told me there are only three interesting things about something sold at auction: where it came from, who bought it, and how much it sold for.

We believe you, but better to say this further into the letter, not at the beginning where space is valuable. Use the first paragraph to explain and sell your offer!

> Dear fellow tax victim:
> Your tax lawyer and accountant don't know your business like you do. They never will.
> Even if they did, they're far too busy to sit and sift through dozens of tax journals, looking for money-saving ideas just for you. They have a hundred clients already.
> And you can't afford to hire a full-time . . .

This lead illustrates the problem of telling a story: It takes forever to tell what is being offered.

THE SECOND SECTION OF THE BODY COPY CONTAINS MAJOR BENEFITS

After we introduce the offer in the first paragraphs, we devote the next few paragraphs to the major benefits. We have already used one major benefit in the headline at the beginning of the letter. Now we will use three or four more that are strong enough to hook the reader emotionally.

■ *KEY POINT:* *Devote the next paragraphs to major benefits.*

Benefits are best used in this position, because by now prospects have read some details about the offer. Now to get more readership, you must show "what's in it for me" again and again. Benefits will draw readers further along in the letter.

■ *KEY POINT:* *Use major benefits to repeatedly show readers what's in it for them.*

Here are some examples of how benefits are developed at this point:

> Because we want to give you more, our magazine is twice the size of any other computing magazine. There is more information, more challenge, more excitement in its pages than you'll find *anywhere*. And—to benefit you fur-

ther—more supplies and equipment than you ever thought existed. Spread before you, so *it's easy to "shop" its pages and find precisely what you want.*

This is the idea, "making it easy to get goodies." Give prospects things that will help them.

It's like your own hardware store! Nuts, bolts, screws, washers, cotter pins in complete size ranges, in bulk quantities. Over 175 dozen fasteners you use for all kinds of jobs—inside and out, on metal and wood, for minor repairs as well as major jobs. And every piece is right at hand, easy to find in the labeled bins. No more mixed-up jar and coffee-can collections for you!

Everything you need for professional-looking jobs in one easy-to-find place!

Excellent: high on "what's in it for me," plus details are thrown in to make benefits legitimate.

Make a dramatic leap in your computer ability. Learn the latest advances in computer technology from our disk magazine. It's perfect if you're just starting with computing and would like to explore new applications. *It will make you a pro* . . . soon your friends will ask you for help.

Brief, but it gives prospects an image of how they will be better off after they subscribe.

This comprehensive, fully indexed manual of customer-pleasing techniques *will make you highly regarded in your company.* When you put into action these new psychological methods to turn negative attitudes into positive ones and ways to make a friend out of even the grouchiest Monday morning complainer, *you will rise to new heights.* In short, this manual will show how to make your entire customer service department one that reflects friendliness and accommodation . . . *allowing you to solve one of the most difficult of business problems.*

This keeps hitting the YOU that's important in showing prospects benefits.

In our new engagement calendar, you will find *ample space to jot down daily appointments,* as well as a *lavish assortment of color photographs* that will brighten every week of your year.

Fifty-three full-color portraits in all! Beautiful in your calendar . . . perfect for informal wall arrangements . . . and a delightful way to learn more about some of nature's wonders.

These two paragraphs attempt to give a personal dimension to the benefits.

This book is especially designed for you. For the busy executive who doesn't have time to read. But must have a continuing source of ideas . . . solutions . . . and, yes, those all-important clippings. The articles are short and to the point. But the ideas are big. Adaptable, usable, and *a time-saving answer to "I don't have time to read."*

Ideas from just about every industry. Marketing innovations and solutions from all over the world. If it worked—it'll be in our book. And in the "Special Reports" you get the thinking and results of today's sales and marketing winners. And in a way that you can absorb a pertinent case history on the run. *You'll still be too busy to read. But now you'll have the ideas and solutions you need.*

Strong benefit copy, lots of "what's in it for me." Also problem magazine and book readership is faced directly, tying prospects more into the product.

This Sourcebook *will increase your earning power and gain the respect of your associates.* Suppose you've been asked to a meeting to discuss ways to speed up cash receipts. In five minutes you can read summaries of 10 to 15 cases that illustrate how other companies have brought in cash faster. Result? You become the resource person for that meeting. Your stature shoots up in the eyes of your peers . . . and in the eyes of your superiors.

This sourcebook *will give you more leisure time for recreation, for constructive thought.* Many people today complain of being swamped with details. Actually, the average businessperson wastes 50% to 60% of his or her time due to lack of organization, to uncertainty in the face of the unfamiliar. The secret of leisure is not to do less work, but to organize work so that you can get more done in less time. This Sourcebook does that for you.

The Sourcebook *will relieve stress.* Most executives I speak with—presidents, owners, and even middle level managers—tell me they feel as if they're living in a pressure cooker. Pressure to get results, and get them fast, leads to stress. Over time, stress can become intolerable, even dangerous to your health, resulting in sleepless nights, loss of appetite, nervousness, irritability . . . a possible breakdown. The what-to-do and how-to-do-it knowledge you will gain in the Sourcebook will allow you to tame the pressures of stress.

Solid what's-in-it-for-me benefits, probably addressed to an individual at a business address. Notice how it gives the emotional benefits of how executives can succeed and look better with peers—important! Also notice that these benefits are specific to the product, being less important than the secondary benefits of saving time and money.

DESCRIBE WHAT IS BEING OFFERED

Description bolsters what we say about benefits. It also ties prospects to the product or service by telling them what its features will do for them, all in the hope of moving prospects further along toward making a decision and acting on it.

■ *KEY POINT: Description supports benefits and helps tie prospects to the product.*

We use description to make our products come alive. Remember, people can't see or feel what we are offering, so we need to use tangible, physical, almost elemental language to describe. We want to tell them what it looks like. Not just green, but mustard green—there's a big difference. If you say it's 8 inches by 12 inches by 15 inches, add "about the size of a breadbox." Now the prospect knows what you're talking about.

■ *KEY POINT: Description gives the physical feel of a product.*

We also use description to tell prospects what they will get and how to use what we are selling. Here are some examples of description:

> You get a heavy-duty polystyrene storage cabinet complete with 25 slide-out bins, bin dividers, and preprinted labels.
> Just look at the variety! Fasteners "made to order" for car repairs, home and shop projects, woodworking, office maintenance, appliance repairs—you name it! Diameters from pencil point #6 to a big 5/16 inch. Lengths from 3/8 inch to a full 1½ inches. Coarse and fine threads (from 18 per inch to 32 per inch). Flat, round, pan, and hex heads . . . plus hex nuts to fit everything. A complete selection of fasteners all made of *standard #2 grade steel*, zinc plated for rust resistance.

This gives good detail on what is offered. It gives a feel for bolt and thread sizes.

> Each superb volume measures 7⅛ inches by 10¼ inches and has 200 or more pages. The set features scores of paintings and sketches and numerous maps. And you'll really enjoy the many keepsake photographs, including rare daguerreotypes that recall the days of the Civil War and the Old West . . . full-color photographs that guide you to famous historical sites . . . striking

portraits and telling biographies of each of our country's Presidents, from George Washington to . . .

. . . Get to know the young, freckle-faced Tom Jefferson; the untidily dressed Patrick Henry; that towering, tight-lipped planter, George Washington; . . . the young Indian woman known as Sacajawea; an assortment of rawhide-tough mountain men with such names as Tom "Broken Hand" Fitzpatrick, Jedediah Smith . . .

We can almost feel the book, its pages afire with exciting history.

Wild Places in North America is spiral bound, is printed on heavy gloss stock, measures 8¾ inches by 7½ inches, and contains *a full page for each week's appointments* faced by a full-page photograph. In addition, each photo is described in a lively, informative way by naturalist Dr. Robert O. . . .

This description makes the product seem tangible. It gives us something we can visualize in our mind's eye.

The VITA-CRUSH 460's patented splash-guard dome top is always open for easy addition. Processing is done by patented reversing blades which are able at the simple flip of a lever to smash into foods with up to 530 mph head-on impact, which is many times harder than possible with any one-way appliance . . . with its controlled impact you can heat and cook gravy, puddings, white sauce, and soups by molecular friction. It is impossible to burn, scorch, lump, or curdle foods with this process. . . .

The complete machine, including its 72-ounce stainless-steel concussion chamber with unlimited capacity and its 7¼-inch adapted saw motor, carries a five-year replacement parts guarantee. This demonstrates that in the home, the VITA-CRUSH 460 provides strength and usability far in excess of that exhibited by the ordinary home appliance.

We believe these claims. We wouldn't want to get a hand caught inside this monster. We understand that it's an effective machine from this excellent description, which lets us visualize it.

As we approach midsummer, the Met will mark the end of its first century and the beginning of its second. Our fiscal year ends shortly and the company begins rehearsals for the historic 1983–1984 Centennial Season in August. The backstage areas, craft shops, and rehearsal rooms will come alive with the work of the Met's artists, and production would not be possible without the contributions of the Met's growing family of donors.

Givers to this worthy cause can see exactly what they are supporting.

LOAD COPY WITH SECONDARY AND COMPARATIVE BENEFITS

Next in our sales letter we want to include the secondary and comparative benefits that remain after we use the top three or four in the headline and start of the body copy. This is where letters can get long.

■ *KEY POINT: Secondary benefits often add length to the sales message.*

This is also where we compare the advantages of our product or service with those of the competition and begin "bribing" our prospects with sweeteners.

Here are some examples of secondary and comparative benefits:

> When you mail the reservation card, get set for a magazine that covers the waterfront. Each issue averages 16 full length features . . . six reviews of new hardware and software . . . 10 regular features you won't find anywhere else . . .
>
> Who writes our magazine? Well, that's our "secret weapon." They are *not* reporters, not journalists. They are savvy, sophisticated, skeptical *computer specialists* who know exactly how to tear down, customize, design, build, and program the hardware and software they write about.
>
> And when it comes to new developments, our wide exposure means that you get the news first from manufacturers and designers. So you learn what's new fast. Here's what you missed in a recent issue: (. . . *and a long list of secondary benefits follows*).

This hits the points that give prospects additional reasons to buy. It is the place to "bulk up" on benefits.

> It happens to everyone. A project takes so many fasteners of one type that even with the Nut & Bolt Kit you run low. No problem! No need to make a special trip to the hardware store and pay those high prices, either. We include a refill label with your Kit so you can order any type or size—any time. And at our *dollar-stretching discount prices*, like these . . .
>
> 100 Machine screws #6-32 × 1". Average retail price: $2.25. Our price: $0.91.
>
> 100 Internal tooth washers #6. Average retail price: $1.21. Our price: $0.29.
>
> Take advantage of this money-saving offer and I'll send you THREE VALUABLE FREE GIFTS! A wall-size specification chart AND a nut and bolt

gauge (so you know exactly what type and size fastener to use) . . . PLUS a three angle level. All three are yours to keep, FREE. . . .

Secondary benefits are combined with comparative benefits and sweeteners. This example illustrates the point that often prospects buy because they perceive the sweeteners as quite valuable.

Everything is ready for you. All programs have been developed by expert programmers and selected by the editors of the *DISK MAGAZINE*. The accompanying 60-page *User Manual* is written in clear, concise, easy-to-understand terms. You'll be able to try programs immediately and see how useful they really are. Think of the time you'll save—

- No listing to be typed into the computer. Just insert the disk and go!
- The latest software developments will be ready at your fingertips.

. . . (*and on and on*)

You can see that in selling certain products by mail, it's not hard to write four- or five-page letters.

It will recommend ways to organize your department with streamlined efficiency, better communication, and repeat business. And, to make certain your "encyclopedia" is never out of date, we will offer you periodic updates on new techniques and federal regulations that affect your dynamic field. These are sent to you automatically and on an approval basis.

Secondary benefits here are not strongly worded, but are consistent with the product.

The Sourcebook is designed to fit on your desk, or in a bookshelf within easy reach. As questions and problems come up, you'll reach for the Sourcebook, identify the subject area, and find approaches used by executives who hold positions just like yours. . . . The Sourcebook tells you how to raise quick cash by borrowing on your hidden assets; how cash forecasting helps you make purchasing, capital investment, and marketing decisions; what venture capitalists are really looking for before they invest, among others . . .

The Sourcebook *saves you time*. . . . Suppose you want to find a better way to manage seasonal up's and down's of cash receipts. You turn to the. . . . Your eye quickly spots a 30-second summary of the case.

The Sourcebook *makes you money*. . . . You want to see how pricing can help boost profits. Turn to the tab. . . . You'll find literally dozens of profit-making ideas.

> The Sourcebook *saves you money*. . . . It is jam packed with successful pro-
> grams that companies are using right now . . . as you read this . . . that are
> saving them thousands of dollars. For example, . . .
> And that's not all. Two other time savers . . .(*the list goes on*).

Secondary benefits can tell prospects how to use something, as well
as what they will get. It is often effective to describe secondary benefits
in the form of a list such as in the preceding example. Also compare
these secondary benefits with this product's primary benefits, quoted
earlier in the chapter. "Saving time and money" are secondary to the
enhanced esteem, recognition, and leisure offered as primary benefits.
People can get tired of hearing about saving time and money; try to be
different.

> You'll never have to "fly by the seat of your pants" again. In addition to
> your 12 monthly news and feature issues, you'll receive two special reports
> and four surveys: . . . Each survey is designed for the busy executive like
> yourself. All the facts and figures. All the background and experience factors.
> The kind of information you must have . . . in a format you can conveniently
> use. Everything you need to start and implement your sales and marketing
> plans. Everything you need to know how to keep selling costs down. All the
> latest information you must have to ensure that you're dealing with reality.

Solid secondary benefits with sweeteners thrown in. The actual letter
is five pages long, and three have this kind of copy.

> This book will give you a concise summary of all the new tax angles found
> in the nation's press. That includes all the famous tax reports AND thousands
> of dollars worth of *non-tax* publications, both well-known and little-known
> financial letters whose pages contain tax gems you'll seldom see elsewhere.
> For example . . .
>
> ● Two simple tax techniques that can move your interest income into
> the next year.
> ● Five examples of cash income you *need not report* to the IRS—all legal!
> ● New tax law that permits you to write off $5,000 in new equipment
> purchases immediately.
> ● New type of tax-exempt security that's *better* than a municipal bond.
> ● . . . (and the list goes on for 15 more "bullets.")

Prefacing secondary benefits in a list with "bullets" is a popular way
to draw prospects' attention.

That's why the *Digest* tells in over 175 pages each month about auction and show reports, from Texas to New York to Canada, pictures, prices, and straight talk about the market for American antiques and art, in-depth, literate, original, authoritative writing by the best reporters.

But that's not all you'll find in each monthly issue—advertisements. Over 300 of America's best dealers, many of whom don't advertise anywhere else, offer their best to you in the pages of the *Digest*, often illustrated with lavish pictures. Each issue is truly a shopping guide for the best in Americana—the things made by and for Americans in years gone by.

Inside is your free guide to record American auction prices. It's a condensation of a seven-page illustrated article from the May issue. You'll see the wide range and careful attention to detail that's typical of our coverage of the Americana market.

This shows the no-nonsense secondary benefits offered by this magazine.

If you order a VITA-CRUSH 460, you are in for a marvelous, enlightening, and joyfully different experience. The VITA-CRUSH 460 is the modern and ideal appliance for our changing times. It's certainly great in times of shortages and high food and labor prices, and for the fast pace at which we live. It is different from anything that anyone has ever had the privilege of using; so don't use it or judge it by comparing it with any blender, juice extractor, cake mixer, ordinary food processor, or other appliance. There is no other appliance like it! Use it hard! Try everything! Juicing, cooking, bread baking, and freezing. I am sure you will become one of the thousands of VITA-CRUSH 460 enthusiasts, too.

Notice how these secondary benefits are of less importance than this product's primary ones, discussed earlier.

Over the course of the year we appeal to you a number of times to help the Met through the Metropolitan Opera Fund, so that we can continue to bring you opera at the Met's best, including our annual series of radio and television broadcasts. And with your help we are completing another successful year. . . .

To express our appreciation for your gift of $25 to the Fund, we would like to send you a special gift from the Met—your choice of a Centennial Wall Calendar, featuring full-color photos of the Met's most magnificent productions, or a copy of the Centennial Season Book, giving you background information on the season's repertory and new productions, stories of the operas, an artists' roster, and a capsule history of the Met's first 100 years.

If your contribution is $50, . . . $125 . . . (the sweetener list goes on, too.)

Secondary benefits are combined with sweeteners for donations received. Often secondary benefits seem to be primary ones, but those here are secondary to the emotional benefit of participating in the Met's success.

SUPPORT MATERIAL BACKS UP BENEFITS WITH PROOF

Support is one of the most important parts of a sales letter. If we're going to get sales, we have to prove what we say. Proof is a major factor in relieving the risk prospects may feel about responding to our offer. We must offer proof, either by direct evidence or by objective testimony.

■ *KEY POINT:*   *Sales copy must offer proof.*

Here are some examples of proof in letter copy:

> There must be a reason why we have grown 300% in just three years. Sure. More and more people like you have discovered us . . . encouraged us . . . and—most important—stayed with the publication. I think you will too, once you've seen it . . .
> . . . You know, 75% of our readers actually *save every* issue for future reference! Doesn't that say a lot about our magazine and its probable worth to you?

Only generalized proof is given here, in the implication that heavy readership supports the magazine. Direct testimony would be better, but it is difficult to work it into a short letter.

> Many of our more than 20,000 subscribers have been able to cut their taxes by 40% to 50%. Some have seen their usual tax refund balloon 10 times, 15 times, or 25 times . . .

This generalized market sampling by the company is nothing more than anecdotal. But it's probably the best this copywriter had.

> Three million people can't be wrong. Here's what one of them said:
> "No longer do I have to delay a Sunday afternoon project until the hard-

ware store is open because I am missing a critical bolt. . . . I have it at my fingertips, well organized and clearly marked. . . . In my opinion, anyone who ever picks up a screwdriver needs your work kit."

Testimony from an individual user is hard to beat.

. . . a few words from some of the well-known sales and marketing executives:

"Today, I introduced our Computer-Assisted Management Program . . . and recalled how I got the seed for the idea. It came from a Special Report. Now my salespeople have more time to put their best efforts against decision makers with the most potential business. . . ." (signed)

"Your November 12th issue now weighs about 25 pounds with all the paper clips I added to it, indicating articles I should reread, copy, and send to my other people." (signed)

Good testimony: specific to the product, sincere, and of course, signed by the user.

In the illustrated four-page introduction to *Wild Places of North America*, Mrs. Lyndon B. Johnson writes:

"Among the many wild lands, a few exert a special pull on us that we cannot fully explain. . . . Each of us tends to have a deep sense of personal geography. . . . We form these images while we are young. Wherever we live, we are only a memory away from that place. . . . There was a certain cast of light, a length of day, a flavor and a fragrance to the weather. . . ."

Having access to a famous name adds credibility, particularly if, like Mrs. Johnson, the person has taken part in the product or service.

GUARANTEE THE OFFER

After we give support for or proof of our offer, we must guarantee it. This is further proof that what we say is true, and reinforces the lack of risk. To succeed, direct mail must be risk free, and we must emphasize this in our sales letter.

■ *KEY POINT: A written guarantee relieves risk.*

Here are some examples of how guarantees are written in letter copy:

If you agree that our magazine is for you, just honor our invoice. Start enjoying it every month. If you don't agree—and it's entirely up to you— then write "cancel" on the invoice and shoot it back to us. That will be the end of that. *Naturally, the free current issue is yours to keep.* And we'll *still* thank you for giving us a try!

Nice relaxed way to offer a guarantee in a short letter. Hard to go wrong with this one.

TEN-DAY FREE TRIAL EXAMINATION. . . . If you decide to keep it, just honor our invoice for $34.95, plus postage and handling. Otherwise, return it and owe nothing.

Typical of many single-page letters with guarantees.

DON'T JUST THINK OF THE TIME AND MONEY YOU'LL SAVE— ORDER NOW! YOU ALSO GET AN IRONCLAD MONEY-BACK GUARAN- TEE!

******

PLUS . . . A MONEY-BACK GUARANTEE! I really do believe in our prod- ucts. I also believe in going out of my way to make sure you're satisfied. That's why I offer you a 100% money-back guarantee. If you're not pleased with your Nut & Bolt Kit, if it doesn't save you a lot of time and money, just return it. You'll get a full refund, including shipping and handling charges.
With a guarantee like this, you've got nothing to lose, everything to gain. So take the time to order now.
If you aren't 100% satisfied with your Kit, return it. You'll get a prompt full refund. *I guarantee it.*

******

Three guarantees in one two-page lettter. No question about it, the guarantee is clear.

If you ever wish to cancel your subscription, simply return the most recent disk in its sealed package and you will receive a full refund for this copy and on all unmailed issues.
Simple but clear. Probably the best that can be offered for this type of product.

Our Guarantee . . .
If the Sourcebook is not all that I say it is, please let me know within 30 days. I
will see that a refund is sent immediately, or a credit is given if you charged it
to your credit card. No questions asked.
    You could hardly ask for a better offer than that. So why don't you mail
your acceptance?

It's a good idea to mention credit cards in the guarantee. Many people
order this way but worry about complications and delays in having their
accounts credited if they want a refund.

Your No-Risk Guarantee
    1. *You will save in taxes at least 10 times* more than you paid for your sub-
scription. If at any time you don't think the *Digest* is living up to this promise,
we'll refund the remaining portion of what you paid.
    2. If you should decide to cancel *before your third issue*, you'll receive *all* of
what you paid, every penny. What could be more foolproof—and fair?

A little extra detail in writing a guarantee can make it seem to be more
important in the eyes of prospects. Numbering reinforces the perception
of importance.

SUMMARIZE THE OFFER

After assuring prospects that your offer is guaranteed, summarize the
offer. Clear up any ambiguity about what they will get and what they
must do to get it. This is also where you tell them why you offer the best
deal in the marketplace.

■ *KEY POINT: Summarize the offer to clear up any ambiguity.*

To receive the hardware kit with over 2100 fasteners and the cabinet, just
fill in the enclosed Order Card and mail it with your check, money order, or
company purchase order for $19.95 plus $3.90 shipping and handling . . . or
charge it to your VISA, MasterCard, American Express, Diners Club, or Carte
Blanche account.

More than adequate. It reminds prospects of what they are going to get and tells them what they have to give up to get it, as well as how to proceed.

> To take advantage of our special no-risk offer, just return the enclosed reservation card to start your introductory subscription to *Disk Magazine* for the special price of $119 (less than $20 per issue), a 34% discount off the full price.
> See for yourself why it's the best thing around.

The basic details of what prospects will pay and what they will get, near the end of the letter as a reminder

> To receive your superb six-volume *Land of Liberty* set for free examination, simply return the enclosed reservation card. Send no money now. When your books arrive in July, decide *then* whether you wish to keep the set. If not completely satisfied, you may return all six volumes without payment.
> If you decide to keep the set, *pay the surprisingly low price of $36.95 for all six books*—little more than you might expect to pay for just one volume of far less scope and with far fewer illustrations! You also have the option of paying in three easy installments.
> But please act quickly, because the supply is limited. So popular are these six titles that more than 2 million have been purchased to date.

Excellent. We are reminded of what the offer is, of the guarantee, what it costs, and finally how great it is.

> Value-priced at only $6.95, the 1984 National Engagement Calendar *costs you even less when you order two or more!* The enclosed Order Form contains a MULTIPLE-SALES discount table which lists a breakdown of the savings you can enjoy.

Like the last example, this summarizes cost and the offer again.

> *Here's an offer too good to refuse.*
> You can see that the Sourcebook is a unique way to save you time, help you make money, and cut costs.
> It's hard to measure the value of this extraordinary new tool until you have had a chance to use it. Its price—$69.95 (including air mail postage and handling). You can pay by check or, for your convenience, charge to your American Express, VISA, Diners Club, or MasterCard.

Along with product and price, this summary, like many others, mentions easy methods of paying.

The *Software Vendor's Directory* is the single source of information about 21,000 software programs for microcomputers. . . . It's just $29.95 (plus $2.50 postage and handling)—for a quick and easy reference resource that's guaranteed to save you hours. And help you make informed software and hardware purchases.

Brief but to the point. The main thing is to put the offer and how much it costs near the end of the letter in capsule form.

ASK PROSPECTS TO RESPOND

One basic principle of selling is to ask the prospect to buy. Whether we are face to face or using direct mail, it is crucial that we ask for the response. Often a sale will evaporate because it isn't clear that the prospect must act, and in a certain way.

■ *KEY POINT: Always ask prospects for a response.*

Asking for a response, or "closing" the prospect, can be used several times in each direct mail offer. Some letters have "trial closes" as often as once a page in the sales message. For example, on the first page you can say, "Decide today if you will take advantage of this offer and be the first to understand. . . ." Then you can follow with more "decision prompts" on every page.

■ *KEY POINT: Ask for a response often.*

We should also make responding easy by offering facilitators such as easy-to-fill-out response forms, self-addressed stamped envelopes and return cards, and other devices.

■ *KEY POINT: Facilitators help make responding easier.*

See our magazine and evaluate it from cover to cover without spending a cent. Without the slightest risk. Just by *mailing the card enclosed.* You'll have the current issue in your hands soon. . . .

It's crucial to ask for the order.

With our money-back guarantee, you've got nothing to lose, everything to gain. So take time to order now. When you do, check your gift list. Chances are friends and relatives will appreciate this "hardware store" as much as you. (Check your order card—and save even more when you order in quantity.)

Ask for one order, and then for quantity orders, too.

Send us your order and see how easily you can expand the use of your computer. When you receive your Premier Issue of *Disk Magazine,* try it . . . test it . . . see for yourself.

You can remind prospects of what they are getting when you ask for their order.

Let me prove how profitable and effective this remarkable volume will make your customer service operation. Just return this letter today, with your initials below, and I'll send the encyclopedia to you at once for the modest cost of just $34.95. . . .

Ask for orders by using the easy "facilitator" of having the prospect initial and return the letter.

I'm sure you'd like to receive the Americana magazine each month, and you can—with just one toll-free call. Here's the number. . .

Making the order easy with a toll-free telephone number encourages fast action.

TELL PROSPECTS WHY THEY SHOULD ACT NOW

The last paragraph of your letter should tell prospects why they must act now. Direct mail is a NOW decision, not one to put off until tomorrow. You want prospects to make their decision and act on it immediately. In some cases, sweeteners and facilitators can convince prospects to respond immediately.

Give them reasons why they should act now and not delay.

■ *KEY POINT: Close your letter by telling prospects to act NOW and giving them reasons.*

    The Special Discount only applies if we receive your order before March 15. So right now, while it's before you, slip out the card below. Peel off the token, place it on the "yes" circle, and drop it into the mail. It's already addressed. Get set to enjoy your current issue—soon!

Create pressure for the prospect to act NOW, while the discount is in effect.

    Remember, the Nut & Bolt Kit is a lot for the money. Mail your order today. . . . I can't guarantee prompt delivery if you delay ordering.

Good, it ties the product into an immediate response.

    With the *Disk Magazine* you'll save hundreds of dollars on your computer software needs this next month. But only if you act now. Start it coming your way today.

Tie in the benefit of saving money if the prospect orders now.

    But please act quickly, because the supply is limited. So popular are these titles that more than 2 million have been purchased to date.
    To assure yourself of the entire set at a saving of more than 10%, mail your Reservation Card today! And take advantage of this great book bargain celebrating the enduring value of our American heritage.

This uses money and scarcity as reasons to act now. It also plucks at readers' patriotic heart strings.

    With a guarantee of an immediate refund if the Sourcebook is not everything I say it is, how could you go wrong? You could hardly ask for a better offer than that. So why don't you mail your acceptance card today?
    And don't forget that if you order within 15 days, you'll receive free. . .

Good, but it's better to tie reasons for ordering now to the product or benefit, rather than to the guarantee alone.

You don't owe the government any more in taxes than you are required to pay by law. If you order the *Tax Digest* before this upcoming tax season, you can save over 10 times what you will pay for it. So help yourself and the economy—cut your taxes and be proud of it! But you can only do it if you have these money-saving ideas in your hands NOW. The tax money you save is yours, don't lose it. Subscribe today!

It doesn't hurt to come on strong when asking for a response on a pocketbook issue like this one.

Please note the time limit on the coupon and be sure to get your order in before it expires. We wouldn't want you to be disappointed. Be sure and fill out and return the coupon today.

Using a time-limited discount as a facilitator to get the prospect to act now often works.

ADDITIONAL HINTS FOR LETTERS

In addition to the preceding strategies for writing sales letters, here are some other hints. First, use sweeteners and facilitators as often as you need to to buy readership, enhance benefits, and encourage response. "If you order now get a FREE Wall Anchor Set!" "Buy now and receive '21 Ways to Improve Cash Flow.'" "Subscribe and we'll send you a FREE copy of 'Dynamite Your Taxes Now.'" "As part of your subscription, you'll receive four surveys, PLUS. . ." "With your gift of $25 or more, you'll receive *Opera News* magazine." "Mail the self-addressed and stamped reservation card today." "Call our toll-free number right now." These can all reinforce the sales message.

■ *KEY POINT: Use sweeteners and facilitators to buy readership and encourage response.*

Second, once or twice on every page of your letter tell readers to read the copy. "Read here how to. . . ," "Read how these benefits can help you. . . ," "Read below to find. . . ," "See in this paragraph how you can save. . . ," are only some of the phrases you can use to maintain readership.

■ *KEY POINT: Ask prospects frequently to read the copy.*

Third, your letter copy should refer to other parts of the mailing piece. Tell prospects to read the brochure, response card, testimonial, or other literature included in your letter. "You'll find further information about each of these books in the enclosed brochure," "Take a few minutes to review the enclosed flyer," "Note the special offer on the coupon," "With this letter is your free guide. . . ," "See the back of this letter and the enclosed subscription card for details," are some examples.

■ *KEY POINT: In the letter refer to other parts of the mailing package.*

TWELVE-POINT SUMMARY OF HOW TO WRITE A SALES LETTER

1. Have the headline describe a major benefit.
2. Write the postscript second, because prospects often read it first.
3. Choose the proper salutation for prospects.
4. State the offer in the first paragraph of the body copy.
5. Highlight the major benefits next.
6. Add description to enhance the benefits.
7. Load copy with secondary and comparative benefits.
8. Back up benefits with proofs and testimonials.
9. Guarantee the offer.
10. Summarize the offer.
11. Ask prospects to respond.
12. Tell prospects why they must act now.

The last three steps are critical to direct mail success. In Step 10, "summarize the offer," tell your prospects what the deal is and what they must do to get the product or service. In Step 11, "ask prospects to respond," you tell them how they can get in on the deal. And in Step 12, "tell prospects why they must act now," you give them the reasons for acting now. This is a natural flow: what is needed to act, how to act, and why to act now.

DESIGNING AND LAYING OUT THE DIRECT MAIL LETTER 8

In this chapter we will learn how design and layout, as well as copy, can increase readership of our sales letter. All the basic elements of design, from paper color to placement of copy, can buy us more readership.

EVERY ELEMENT OF DESIGN AND LAYOUT IS IMPORTANT

Our goal in designing direct mail letters is to gain readership, a response, and a sale. But given the resistance people have to advertising, we must be good at presenting our offer. The design and layout we use in our letters can draw readers in and get them to focus on our sales message.

■ *CAUTION NOTE:* *Design is critical in overcoming readers' resistance.*

All the factors to be discussed here—paper and ink color, typeface and style, letterhead and subheads, highlighting, paper size, and copy placement—play an important part in making it easy for prospects to read the copy we have written. Design elements can also be used to gain immediate decisions. No matter how good our copy is, we can lose responses if the copy is not presented so readers can understand what they have to do.

■ *KEY POINT:* *Design is an essential part of making it easy for prospects to respond.*

Our twofold aim of gaining readership and a response can be enhanced by careful attention to every element of design and layout in our letter.

The first thing to keep in mind, however, is that designing a direct mail sales letter is vastly different from designing display or awareness advertisements. In direct mail, the visual attractiveness found so often in awareness advertising is far less important. In fact, in direct mail, design can often interfere with readership if it competes with sales copy. Design in direct mail must never be flashy or call attention to itself. It must do only two things: promote readership of copy and prompt prospects into making a favorable decision on which they will act NOW.

■ *CAUTION NOTE:* *Good design in direct mail does not mean visual attractiveness.*

■ *KEY POINT:* *In direct mail, subdued design best promotes readership and response.*

CHOOSE PAPER THAT GIVES HIGHEST CONTRAST WITH INK COLOR

In designing our letter, we should first decide what kind of paper to use. Since readability is crucial, we need the best visual contrast between the color and finish of the paper and the color of the ink we will use for our message. Thus we should use as light a paper as possible to provide contrast with the chosen ink color. This contrast enhances the readability of our sales message.

■ *CAUTION NOTE:* *The colors of paper and ink must contrast for readability.*

The best choice for paper is thus pure white or light cream-colored stock, like cream ivory or antique white. White obviously contrasts well with black ink. Cream-colored paper also contrasts well with black or even slightly lighter ink, such as blue or blue-black.

■ *KEY POINT:* *White or cream-colored paper provides highest contrast.*

Avoid paper and ink colors that are similar; coordinated colors, no matter how light or dark, do not usually have enough contrast for easy reading. Avoid using bright white paper, too; it is hard on the eyes and looks like junk mail to prospects.

■ *CAUTION NOTE: Avoid using coordinated colors.*

Other paper colors to stay away from are earth colors like brown, yellow, rust, dull orange, red, and mustard color. They too often convey a "dirty" color and look musty when used for stationery. And because they have a psychological connotation of slowness and inactivity, they don't encourage swift response.

■ *CAUTION NOTE: Earth colors are not psychologically exciting.*

Also avoid purples and violets, which have been overused in direct mail.

An excellent way to gauge paper color is to examine the direct mail you receive yourself. You will see that the better companies use soft white or cream-colored stock, while the one-time grapefruit squeezer offer is more likely to be made on flashy stock.

INK COLOR MUST PROVIDE CONTRAST TO PROMOTE READERSHIP

Our choice of ink color depends on the color of the paper. With a white or light-cream paper, black or dark-blue ink offers the most contrast. And contrast, if not harsh or glaring, promotes readership.

■ *CAUTION NOTE: Ink color must provide contrast.*

Avoid combinations like medium-brown ink on buff-colored paper. Coordinated colors won't inspire readership, let alone response, from your prospects. Instead they will put readers to sleep, because they are psychologically boring.

We often see coordinated color combinations in fund-raising mail, when the writers are reluctant to ask too firmly for a donation. They probably wish to be "tasteful" or "classy." Since you have only today to ask the question, don't be weak about it. Even the Metropolitan Museum doesn't pussyfoot around when it comes to asking for money.

■ *CAUTION NOTE: Don't use coordinated ink and paper colors.*

Black and dark shades of blue, maroon, and green give enough color contrast to communicate the message. Sometimes other design elements, such as visually oriented headlines, perhaps combined with pictures or line drawings, are done in full and lighter color. But in this case, the colored designs are used to gain attention and get the copy read.

■ *KEY POINT: Use black or a dark shade of blue ink for most copy.*

Once you have narrowed the range of what works and what does not, the choices become more subtle. For example, white is not just white, it is either warm or cool. If we combine a warm-white paper with a dark-brown ink, we cut down on contrast, but not enough to lose readership. If we use a cool-white paper, a dark-maroon ink provides dramatic contrast.

Consider your product or service when choosing paper and ink colors. If the mailing is for a charitable institution and you want a firm but dignified request, use a low-contrast combination. If you are selling a low-cost product and want to create some excitement, go for higher contrast.

■ *KEY POINT: The final choice of ink and paper color is often subtle.*

PAPER COMES IN DIFFERENT FINISHES, TEXTURES, AND WEIGHTS

There are other decisions to make about paper. Paper for our needs is either coated or uncoated. Coated paper has a hard, polished surface texture. It is opaque and often used when high-quality color photographs are incorporated into the piece. But its glossy surface reflects light into the eyes, which makes reading more difficult. Also it costs more than uncoated paper.

■ *CAUTION NOTE:*   *Coated paper is good for pictures but bad for reading.*

Uncoated paper is less opaque than coated paper and has a matte (without luster) slightly rough finish. It is more than adequate for printing and does not reflect light. If you are using special color designs, consider plain, uncoated paper with a nonglare finish, as it is best and least expensive for printing text.

■ *KEY POINT:*   *Uncoated matte-finish paper holds ink well and does not cause glare.*

Uncoated paper that has been "burnished" under high-speed rollers on a special paper-making machine has been treated to not absorb ink or reflect glare. Use a hard-finished version of uncoated paper if you are planning a special multicolor headline or other visually oriented design.

■ *KEY POINT:*   *Use burnished paper when a hard finish is needed for color or photos.*

Classic laid, a textured finish, is also a good choice for marketing relatively expensive products or services. It simulates more expensive rag-content paper. Because of its rough texture, this paper does not take multicolor designs as well as coated paper, but it is a good alternative to standard coated paper if you are selling something unique and wish to draw attention to it.

■ *KEY POINT:*   *Textured or rough-finish paper conveys an impression of quality.*

We must also decide what weight paper to use. Here the mailing costs set by the U.S. Postal Service can affect our choice. For example, most good-quality papers we would use are of 20 to 24 pound weight. But if we want to keep the total weight of our mailing package, including brochure and response device, under 1 ounce, we may need to choose a thinner, more transparent paper (16 or 20 pounds) for the letter.

■ *KEY POINT:*   *The weight of the paper chosen is affected by the quality needed and by postal rates.*

Most evidence indicates that people do not notice if paper is cheap or flimsy. However, use your judgment. Your choice should depend on the decision you want prospects to make. If you are selling an expensive product or service, consider a paper quality that conveys this impression; if a magazine subscription or $29.95 kit of hand tools, go for the simplicity of standard uncoated paper.

■ *KEY POINT:* *The decision about paper weight and quality is based partly on the product being sold.*

In most mailing campaigns, your two major criteria are a paper's ability to accept ink and its lack of glare.

■ *KEY POINT:* *Choose paper by its ability to accept ink and reflect light.*

WHAT STYLE AND SIZE TYPEFACE DO WE USE?

There is little argument about the best typeface to use in direct mail letters: a style that duplicates standard typewriter type. We want to use a typeface that is familiar, because our primary goal is legibility, and legibility encourages readership. Our letter need not look memorable. Unlike in awareness advertising, in direct mail we do not care if our product is remembered. We want a decision now, and we want our copy to be easy to read.

■ *CAUTION NOTE:* *In selecting the typeface, seek legibility of the letter, not memorability.*

We use a typewriter typeface for our letter and save special type for our brochure and response device. You may well decide, as many sellers do, to simply type your letter copy on your office typewriter and give it to your printer, who will print it on the paper you have chosen.

But not any type style will do. You must use a *serif* typeface, that is, one with the "feet" on the top and bottom of individual letters (Figure 8.1). Serifs encourage a reader's eye to move horizontally across the copy, which is what you want.

**REAL ESTATE
DATA PUBLISHING**

PO Box 885 • Framingham, MA 01701 • 617-655-4000

September 16, 1983

James Lumley, Realtor
57 South Valley Rd.
Pelham, MA   01002

Dear Realtor:

If you survived the past years of high interest rates, scarce
mortgage money and buyers who didn't qualify, it's probably
because you made some wise decisions, were well-organized and
offered a premium service.

Our customers are the top real estate professionals in Massachusetts who, not only survived, but continued to grow.

They tell us the REDP Advantage helped them succeed!

The REDP Advantage is a $45 investment that brings you 12 monthly
supplements of the Transfer Directory listing every property
transfer in your town.

The REDP Advantage is a comparable sales file that lists all
your sales, all MLS sales - plus, the balance of property
transfers that you or your staff have been searching for.

REAL ESTATE DATA PUBLISHING has been providing this valuable
reporting service since 1971, and each year our client base has
grown as more successful firms have discovered the REDP Advantage.

If you are one of those top real estate professionals in Massachusetts, then you should gain the REDP Advantage by ordering the
Transfer Directory today.

We look forward to helping you succeed.

Respectfully,

David B. Hamilton, President

Figure 8.1 Typewriter-style pica type with serifs that moves the eye horizontally. (Courtesy Real Estate Data Publishing)

You must also use a large, readable type size—*pica,* which has 10 characters per inch. *Do not use elite,* which crams in 12 characters per inch.

■ *KEY POINT: Use typewriter-style print in "pica" size with "serifs."*

USE THE LETTERHEAD TO DELIVER THE SALES MESSAGE

The reader's eye will go first to the top of the page. Do not waste this space by using your company name or letterhead there. Instead use a sales message that stresses a benefit of your offer. "Advanced Strategies for Successful Investing," or better still, "How You Can Save Money for Your Children's Education by These Advanced Strategies," works better than the company name. This is especially strong because it puts a benefit right at the top of the letter.

■ *CAUTION NOTE: Don't waste letterhead space by putting your company name there.*

■ *KEY POINT: Create special "letterheads" that sell.*

A letterhead used this way is like a headline, but it is usually shorter, even when stressing a benefit. For example, "Just Published . . . How to Make Your Advertising Make Money" leads off a letter without a company name (Figure 8.2). It is also short. The copy that follows contains a number of subheads that accentuate major benefits.

■ *KEY POINT: A headline can be used in the letterhead space.*

Often the name of the product is intrinsic and specific to the offer. When the *Wall Street Journal* is at the top of the letter, we can make a pretty good guess about what is being offered. The same is true for products of the Kiplinger Company. The corporate name is nowhere to be seen. If the company is marketing its *Washington Letter,* the letterhead is "The *Kiplinger Washington Letter."* We know exactly who the company is and what it offers. When we see the letterhead of *Fortune, National*

Just published . . .

HOW TO MAKE YOUR
ADVERTISING MAKE MONEY

A clear, concise guide to effective advertising . . .   *by John*
                                                Caples

* a collection of hundreds of words, phrases, sentences, headlines and copy you can use to take the guesswork out of your advertising

* a source of dozens of case histories, based on successful advertising created for many of the world's major consumer and industrial companies

* an idea treasury—hundreds of ready-to-use ideas— plus the coaching you can use to brainstorm new ideas for virtually any product or service

* a sourcebook of direct mail strategy that shows you how to plan, produce and evaluate any campaign— for any market

* a collection of sales appeals that work now and will work forever

* plus the insight of a successful writer and businessman who has helped thousands of people and companies to make millions with effective advertising

Dear Advertising Professional:

    These are just a few of the wide ranging subjects that are covered in John Caples' new book. In clear, conversational style, Caples gives you the guidance and insight he has provided to his clients and fellow advertising professionals for 50 years. In a single volume, he tells you how to write sentences that sell.... how to write headlines that attract attention.....how to write sales letters that pull orders, list-after-list.....how to find advertising ideas.....plus much more.

    Because of your keen interest in making advertising work, I'm sure that you will want to review this book. Therefore, I invite you to see it and use it for 30 day, without charge.

    The product of a lifetime of active research and practical experience with some of the world's most prestigious companies, this book is John Caples' crowning achievement. Here are just a few of the secrets he reveals.....

        * 106 ads that have made fortunes * How to use mail order techniques to multiply the strength of other advertising * How to write successful small space ads * Ten ways to begin a sales letter * Six ways to ask for the order * Six ways to multiply the effectiveness of any size ad budget * The most successful sales letters ever written * Twelve ways to find advertising ideas, and how to put them to use * The secrets of top advertising professionals * plus much more

                          please turn to the back page........

Figure 8.2 See how this big, bold headline is used as a letterhead to deliver the sales message—the major benefit—and is followed by many subheads before the body copy starts. (Courtesy Prentice-Hall)

147

Geographic, or *Garden Way Carts* we know what we are getting. The message is inherent in the name.

■ *KEY POINT: Company names make good letterheads to describe the product or service.*

Some companies have their name on the letterhead but "bury" it, using a bold and prominent sales message as well (Figure 8.3). (The message should be on the left, the company name on the right, as in this example, because that's how we read.)

■ *KEY POINT: Some companies combine their name and a headline to start the letter.*

Other companies have redesigned their logo so it incorporates their selling message, or they develop a logo that supports their sales message.

■ *KEY POINT: Use your logo to identify your sales message.*

Remember, the area at the top of the letter catches the reader's eye before anything else. Use it to promote your selling message by highlighting a benefit.

BOLD TYPE EMPHASIZES THE HEADLINE AND SUBHEADS

We can use many graphic devices to emphasize parts of our sales message. Because we want to organize our material to make the maximum impact on readers, we design our letter so graphics emphasize key parts. Bold print, underlining, italics, asterisks, reverse background (white on black), color, and even hand-written notes are some ways we do this.

■ *KEY POINT: Graphic devices emphasize key parts of copy.*

For example, letterheads or headlines are often set in large, boldface characters, in a type style that differs from the "typewriter" style of the

Fact or Fiction?

You'll find the answers below—along with a FREE TRIAL offer from OMNI!

OMNI
1965 BROADWAY, NEW YORK, NY 10023—5965

Dear Reader:

Imagine a noseless man with sealed lips and crocodile skin, a creature perfectly adapted for survival in the frozen vacuum of space.

In the not-too-distant future genetic engineers may be able to sit down at computer consoles and type in the DNA codes for these and other beings designed to explore distant planets...

Science fiction?

Or science fact?

Maybe both. And only in OMNI will you find a blend of top-notch science-fiction stories by Stanislaw Lem, Harlan Ellison, and Robert Silverberg--and scientifically accurate articles on biomedicine, astronomy, the environment, computers that animate movies, electronic spying, or genetic engineering.

> If you are fascinated by the future, mesmerized by modern technology, and if you love to speculate on the world of tommorrow, I would like to invite you to receive a FREE TRIAL ISSUE of OMNI--yours to examine with absolutely no risk!

This is your chance to get to know OMNI, the only magazine

(please turn page)

1

Figure 8.3 The company name is small an unobtrusive on the right. The letterhead starts on the left with a prominent benefit. (Courtesy *Omni* magazine) body copy. Because they are set in bold type they are clearly identified. Headings should also be surrounded with enough white space so they stand out, so that the reader's eye is caught by the first of our key selling benefits.

■ *KEY POINT:*   *Use boldface type to identify the major headline and benefit.*

Subheads about primary or secondary benefits can also be in boldface type but should not be as large as the main headline. Even when subheads stand alone in front of the text that explains them, they are usually printed in the same type size as the rest of the body copy.

UNDERLINING DRAWS ATTENTION TO KEY WORDS WITHIN THE COPY

Underlining is used to draw attention to words or whole phrases in sentences. "But this one is <u>yours now for just $3.95</u> with a no-risk . . . ," "If money is the only reason you've held off buying, <u>I have good news</u>," or "<u>I guarantee you will save</u> at least 10 times the $8.97 <u>dues within the first 90 days</u>" are examples of how underlining identifies key parts of the selling message.

Magazine titles, when they appear in the text, are often emphasized with underlining, for example, "Come to the pages of <u>Vanity Fair</u> and meet . . ." Subheads can also be identified by underlining, for example, "But that's not all! You also get. . ."

Underlining is the most commonly used graphic device to emphasize major sales points (Figure 8.4). It may even be used once or twice in every paragraph. (It should not be overused, however.) Underlining makes it obvious that the letter was composed on a typewriter; its use is similar to how people accentuate points in letters to friends.

■ *KEY POINT:*   *Underlining is the most effective device for attracting attention.*

DARTNELL
Publishers Serving Business Since 1917
4660 N. Ravenswood Ave.
Chicago, Illinois 60640

```
* * * * * * * * * * * * * * * * * * * * * * * * *
```

                    ANNOUNCING ... a new, low-cost program
                    to help you guard your best source of
                    future business from today's cutthroat
                                        competition!

        * * * * * *   * * * * * *

        It's a well-known fact. The best ... the fastest ... the most
effective way to increase sales is to sell more to your present customers.
They have faith in your salespeople. In your firm. In your products.
And, in the service you provide.

        No doubt you have invested thousands to train your salespeople.
Doesn't it make sense to invest something in the people who have in-
valuable insight into your customers' needs and have a big impact on
your future sales -- your field service reps? When you think about it,
they are your second sales force! Here's how to put them to good use.

        Dartnell has developed a new program to help your field service
reps become more aware of your customers and their needs. To help them
build a lasting impression of courteous, quality service.

        A practical program to help your field service reps lay the
groundwork for your salespeople to sell more to your present customers
... and reduce skyrocketing sales costs. To help your reps build the
kind of loyalty that discourages competition -- virtually guarantees
you growing sales and profits.

        I'm referring to Dartnell's ...

                        FIELD SERVICE PLANNER

        ... which provides your field service reps with an easy means
of setting goals. Plus, a foolproof system for reaching them. As well
as an effective means of building a favorable impression of your firm in
the customer's mind that will result in new, high-profit business.

        Here's how it works. Each month your field service reps receive
a new Dartnell FIELD SERVICE PLANNER that brings them:

        1. a fold-out planning calendar which acts
            as a fail-safe reminder system to insure
            your reps are managing their time properly.
            A prime ingredient in providing outstanding
            service ... and building future sales.

        2. a daily memo book section which provides
            your reps with plenty of space for writing
            all their important notes. (It eliminates
            the need to carry a pocketful of loose, un-

                        please turn page for FREE-Trial offer ...

Figure 8.4 Underlining draws the reader's eyes to all the key benefits of the offer, even to the free trial. (Courtesy Dartnell Corporation)

151

organized pieces of paper that can be lost.)
A vital feature in any business building
program.

3. <u>a short refresher training article</u> that dis-
    cusses good customer relations principles.
    (i.e. "Handling Customer Complaints," "How
    To Ask Questions," "Time and Schedule
    Organization," "Customer Courtesy".) And,
    supplies your reps with practical tips about
    dealing with various types of customers.

4. <u>PLUS ... at least one full page for recording</u>
    -- Warranty Information, Service Rates,
    Maintenance Agreements Sold This Month,
    Supplies Sold This Month, Parts Used This
    Month, Summary of Month's Expenses, Advance
    Schedule of Calls - and more.

Your reps will welcome Dartnell's new FIELD SERVICE PLANNER
because it provides them with a central source to refer to: in planning
their daily work ... in keeping on schedule ... in reaching production
goals ... in building efficiency and good customer relations.

Try It For 30 Days ... <u>FREE!</u>   But don't take my word for it. See
Mail Your Enclosed "No Obligation"   for yourself the dramatic results
Certificate - Today.   your field service reps can accomplish
                                       in just 30 short days. At no cost,
no obligation, let each of your reps try Dartnell's new FIELD SERVICE PLANNER
... <u>free for 30 days</u>. Simply fill in and mail your enclosed <u>FREE</u>-Trial
Certificate. By return mail, you'll receive a copy of Dartnell's new FIELD
SERVICE PLANNER for each of your field service reps.

During the next month, let each of your reps put Dartnell's PLANNER
to the test by using it daily in his work. Then ... and only then, decide
whether you wish to continue. There is no cost. No obligation for trying.

Do it now, while you're thinking about it. Complete and mail your
<u>FREE</u>-Trial Certificate. And, start enjoying increased output, efficiency,
sales and profits. Remember, it costs nothing to try!

                        Sincerely,

                        George Economos

                        George Economos
                        for Dartnell

P.S. Please take a few minutes to review the enclosed FIELD SERVICE
      PLANNER. Note how it is designed to organize your rep's efforts,
      simplify his work and build good customer relations. Then, on
      your no-obligation, <u>FREE</u>-Trial Certificate, write in how many
      PLANNERS you wish to try <u>FREE</u> for 30 days and mail it. We'll do
      the rest.

Figure 8.4 (Continued)

OTHER GRAPHIC DEVICES THAT ENHANCE COPY

Italics are used in much the same way as underlining. For example, "You pay less than 93¢, that's *only $24 for the six months just ahead.*" However, italics is a change in the style of type and its use makes it obvious that the letter was not typed on a keyboard. This is also true for use of different ink colors to draw attention to parts of the text. Though neither device is offensive to readers, use of both should be limited.

■ *CAUTION NOTE: Use italics sparingly for emphasis.*

Asterisks are used to identify subheads, secondary benefits, or almost any kind of information that can be presented in a list. Occasionally asterisks are printed in a color different from the body text.

■ *KEY POINT: Use asterisks to identify lists of material.*

Hand-written messages are dramatic devices because they make the reader aware that a real person wrote the message. This increases the reader's emotional involvement with the message. Not everything must be straight text in a letter.

■ *KEY POINT: Hand-written messages gain readers' attention.*

Line drawings of benefits can add to the reader's understanding by showing how something works or how it's constructed. Drawings are valid devices if they contribute to helping prospects make a decision and act on it. Photographs are similar. You don't always need to reserve these for the brochure; often they can help prospects understand the offer, and thus encourage a decision.

■ *KEY POINT: Photographs and line drawings can add to understanding.*

■ *CAUTION NOTE: Use graphic device only if it helps the prospect to make a decision.*

We must remember, however, that graphic devices used in the body of the text must refer to the essentials of a particular paragraph or section of text. Underlining, for example, must draw the eye not only to the most important section of text but to the best place to start reading in the paragraph.

The most successful direct mail letters are designed so that if prospects read only the underlined or highlighted sections they will know what is being offered and how to respond. In this way, buyers who won't read the copy completely still know enough to make a decision and respond.

■ *KEY POINT:*   *Graphic devices are powerful ways to draw the eye.*

■ *KEY POINT:*   *Graphic devices should summarize everything prospects need to make a decision.*

Figures 8.5 and 8.6 show the uses of letterheads and headlines and other graphic devices to draw the prospect's eye.

VARYING THE SIZE OF PAGES ALLOWS YOU TO BE DIFFERENT

As we saw in the last chapter, effective sales letters are often long. Text length affects the size of the page and the number of pages. Most sales letters are the standard letter size of 8½ inches by 11 inches. Some mimic the more "personal" correspondence size of 7 inches by 10½ inches. We are most used to the standard size, which gives us more space to write long copy. However, since standard size is used so much by direct mailers, prospects also identify it as a sales message. The smaller-size paper resembles the stationery many prospects use for their personal correspondence.

■ *KEY POINT:*   *Standard- and "personal"-size pages are both appropriate for letters.*

The smaller-size paper is often used by fund raisers who want their appeals to be more personal than messages selling products. We can also vary paper size from mailing to mailing. Because we must make frequent contact with prospects, our mailings must look different. Changing the size of the letter is one way to create that difference.

■ *KEY POINT:*   *Vary the paper size when making a series of mailings.*

2 Disk Drive, P.O. Box 4004, Sidney, OH 45365

CHARTER FREE ISSUE OFFER

Announcing a new magazine
for personal computing users . . .
   SOFTWARE SUPERMARKET
. . . the best solution to software confusion!

Dear Reader:

    What program are you going to watch on your personal
computer tonight? Of all the software compatible with your
computer, is it the best of its kind? Could you have had
a better program for less money?

    Is there software on the market right now that would
fit your needs perfectly ... if you only knew about it?
Are you having trouble keeping up with the proliferation of
software packages available? Are you even hearing about the
bargain software?

    If you're a little confused, it's no wonder! There's
been an explosion in the development of personal computers
and their software. And after any explosion, a shambles and
confusion are bound to follow.

    You need someone to make order out of the software chaos.
Someone to fill in the missing pieces. Someone to give you
the facts about software. You need Software Supermarket!

    FREE CHARTER ISSUE. We've reserved a free copy of
Software Supermarket's Charter issue for you. No
risk. No obligation to continue. Just a perfect
opportunity to see for yourself that Software
Supermarket is the solution to your software confusion!

    Take a pre-publication glimpse at some of the practical,
helpful articles scheduled for the Charter issue ...

(over, please)

Figure 8.5 The eye is strongly attracted to this hand-written note. A major
benefit is used as the headline. (Courtesy Software Supermarket)

VANITY FAIR

The Condé Nast Publications Inc.

350 Madison Avenue, New York, NY 10017

Dear Reader:

Running down the margins of this letter --
some of today's most fascinating artists.

People who, with stunning twists of words,
with rhyme, with wit, sometimes with raucous
humor, with a combination of sounds perhaps,
or movements, a splash of color, a seductive
play of light and shadow, capture, communicate,
and contribute to the sparkle and excitement
of our time.

Their pictures, reprinted here, have recently
been a part of the first issues of a wonderful
new magazine. Vanity Fair.

Vanity Fair is a monthly panorama of today's
most exciting art and literature, theater,
film, music, dance, books and politics, pop
culture, private lives and public events.
It is a magazine of elegance and wit that
alerts its readers to what's worth seeing,
doing, knowing, and talking about.

Admittedly, it is not for everyone. But for
those who relish exceptional reading -- a
literary feast. And for those who delight in
imaginative graphics -- a feast for the eye.

If you count yourself among these, then you
are certain to enjoy our extraordinary new
magazine.

      And this letter is your personal
      invitation to accept a forthcoming
      issue with our compliments.

Come into the pages of Vanity Fair and
meet the poets, playwrights, painters,
photographers, novelists and journalists,
musicians, dancers, actors and actresses who
have been born with gifts to charm, divert,
intrigue, touch, and provoke us.

                              (over, please)

Susan Sarandon,
photograph by Brigitte Lacombe

Vincent Spano,
photograph by Annie Leibovitz

Norman Mailer,
photograph by Annie Leibovitz

Figure 8.6 Look at the power these pictures have to underscore the importance of the message in this letter. (Courtesy *Vanity Fair*)

LAYING OUT THE SALES LETTER

Copy should have a margin of ¾ inch to 1 inch on all four borders. (A specially designed letterhead is used at the top of the page.) The borders need not be as wide as in a standard business letter. We can take some liberty with our borders and approach the edges more, as we strive for a personal, unique approach.

■ *KEY POINT:* *Use adequate margins.*

Even though we want to put lots of copy on the page, this is one occasion when white space is valuable. We double-space lines between paragraphs and highlighted subheads or benefits. If we want to draw attention to a single sentence or phrase, we allow space around it. Like graphic devices, white spaces must draw attention to the right parts of our copy. If copy is crammed, it will go unread. Be forewarned: Keep the pages looking spacious.

■ *KEY POINT:* *Correct spacing draws attention to the right parts of the copy.*

For example, if you are using 8½-inch by 11-inch paper, don't exceed 300 words on the first page and 350 words on subsequent pages. If your paper is 7½ inches by 10½ inches, don't go over 200 words on the first page and 275 thereafter. Otherwise your copy will look crowded.

■ *CAUTION NOTE:* *Limit the number of words on each page to avoid crowding.*

Always leave a *ragged right* border on the right-hand side of the text. Sales letters must imitate, as best they can, personal letters, and few people writing at home use computers to "word process" the text *flush right*. Designers tend to not like rough edges on the right, and you may have to put your foot down and insist, if those helping you design your letter don't agree.

■ *CAUTION NOTE:* *Always use "ragged right," never "flush right."*

You should also indent paragraphs, although this is not as important as using ragged right. Many mailers don't bother to indent because they double-space between paragraphs. But again, you are simulating a personal letter, and most people indent paragraphs. And, if you want to emphasize something important, bring the body of *all* paragraphs to the left (Figure 8.7).

■ *KEY POINT:* **Indenting paragraphs imitates personal letter writing.**

HOW LONG SHOULD THE LETTER BE?

The final answer to this question is another question: How many words do we need to tell our sales story?

Most direct mail letters are two pages long. But it is difficult to get readers to read the second page, even if they only have to turn the paper over. It is even harder to get readers to the last page of a four-page letter.

■ *CAUTION NOTE:* **It's hard to get readers to read a reverse page.**

Consider this: Make what would normally be a two-page letter into a three-page letter. Space the letter out, or write more copy, and use a second piece of paper for the third page. Do this even if the third page is only half a page long.

Why? Because the end of a letter contains so much—the summary of the offer, the close, how to respond, the postscript with the offer again. If the end is on its own page, the facing page of a second sheet, it stands alone and gets more attention. If the end is on the back side of a two-page letter, it's buried.

The same principle holds for four-page letters—the end, the part you most want prospects to read, gets lost. The answer is to condense the letter to three pages or expand it to five.

■ *KEY POINT:* **Make an even number of pages an odd number so the last page is a facing page.**

---

to send you a free sample of the current issue of HIGH TECHNOLOGY, so you can judge for yourself whether you'd like to subscribe.

I'm convinced it will be love at first sight, and that once you see just one issue, you'll never want to be without HIGH TECHNOLOGY.

For here, at last, is a magazine that gives you an easy, convenient way to keep up with the latest and most important breakthroughs in new technologies. HIGH TECHNOLOGY covers them all—from gene splicing to fiber optics...from robotics to thin-film photovoltaic cells...from laser weaponry to magnetic levitation of high-speed trains.

With HIGH TECHNOLOGY, you'll know about the latest advances in computers, space technology, transportation, medical technology, construction, communication, military & aerospace technology, automotive design, the electronic office, new materials, industrial technology, fuels, television & entertainment—every field where technology plays a key role!

You'll see what the new technologies are...how they work...and how they interact. You'll be alerted to future technologies that are now on the drawing boards and in the labs. And you'll see what changes are coming soon for existing technologies.

You'll read about discoveries and experiments that are more fascinating than any science fiction—because they're actually taking place right here and now!

But How Will This Information Benefit You?

...I can think of many ways you'll find this kind of coverage rewarding, but let me cite four benefits that immediately spring to mind...

1. YOU'LL GAIN IDEAS THAT CAN HELP YOU IN YOUR WORK...
    PERHAPS EVEN ADVANCE YOUR CAREER.

If you work in a high tech organization, you know how advances in a totally unrelated field can spark new ideas and breakthroughs in your own.

With HIGH TECHNOLOGY, you can be among the first to spot the possibilities that other technologies hold for your work—and perhaps even use them to forge new breakthroughs of your own.

You'll also be among the first to become acquainted with the most advanced tools, materials, measurement devices and computer programs—not to mention enlightening new theories and concepts—that can further contribute to your work and your career.

2. YOU'LL GET HELP IN GUIDING YOUR ORGANIZATION INTO THE
    FUTURE.

If you are an entrepreneur or manager in a high tech organization, you need the facts, figures and forecasts to appraise specific products, processes, systems and technologies. You need to know how a new tech-

Figure 8.7 A border that measures more than 1 inch, spaces between paragraphs, a ragged-right margin and indented paragraphs. (Courtesy *High Technology*)

HOW DO WE GET READERS TO GO TO THE NEXT PAGE?

Since our sales letters are usually several pages long, how can we lead readers from one page to another? One way is to simply indicate at the bottom of the page, with an arrow or in writing, that they should turn the page over. This message can be typed or handwritten. For example, "(over, please)," "over," or "please go to next page" are all messages that guide readers.

■ *KEY POINT:*   *Tell prospects to turn to the next page.*

Another key device is to split the copy in the middle of a sentence. Readers will go to the next page just to see what you're saying. Use both devices—a preferably handwritten instruction and a split message, when constructing your letter.

■ *KEY POINT:*   *Always split your copy at the bottom of the page.*

Many of the examples in this chapter use messages and split copy to draw readers to the next page.

BUILDING MULTIPAGE LETTERS

You can construct your pages several different ways. One way is to print three pages on two pieces of paper, or five pages on three pieces of paper. You can also fold an 11-inch by 17-inch paper in half like a small brochure and print on three pages, leaving the fourth blank. A smaller-size letter can be made by folding a 10½ by 14-inch paper in half, with copy on three pages. If you use folded pages, you can insert single pieces of paper, which give you two or four more pages for copy. In this way it is easy to construct sales letters of five or seven pages.

■ *KEY POINT:*   *Longer sales letters can be constructed by folding paper pages.*

All of these options are ideal for long sales letters. For shorter copy— under 300 words on a single side of a page—either size will work because prospects can easily see at a glance what's in it for them.

However, with certain types of products such as film processing, in which color is essential, the brochure may be more important than the letter. In such cases, small notepaper size may work best for the letter copy.

DO'S AND DON'TS IN DESIGNING DIRECT MAIL LETTERS

Do's

Use subdued design.

Use light-colored paper for contrast.

Use white or cream-colored paper.

Use black or dark-blue ink.

Use uncoated paper.

Use texture-finished paper for expensive mailings.

Use 20- or 24-pound paper.

Use typewriter-style typeface for body copy.

Use pica 10-pitch type.

Use serif typeface.

Tie benefits into letterhead.

Use benefit for headline.

Make letterhead boldface and prominent.

Make headlines and subheads boldface.

Typeset letterhead and headline.

Print major benefits in boldface.

Underline to draw attention to major selling points.

Use asterisks for lists of benefits.

Add handwritten note for personal touch.

Use line drawings and photographs for realism.

Vary page size in frequent successive mailings.

Maintain ¾-inch to 1-inch margins.

Double-space between paragraphs.

Keep ragged-right style.

Indent paragraphs.

Tell reader to turn page.

Use italics sparingly.

Don'ts

Never use flashy design.

Don't use glossy paper except for photographs.

Don't use coordinated paper and ink colors.

Don't use bright-white paper.

Don't use earth color, such as brown or mustard, for paper.

Don't use purple or violet paper.

Don't use any coated paper that reflects glare.

Don't use flimsy 16-pound paper.

Don't use elite (12-pitch) type size.

Don't use sans serif type style.

Don't use corporate letterhead.

Don't run copy to edge of paper.

Don't cram copy.

Don't exceed 250 to 300 words per page.

Don't use flush-right style.

Don't use flush-left style to start paragraph.

Don't end letter on back page.

WRITING COMPELLING HEADLINES AND COPY FOR BROCHURES 9

In this chapter we will explore how to write headlines and body copy for brochures and how to tie the brochures' sales message to the sales letter.

WHAT IS A DIRECT MAIL BROCHURE?

The brochure is the visual piece of the direct mail package. It contains all the big headlines, photographs, drawings, and details that are not always appropriate in the letter. And although it relies more heavily on design and layout than does the letter, it must still have persuasive copy.

■ *KEY POINT:*   *Brochures are usually more visual than letters.*

■ *CAUTION NOTE:*   *Convincing copy is essential in the brochure.*

Often the brochure is the only piece of a mailing package that prospects may keep. They may read the letter, and glance at the response device and other facilitators, such as testimonial sheets, but they'll keep the brochure.

■ *CAUTION NOTE:*   *The brochure is often the only piece kept by the prospect.*

Since the brochure is the piece most likely to be retained by prospects, it must contain our complete selling message. As we've seen, letters start with a major benefit and a description of what the product or ser-

163

vice offers prospects. It continues with secondary benefits and proof to substantiate them, plus sweeteners to enhance the terms of the offer. It concludes by asking prospects to buy and showing them how easy this is with facilitators like simple order forms and stamped envelopes.

The brochure must do the same. None of the features just mentioned can be left out, because the brochure is another chance to show prospects what they will get out of the offer and what they must do or give up to get it.

■ *CAUTION NOTE: The brochure must contain the complete selling message.*

Never split up sales elements of your offer between your letter and your brochure. The brochure must stand on its own, with each crucial sales element doing its job. It's true that you may present more details of the product in the brochure than in the letter, but you cannot leave anything you said in the letter out of the brochure. In fact, each side of the brochure must have these elements so that they can be seen at any time.

■ *CAUTION NOTE: Never split sales points between parts of the mailing piece.*

HOW DOES THE BROCHURE DIFFER FROM THE LETTER?

The goal of any part of the mailing piece is to get prospects to respond. If we leave out of one part any element covered in another, we jeopardize our success. But if we have already said everything in the letter, how can we write anything new for the brochure?

First, we don't repeat exactly what we said in the letter. We rewrite, so the words do not look or read the same. We repeat the meaning but not the words. We use synonyms to make the old seem new.

■ *CAUTION NOTE: The brochure must carry the same selling message as the letter, without being repetitious.*

Second, we add to the brochure new material and information we were unable to put into the letter. This may be technical information or details on specific features of the product or service.

■ *KEY POINT: Put new material, such as technical information and specific details, into the brochure.*

The letter, by its nature, lets us give something of ourselves to someone. It gives us a measure of intimacy with readers and lets us give them the emotional reasons why they should buy. The brochure is not as personal. It must continue the selling momentum we developed in the letter and back up what we have already said.

To do this, it must expand on the features of our offer. In this sense it is an extension of the letter.

■ *CAUTION NOTE: The brochure is more impersonal than the letter.*

■ *KEY POINT: The brochure continues the selling momentum by expanding on the features of the offer.*

So the brochure is more than a rewrite of the letter. It adds an entirely new dimension to our product and offer.

WHAT DO WE PUT INTO THE BROCHURE?

What goes into a brochure? The first major element is the headline. The headline's job is to attract marginally interested readers by telling them what they can get out of our offer. To do this, headlines are usually long, spelling out not only what is being offered but what buyers must pay and how they order.

■ *KEY POINT: The brochure has a long headline stating the offer and the benefits.*

The headline attracts the reader's eye and guides it to the parts of the body copy that we want read. This is also true of the subheads, which we place strategically to draw the eye. But we cannot separate our discussion of what headlines say from how they are placed in the brochure. The use of underlining, discussed in the last chapter, is similar to what we will now do with the headline and subheads. These identify key features of the offer as well as what is gotten and what is given up.

■ *KEY POINT:*   *The headline draws the eye to major selling points.*

A brochure is a second chance to identify benefits, repeat the offer, and tell how to respond. The brochure lets us present benefits in visual chunks with separate borders, or in striking color, each with its own headline. "Filled with powerful time- and money-saving suggestions," can be followed with those numerous suggestions. "We offer you absolutely FREE use of the exceptional tool for 30 days," can be elaborated on for five paragraphs.

■ *KEY POINT:*   *Body copy in the brochure allows an expansion of benefits.*

Photographs fit the format of the brochure better than that of the letter. Photographs that show the product or service being used by prospects buy readership and attention. Prospects read captions, and their eye is drawn to the sections we want read next.

■ *KEY POINT:*   *Photographs show prospects how the product is used.*
■ *KEY POINT:*   *Photographs buy readership for captions.*
■ *KEY POINT:*   *Photographs draw the reader's eye to key parts of the copy.*

Brochures also let us elaborate on the proofs we offer to back up our claims. They give us more space than tables, charts, graphs, and other visual presentations to clinch arguments.

■ *KEY POINT:*   *The brochure allows space for expanded proof, to weight the sales argument.*

The brochure is also an excellent place to list the testimonials we have collected. We can include only two or three in the letter, but in the brochure we can use a dozen or more. We can do this not only because we have more space, but also because we are less tied to the particular theme we developed in the letter. In the brochure we can give our testimonials their own separate section and let them do their job by themselves.

■ *KEY POINT:*   *The brochure allows space for more testimonials.*

The brochure also lets us describe many more details of the product or service than we could in the letter. For example, if we are selling a subscription service, we might give extensive information of what is included. In a home tool kit, we could include a complete listing of each kind of tool, nut, and bolt; if a fund-raising campaign, a detailed description of how the funds are used.

■ *KEY POINT:*   *The brochure allows space for more numerous details than does the letter.*

A brochure's body copy can offer information about our company, to lend more credibility to our offer. A firm marketing special plates for collectors can tell prospects about its 140 years of experience in modeling and firing ceramics. The publisher of a training guide can tell prospects about the author's or editor's background. The brochure gives information that might be too long or inappropriate for the intimacy required in a letter.

■ *KEY POINT:*   *The brochure allows detail on how the product was made and who produced it.*

HOW DO WE WRITE THE HEADLINE FOR THE BROCHURE?

The headline is the focal point of the brochure because it must draw and hold the attention of prospects.

Several kinds of headlines can be written for the brochure. The first is the *benefit headline*, which makes a personal appeal to prospects' self-interest. This is the easiest kind of headline for prospects to understand—it tells them what's in it for them. On a personal level it buys readership, because it shows direct benefits to prospects.

Examples are:

> HERE'S THE AMAZING EXERCISE BICYCLE THAT CAN
> PROLONG YOUR LIFE

MODERN LOVE STORIES FOR READERS WHO WANT TO EXPERIENCE
FIRSTHAND ALL THE EXCITEMENT, PASSION, AND PURE JOY OF LOVE

AMERICA'S TOP ARTISTS SHOW YOU HOW THEY CREATE THEIR WORK
WITH PRACTICAL STEP-BY-STEP INSTRUCTION

GIVE YOUR CHILDREN A LIFELONG ADVANTAGE . . . START THEM OFF
WITH A LOVE OF READING! THESE FOUR BRIGHT NEW BOOKS WILL
DELIGHT YOUR YOUNGSTERS WITH REAL-LIFE ANIMAL WONDERS!

NOW—YOU CAN DISCOVER HUNDREDS OF IDEAS TO EXPRESS YOUR
STYLE OF LIVING—YOUR WAY OF WORKING . . . EVERYTHING YOU'LL
NEED TO MAKE YOUR OFFICE A SHOWPLACE OF TASTE AND EFFICIENCY

TAKE A GIANT STEP INTO THE FUTURE TO GET WHAT YOU WANT—A
SUCCESSFUL BUSINESS OF YOUR OWN, THE OPPORTUNITY TO GROW,
FINANCIAL SECURITY FOR YOUR FAMILY

The second type of headline is the *all-inclusive headline*. Here the headline tries to maximize sales impact by summarizing all elements of the
offer: benefits, description, proof, risk relieving, and response, plus any
extras that enhance the offer. But the job of packing all this in a successful headline is not easy.

For example:

THE SUPER-SAVER GUARANTEED-ACCEPTED GROUP TERM LIFE PLAN
PAYS UP TO $5000 CASH FOR EVERY UNIT AT JUST $1 A WEEK . . . UP TO
$20,000 CASH FOR JUST $4 A WEEK . . . AND YOU CAN'T BE TURNED
DOWN, IF YOU ARE 50 TO 79 YEARS OLD"

SEVEN STAR—THE COMPLETE TIME-MANAGEMENT SYSTEM THAT FITS IN
YOUR POCKET. A PLANNER, EXPENSE BOOK, ADDRESS BOOK,
NOTEBOOK, ALL-IN-ONE FOR $19.75.

YOU CAN USE THE GARDEN WAY CART ON YOUR TOUGHEST AND
HEAVIEST CHORES WITHOUT RISKING A PENNY . . . BECAUSE IF IT'S NOT
THE BEST OUTDOOR TOOL YOU'VE EVER OWNED—WE'LL BUY IT BACK!"

LET US PROVE HOW INCREDIBLY EASY IT IS TO SAVE 30%–70% ALMOST
EVERY TIME YOU PLAY . . . WITHOUT THE INCONVENIENT RESTRICTIONS
NORMALLY ASSOCIATED WITH DISCOUNT AIR TRAVEL

THE NUT & BOLT SHOP: OVER 175 DOZEN (2101) INDUSTRIAL GRADE
FASTENERS IN A SIZE-BY-SIZE SELECTION . . . PLUS HEAVY-DUTY CABINET
ORGANIZER . . . ALL FOR LESS THAN $20

The third type of headline is the *involver headline*. The involver headline gets prospects to remember a major benefit by involving them in the

use of the product or service. It asks them to do something, and this involves them in the sales message; for example, scratching a paper patch to release the smell of perfume.

TAKE THIS SIMPLE TEST TO SEE IF YOU CAN WIN A FORTUNE

NOW . . . INSTEAD OF TAKING CHANCES, CHECK THE RATINGS BELOW
BEFORE YOU BUY

A fourth kind of headline is the *curiosity headline*. This headline is designed to pique curiosity about the product. It can tantalize prospects to read more of the copy. The key point is that the headline must be connected to the product in some way to arouse the interest of the right prospects. "They laughed when I sat down at the piano" is a good example.

One caution with any headline that provokes curiosity is that it must not entertain people. As we saw earlier, humor can take people away from the sales message. And sometimes, like the example just quoted, it can be remembered long after the product is forgotten. So be warned, Avoid using a curiosity-provoking headline unless it is specifically tied to the product or a major benefit, because such a headline, like a humorous one, can detract from the primary message it contains.

■ *CAUTION NOTE: Don't use headlines to entertain.*

Here are some examples of successful curiosity-provoking headlines that are tied to products:

BUYING COMPUTER SOFTWARE WITHOUT SEEING A DEMONSTRATION IS
LIKE BUYING A NEW CAR WITHOUT TAKING A TEST DRIVE

WHEN GRANDMA WAS A GIRL, GE PROBABLY BUILT HER FIRST WASHER

MY FIRST REACTION WAS . . . WHY FOR HEAVEN'S SAKE DOES ANYONE
NEED A CART THIS BIG?"

FABULOUS! TWENTY-SEVEN NEW WAYS TO MAKE YOUR GUESTS SAY IT

WHAT'S HOT AND WHAT'S NOT?

A fifth kind of headline is the *newness headline*, which implies that there is something new about your product or service, something people have never heard about before. Such headlines usually use words like "announcing," "introducing," "just published," "for the first time," or "just released."

For example:

INTRODUCING MASTER SALESMANSHIP—A BRAND NEW SALES BULLETIN
THAT HELPS YOUR SALES FORCE DO THE JOB YOU EXPECT OF THEM
EVERY DAY.

INTRODUCING THE REVOLUTIONARY, NEW SCIENTIFIC BREAKTHROUGH
THAT SHOWS YOU HOW TO ACQUIRE THE HABITS, ATTITUDES,
CHARACTERISTICS, AND SKILLS OF THE WORLD'S GREATEST ACHIEVERS.

A sixth type is a *value headline*, which suggests that prospects will get something of direct value from an offer. This could be either money or how-to help. Words like "become," "get," "how you can," and "how to" are common in value headlines.

Examples are:

HERE'S WHAT MY MONEY-MAKING PLAN WILL DO FOR YOU

READ THIS FOR THE 10 FINANCIAL SECRETS OF THE UNIVERSE

ONE MORNING MY AUNT HILDA GAVE ME THIS STOCK TIP . . . SO THIS
YEAR I GAVE HER A MERCEDES

The seventh type is a *question headline*, which attempts to arouse interest by asking questions readers will be unable to resist answering. Headlines that ask questions usually work only with prospects who are already interested in the offer.

The question should never be negative or have a negative connotation. "Have you got cancer yet?" or "Have you had your first coronary yet?" will not motivate prospects to read copy. Quite the reverse.

■ *CAUTION NOTE: Avoid negative questions in headlines.*

If you use questions, target them to a specific group of prospects from whom you want a response. The following are examples of successful question headlines:

DO YOU KNOW WHAT MAY PUT YOU IN THE TOP 5% IN THE NEXT 60
DAYS?

WILL SOMEONE PLEASE TELL ME WHAT AN APPLE III CAN DO?

DID YOU KNOW YOU COULD SAVE HUNDREDS OF DOLLARS IN HEATING COSTS THIS SEASON?

ISN'T IT TRUE THAT MANY PEOPLE TRY LOW-TAR CIGARETTES AND JUST AREN'T SATISFIED?

The eighth type of headline is the *knowledge headline,* which implies that readers will gain knowledge. It tries to convince prospects that the product contains the secret of the ages. "All you have to do is. . ." It also implies that the particular offer is the way to do something. If prospects want the secret, they must buy what is offered. Numbers often work well here.

For example:

FIVE WAYS FOR REDUCING HEATING COSTS

TEN WAYS TO CLEAR DANDELION WEEDS

WITH THESE FIVE POINTS YOU WILL LEARN

NOW . . . ALL THE SCIENCE AND TECHNOLOGY OF MAN'S GREATEST INVENTIONS . . . PRESENTED IN THIS LAVISHLY ILLUSTRATED "HOW IT WORKS" ENCYCLOPEDIA

HOW TO READ 2000 PAGES IN LESS THAN HALF AN HOUR

12 FASCINATING PREDICTIONS FROM THE FRONTIERS OF HIGH TECHNOLOGY

168 OF THE BEST-KEPT SALES-CLOSING SECRETS IN AMERICA

27 EXAMPLES OF HOW SMALL BUSINESS TAX CONTROL CAN HELP YOU SLASH TAXES AND AVOID TAX TRAPS

These all give numbered ways readers will gain knowledge.
One example of a long knowledge headline is:

A MAGNIFICENT BLEND OF BEAUTY AND BRAINS, MAGIC AND MEANING, STYLE AND SUBSTANCE . . . THE FIRST AND ONLY MAGAZINE THAT HELPS YOU BETTER UNDERSTAND AND APPRECIATE *ALL* DIMENSIONS OF THE VISUAL ARTS . . . COME WITH US AND EXPERIENCE THIS MARVELOUSLY BRIGHT, PROVOCATIVE, EXCITING TOUR OF THE PAST, PRESENT, AND FUTURE OF ART—STARTING WITH YOUR FREE PREMIERE ISSUE.

It promises prospects understanding and knowledge about many aspects of art.

No matter what kind of headline we use, its purpose is to gain readership of the brochure's copy. The headline cannot tell the whole selling story. We use it to draw prospects into our story, where our copy persuades. It is our copy that brings us face to face (almost) with our prospects.

HEADLINES TO AVOID

Here are some examples of headlines to stay away from:

ABC CLEARINGHOUSE DIRECTORY HAS IT ALL!

The trouble with short headlines is that they can't say enough to grab the reader. This headline isn't able to offer proof for this extravagant claim.

NOW . . . AN ENTHRALLING, STIMULATING FILM TO MAKE YOUR NEXT
SALES MEETING UNFORGETTABLE!

Again, a strong claim but no proof. Also the headline is oriented to subjective claims of the product and does not inquire as to the reader's needs.

IT'S A SURPRISING, PROVOCATIVE, HUMANLY ELEGANT WORLD FILLED
WITH GLORIOUS OPTIONS

These words attempt to tell us something without showing us. It is showing that gives veracity and makes us believe.

WINNING TACTICS FOR IMPROVING CUSTOMER RELATIONS

A sleepy title like this won't intrigue prospects. It won't buy more readership even from prospects who should be interested.

WHERE CAN YOU GET COMPREHENSIVE, FAST, OBJECTIVE INFORMATION
ABOUT PERSONAL COMPUTING?

Abstract, generalized words are used in this headline. This illustrates a problem most short headlines have: Because they are short they must use generalized words. But generalizations fail to make an emotional impact on readers.

THE ULTIMATE IN EASE, EFFICIENCY, AND ECONOMY

Again, too general. This does not make us feel, it just "tells" us.

AGLOW WITH ACHIEVEMENT. GLOBAL IN SCOPE. CRACKLING WITH
NEWS, OPINION, CONTROVERSY, SURPRISE

Better than the last, but we still don't feel it. The copywriter mistakenly used adjectives to describe. Nouns are better—they name things. At best, adjectives only modify a noun's meaning.

FROM NOW ON, LET US BE YOUR CLEAR AND COMPREHENSIVE GUIDE TO
THINGS OF ENDURING VALUE AND BEAUTY

The word "comprehensive" should be banned from advertising, certainly from selling by direct mail. It's a mushy word, because readers must stop for a split second to try to figure out what is meant. Also this headline asks for but does not show.

STRATEGIES FOR CREATING SUCCESSFUL HEADLINES

In writing the headline, it helps to establish an overall guideline. For example, if the price for our product is particularly low, we might feature this fact in the headline. Price can be a major reason people buy some products, particularly consumer goods. Price is often less important with magazines and books, because all of the same type tend to be about the same price. But if our safari bush jacket is competing against similar jackets from six other companies, we must make it stand out from the herd. If price is the difference, we put it into the headline.

If price is what people want to know, it is best to deal with it right in the beginning, in the headline. In fact, if our product is not visibly different from our competitors' products except for price, prospects won't slog through our copy looking for the price. They'll go to the postscript on the letter, or the order form on the response card, and assure themselves the price is acceptable. Then, and only then, will they read the copy. So if the price is different, we'll headline the brochure with it.

■ *CAUTION NOTE:* *If price is a concern to buyers, deal with it in the headline.*

Discount offers are related to price. Some people will buy almost anything if it's available at a lower than normal price. They are not committed buyers, because they won't buy at full price, but with many people watching their budget, lower prices can often sell products. Discounts are an excellent way for catalog marketers to begin a relationship with customers. The danger, however, is that this may lead prospects to believe everything is on sale once a year, which can undercut sales at regular prices.

■ *KEY POINT:* *Discounting can be used to gain customers who might not buy otherwise.*

■ *CAUTION NOTE:* *Limit discounting to certain products.*

Another strategy is to offer something free. Everyone likes to get something free, even corporations. If you have some special information, such as a booklet giving nine valuable tips on how to buy software, offer it to a prospect free. What does this do for you? It begins a relationship. It gives you a lead with someone who may be interested in your product. You haven't found out if the person has the need or the money yet, but you've identified a prospect out of the mass of suspects.

■ *KEY POINT:* *If you are out to gain leads, offer something free in your headline.*

Another excellent strategy is to promote the "quick and easy" way your product or service will get the job done. We are an impatient people. We like to get things done in a quick and easy manner. When getting a job done quick and easy is a suitable promise for your product, it's a good strategy. For example, a handy-dandy tool kit offering might emphasize how quickly home repairs can be done, how easily they will be done with the rubber-handled plier assortment. Any time you can position your product so that it can be perceived by prospects as helping them get something done hasslefree and allowing them more free time to pursue other interests, consider the "quick and easy" strategy. It's been used for years and still works.

■ *KEY POINT:* *"Quick and easy" is a good headline strategy.*

A similar strategy is to show prospects how to do something. Most of us are practical and would like to know "how to build a porch," "how to save $5000 in taxes this year," or "how to make money in the stock market." This headline strategy offers solutions to problems—and that's what we're trying to do in direct mail.

■ *KEY POINT:* *Use headlines to show solutions to problems.*

If any one headline strategy can be considered best or most effective, it is probably the one that builds the headline around a summary of the entire offer. You will find by experience that benefit-packed headlines that give details of offers can win surprising results.

■ *KEY POINT:* *The best overall headline strategy is to have the headline summarize the entire offer.*

WRITING BODY COPY FOR BROCHURES

In the brochure, body copy does not have the same importance as it does in the letter. The brochure is a less "personal" message; it gives another version of the sales story contained in the letter and tries to reinforce the letter so as to get a decision from the prospect.

■ *CAUTION NOTE:* *Brochures are more impersonal than letters.*

■ *KEY POINT:* *The body copy in the brochure broadens the letter's ability to get a decision.*

For example, the brochure allows us to present multiple proofs: photographs of prospects happily using the product, graphs and charts comparing our product with others, pictures of the product itself, extensive testimonials verifying customer satisfaction, and detailed descriptions of how the product is made and how it works.

Remember, the brochure elaborates on the information in the letter; it can never supplant the letter. In fact, the brochure is the most expendable part of a mailing package. It is often omitted in fund-raising and campaign mailings. The letter is the place for the emotional appeal—and it is emotion that sells. But the brochure can cement the deal with prospects who are willing to read the letter and have made a tentative decision that this is the right product for them.

■ *CAUTION NOTE: A brochure does not have the emotional appeal of a letter.*

■ *KEY POINT: The brochure's purpose is to reinforce a positive decision and cement the deal.*

This is the key: The brochure is for those who have already shown an interest. We write copy for those who have already read our letter, to reinforce a positive decision.

■ *KEY POINT: The brochure's body copy reinforces the prospect's interest.*

Does this mean we can omit in the brochure what we said in the letter? Not at all. We must still give all the benefits, what prospects are going to get, and what they have to give up. We still have to put in how much the product costs and how to respond. We still need to explain all the extras. We still need to make it as easy as possible for prospects to place their order. And we must say all of this differently than we did in the letter.

■ *KEY POINT: The brochure should elaborate on what was said in the letter.*

Brochures are more visually oriented than letters. We start with a big, bold headline, using it and various subheads to lead the reader's eye to the benefits, proofs, details, sweeteners, facilitators, and ordering information. The brochure is graphically oriented. For example, copy about a major benefit will be prefaced by its own headline. Further, we might put the copy in a box and set it against shading inside the box.

■ *KEY POINT: The brochure is a visual piece in which headlines lead the reader's eye to benefits and proofs.*

We can use many graphic techniques to accentuate what we say. In part this gives us an opportunity to repeat what we have said in the letter, but it also gives prospects a way to actually see our product.

Our prospects are part of a picture-oriented and television-raised generation. They need to "see" what they are buying. This is a major reason for use of a brochure in the first place. People can be emotionally turned on by what we say in the intimacy of the letter, but they also want something graphic to show what's in it for them. And that's what we need to know when we write copy for the brochure—how the copy will fit within visual material.

■ *KEY POINT:* **Brochures graphically show the what's-in-it-for-me element.**

Figures 9.1 through 9.3 show examples of brochure copy and how they fit into the overall brochure design. In Figure 9.1, the headline and front copy are packed with major benefits in a visually oriented first page. Figure 9.2 shows how benefit-oriented copy fits on the inside of a brochure.

As we will see in the next chapter, the back page of a brochure does not get high readership. Therefore it might be a good place to put feature-oriented detail about the product, such as the table of contents of a book (Figure 9.3).

As we see in these few examples, the brochure is not as dependent on body copy as is the letter. Body copy is organized by headlines and subheads, in sections that describe benefits. Like the sales letter, the brochure describes important elements of any offer—benefits, description, proof, sweeteners, and facilitators—but whereas the letter presents these elements in a formal, step-by-step way, the brochure is more flexible. It moves the eye around to various subheads, so prospects can choose to read about the benefits that most interest them.

■ *KEY POINT:* **The brochure is a flexible way for the reader to search for particular benefits.**

Because readers do roam around looking for what matters to them, we as copywriters must be sure to connect our headlines and the benefits in the body copy. Also the brochure must contain all ingredients of the offer.

■ *KEY POINT:* **The brochure must have a strong connection between headlines and benefits in the body copy.**

Give your children a lifelong advantage...

You can do nothing more important for young children than to sit down with them and share a good book. That special closeness you nurture... and the curiosity you awaken...build positive attitudes toward learning that will help your youngsters excel throughout their lives.

That's why National Geographic's **Books for Young Explorers** win such wide acclaim, why every new set becomes an instant best-seller!

Enticing, child-tested subjects! To pick the topics for these books, we go straight to our audience of four-to-eight-year-olds. We take their choices, then work with educators and reading specialists to create learning adventures for beginning readers and little listeners.

Brightly illustrated...easy and fun to read! Sparkling color photographs and superbly detailed paintings present rare, closeup views of new friends, new wonders, new worlds. Lively text, tested for readability, appears in large, clear type.

Big books, designed for frequent use! Each 8½-by-11-inch volume has 32 pages, printed on heavy paper, with hard covers and durable binding.

Plus a special bonus! A 16-page, full-color *More About...* booklet for parents and older children comes with each set. It's filled with additional information about each book's subject to help you answer a child's eager questions.

start them off with a love of reading!

Research confirms that positive attitudes toward reading and learning are formed in the home during the early years.

Figure 9.1 Notice how these major benefits tie into the picture; the combination of words and photo make the product come alive. (Courtesy National Geographic Society)

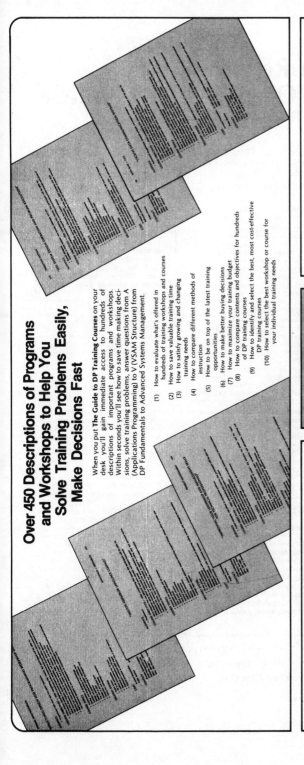

Over 450 Descriptions of Programs and Workshops to Help You Solve Training Problems Easily, Make Decisions Fast

When you put **The Guide to DP Training Courses** on your desk you'll gain immediate access to hundreds of descriptions of important programs and workshops. Within seconds you'll see how to save time making decisions, solve training problems, answer questions from A (Applications Programming) to V (VSAM Structure) from DP Fundamentals to Advanced Systems Management.

(1) How to evaluate what's offered in hundreds of training workshops and courses

(2) How to save valuable training time

(3) How to satisfy growing and changing training needs

(4) How to compare different methods of instruction

(5) How to be on top of the latest training opportunities

(6) How to make better buying decisions

(7) How to maximize your training budget

(8) How to compare contents and objectives for hundreds of DP training courses

(9) How to identify and select the best, most cost-effective DP training courses

(10) How to select the best workshop or course for your individual training needs

FILLED WITH POWERFUL TIME AND MONEY SAVING SUGGESTIONS

See for yourself how this indispensable guide to DP training courses can help you save time and money. It's jam packed with hundreds of course opportunities to help you use your training budget more profitably.

You'll gain immediate access to literally thousands of important facts and information on current DP training, programs and workshops. Within seconds you'll see how to compare the quality of courses offered and select the training methods—lecture, video, workshop, self-study—best suited for your programmers.

For instance . . .

You know how important training is to your business. **The Guide to DP Training Courses** describes over 450 programs and workshops. It gives you the information you need to decide which employees should take what courses. It explains in detail what is offered in each course, how the course is delivered, what its cost—in-house or

public seminar—is, and whom do you contact. If you don't have this important sourcebook you've probably missed out in sending your staff to the right training . . .

Or, spent thousands on the wrong training . . .

We invite you to carefully look through the over 450 DP training programs and workshops detailed in this unique guide. Just one of them could very well be worth many, many times the cost of this book.

Or, solving training problems.

Have you even had a training schedule fall through because an employee couldn't attend a special progam? Take a look at the numerous ways courses and workshops are given here. For example, you might find the proper course for your employee in a self-study format. Next time you run into a training problem you might just be able to boost an employee's DP experience with one of these ideas.

We Offer You Absolutely FREE USE of this Exceptional Tool for 30 Days

You could buy this important NEW sourcebook without even seeing it because it has so many ways it helps you save time and money.

But you really ought to see its value for yourself before you make up your mind. That's why we are sending it out on a 30 day free trial basis to a select number of interested data processing managers and trainers.

Put it on your desk. Use it to solve problems, answer questions, generate new ideas for saving time and money.

Then, if you decide it's not for you, just return it—no explanation is necessary—and owe us nothing. You really can't lose with such an offer. So hurry and mail your card today.

"9 Books in One"

Why collect hundreds of advertising brochures on data training courses when **one source** will do?

The Guide to DP Training Courses pulls together **all** the information you need as a professional involved in training and managing.

This remarkable sourcebook and update service has descriptions of over 450 programs and workshops in nine subject areas which cover the whole realm of data processing training. All courses and workshops are fully described in this one source. It's just like getting **nine**

books in one big, easy-to-use volume. Just as an example, the section on "Data Base" presents over 85 courses in CICS, IMS, VSAM, Concepts and Design, Implementation Fundamentals, Modeling, Resource Management, among others—all offering you the latest information and technique in the data processing training.

In addition, a comprehensive subject index at the end of this indispensible reference tool will help you be on top of these special training opportunities.

Figure 9.2 See how this two-page spread boxes in benefit-oriented copy. (Courtesy Human Resource Development Press)

Nine Reasons Why You Should Own this New Guide to DP Training Courses

Here are nine good reasons why you should keep a copy of the new **Guide to DP Training courses** on your desk. They summarize the massive contents of this remarkable new reference book. You'll use it day after day to answer questions, solve training problems, generate new ideas.

1. **Data Base**
Data Base Fundamentals . . . Data Base Management . . . IMS Data Base Design to Implementation to Debugging to Management to Administration . . . VSAM Programming, Structure, File Design, Performance . . . CICS Command Level Programming, Design, and Debugging . . . Adabas Concepts, Facilities, and Design courses . . . DL/I Programming and Applications . . . How to build and manage an Information Resource Directory among many other DP course offerings.

2. **Programming Languages**
Languages and Operating Systems . . . How languages are used in program design; Advanced Programming Techniques and debugging in Cobol ADA, Assembler, Fortran, JCL, Pascal, PL/I, RPG II, SAS . . . Structured programming Design and Techniques . . Fundamentals of Operating Systems, Development Levels in systems as MVS, FOCUS, CMS, JES3.

3. **Project Management**
Organizational Needs and System Requirements from fundamentals to productivity to leadership skills to long-range planning . . . Developing the On-line Application . . . Control and Security Considerations for Information Systems . . . Making Human Fac-

tors a Reality in Interactive Systems . . . Problem-Solving Leadership Workshop.

4. **Systems Analysis and Design**
Advanced Structure and Design Techniques . . . Systems Analysis . . . Application Software Design . . . Building On-line Applications . . . Designing Security Controls . . . Screen Design . . . Structured Analysis and Design . . . Structured maintenance . . . Quality Assurance . . . Certificate in Information Science.

5. **Systems Programming**
Programming and Modeling Techniques from Entry Level Programming to Advanced Debugging . . . MVS VSAM for System Programmers . . . RDOS System Programming . . . Structured Programming, Analysis, Design, and Testing . . . Systems Programming . . . Basic Systems Programming . . . MVS/SP1.3 Functional Characteristics . . . VSAM for Systems Programmers

6. **Data Communications — Telecommunications**
Components, Systems, and Networks from Design, to Management Concepts to Applications . . . Digital PABX, DPPX Applications, Analysis, and Design . . . Telecommunications Concepts to Management to Network Design . . . SNA Formats and Protocols

. . . **and there's lots more!**
To find the training information you need, simply check the easy to use index and in seconds you'll be able to solve problems . . . answer questions . . . generate creative new ideas.
To order your copy simply mail the postpaid card. This outstanding sourcebook will be yours to examine FREE for 30 days.

7. **User Training**
Courses users can take: DP Fundamentals for End Users . . . DP User Courses . . . Integration of Word Processing and Electronic Data Processing Systems . . . User Documentation . . . Becoming a Word Processing Specialist . . . WP Implementation Workshop . . . WP Management . . . Data Processing using SAS . . . Executive DP Concepts.

8. **Communications Skills**
Communications Skills for DP supervisors, managers and employees . . . Data Processing Communications . . . Improving Managerial Communications . . . Person to Person Communications . . . Active Listening Skills . . . Organizational Communications . . . Business Writing for Data Processing Professionals . . . Writing Strategies for Technical Managers.

9. **Management and Motivation Skills**
Leadership, Productivity, and Supervisory Skills . . . Management and Financial Development Skills . . . Managing and Motivating People . . . Using the Computer as a Management Tool . . . Auditing and Accounting for Non-Financial Managers . . . Financial Information Systems . . . Supervisory Cost Control . . . Developing Business Analysis Skills . . . Situational Leadership . . . Data Processing for the Non-Data Processing Executive . . . Human Relations: Forming Productive Working Relationships . . . Interpersonal Managing Skills . . . Video Instructional Systems . . . Action-Oriented Problem Solving.

ABOUT THE EDITORS . . .

Roger _____, Consulting Editor for the Guide to DP Training Courses is Director of the Corporate Resource Center at the Commercial Union Insurance Company and Chairman of the North American Computer Education Council. He is the Senior Editor of "Quest," a newsletter for the data processing educator. He has written over 100 papers on DP education and adult learning. His experience, includes 20 years of working in the data processing field. He is currently working on the book Microshock: Its Effect on the Workplace and Workforce.
Human Resource Development Press (HRD) has been publishing training and reference books for 10 years. Its staff is composed of experts in publishing, information gathering, and consultants in training.

Figure 9.3 The back page of this brochure gives considerable detail about what is in the book, gives information about the editor, and tells how to order. (Courtesy Human Resource Development Press)

USE OF TESTIMONIALS IN BROCHURES

The brochure is an excellent place to give testimonials that back up claims. Use either a few comments excerpted from customer letters or reprint the full letter.

■ *KEY POINT:* *Testimonials in brochures support benefits.*

An indirect testimonial:

PROVEN TRACK RECORD
You can have confidence in these secrets of closing sales because they represent the culmination of nearly 40 years of research and testing. More than 200,000 copies of this classic were sold in the first four editions.
Now this fifth edition is expanded and filled with techniques that reflect current marketing conditions and growth sectors of the economy. Use this guide with confidence . . . it can more than double your sales income.

The best testimonials we can use are excerpts from signed letters (Figure 9.4).

WHAT SWEETENERS GO INTO BROCHURES?

Sweeteners, the extras prospects get for responding to our offer, are given to add weight to our side of the argument. The "handy wall chart" and "pocket sizing tool" that we give away when we sell our 2101 nuts and bolts are what make our products different from products sold at the local hardware store.

■ *KEY POINT:* *Sweeteners in brochures weight our side of the argument.*

Sweeteners are particularly important when the product or service is available locally and price is not an advantage. The nut and bolt set can often be bought at the local flea market at half the price, but without the wall chart. Prospects will think "Gee, that chart would give me some other ideas of how I can use. . ." That's how sweeteners work best—

Comments from some of our millions of satisfied customers

THE WORLD'S SAFEST MACHINE!

Every year around this time I Thank God for my VITA-MIX. I have a little story to tell you. Well, it happened a year ago this month. I buy pumpkins, clean, cook and puree them for fresh pumpkin pie. Well, this one day I went to use my VITA-MIX; I plugged it in not knowing it was turned on or that there was anything in it. To my surprise there was shooting all over my kitchen.

Thank God no one got hurt. I got up enough nerve to unplug it and inside was an empty box that had Hi-Speed 22 short bullets. My VITA-MIX has a few dents in it but it still works as good as new. I sure am glad my husband isn't a pennypincher or I'd be dead. I just thought you would like to hear my little story. Thank you for making a Great VITA-MIX; I wouldn't know what to do without it.

Mrs. N.C., VT

WOULD LIKE TO BE OUR AGENT

I sure like my VITA-MIX and have been responsible for the sale of three of them, two direct from your factory and one purchased by my son from a Health Food Store.

If I were only 75 instead of 82 years old, I would be asking to be one of your agents!

S.F.T., Quartzsite, AZ

TOTAL JUICE — "FEELS NUTRITIONAL DIFFERENCE IN A FEW DAYS"

I am enjoying a glass of miscellaneous Total fruit juice again this morning. A truly pleasant way to begin a day and sip right on thru it! And I can already, after only a few days, feel the nutritional difference, and the positive physical changes. I have only ventured thus far into ice cream and soup - more to come. All well worth the two years waiting and several friends are already talking about getting their own VITA-MIX.

Thank you for such a wonderful product. I look forward to using and enjoying it for many years to come.

A smiling P.R.S., Ann Arbor, MI

"LOVES CUCUMBER VITA-MIX® SOUP"

We have made several of the soup recipes and have enjoyed them very much, especially the cucumber soup, as we had an abundant crop of cukes from our garden this year, it was a tasty way to enjoy them.

C.S., Nashville, TN

"IT IS EVERYTHING ADVERTISED"

I have had my "3600" for several weeks now and am highly pleased! It is everything that you advertised.

G.G., La Crescenta, CA

A PERSONAL TESTIMONIAL

We personally grind our own wheat and other grains for bread, pancakes, cereals, muffins, pies, cakes and even flour fine enough for angel foods. This is our only source of flour. Last month my wife and I emptied and ate one 45 lb. container of VITA-MIX wheat. In a year's time we save hundreds of dollars and live on much better food.

B.B., Cleveland, OH

THE VITA-MIX® IS A WONDERFUL GRAIN GRINDER, BREAD MIXER, JUICER, ETC.

I love my VITA-MIX 3600. A lot of my friends have grain grinders and needing one myself to grind up the wheat I had stored, I looked at seven different models. The day I was going to purchase a grinder I saw an ad for a VITA-MIX. Not believing one appliance could do everything the VITA-MIX claimed to do, I was informed that the VITA-MIX was being demonstrated at a local fair. I found out that not only could the VITA-MIX do what they claimed, but do it fast.

My breads are wonderful (my husband likes to make bread also), we make our own pancakes, muffins, cakes, etc. from our stored wheat. We make our juices, soups, cole slaw, grind our meat and my favorite part is the fresh homemade ice cream from our frozen fruits. It's great.

J.B., Ogden, UT

Some like VITA-MIX® so much they even write poems about it

"AN ODE TO A FINE MACHINE"

"A machine that knows all the tricks,
Is a machine that is called the 3600 VITA-MIX.
It grinds and blends and even stews;
Yes, it's the best machine for any family to use.

I've made bread, soup and ice cream, too
It does all the things no other machine can do.
If you doubt what I say to be true;
Try it for yourself, and it will convince you.

The 3600 VITA-MIX is really and truly fine;
It makes juices, slaw, salads and wine.
It's the only machine made of its kind,
I'm really glad that this VITA-MIX is mine.

My health is so improved, I feel like a king,
Come on, folks, and get in the swing!
Buy the 3600 mixer and do your own thing,
You'll be glad you did and do a ring-a-ding ding.

When you are gloomy from day to day,
Your 3600 VITA-MIX will drive the blues away.
When times are sad and you're feeling bad,
Use your VITA-MIX and you'll feel glad.

With this mixer, you're the master of your fate,
Why not buy one now ere it is too late?
If to your friends you would be true,
Just tell them what the 3600 mixer will do."

A.W.H., Chicago, IL

3V

Figure 9.4 You can't get better testimonials than favorable comments with signatures. (Courtesy VITA-MIX Corporation) they should be so allied to the product that buyers cannot visualize using the product without them.

■ *KEY POINT:* *Sweeteners can help when price is a problem.*

Sometimes sweeteners are touted so heavily it's hard to tell the product from the gift. As we can see in Figure 9-5 one has to think twice to realize that the book that is a free gift is not the offer itself. In this case the copy makes the "extra" book so desirable. However the gift does buttress our sales argument and helps to knock out the competition. That's why we offer them—they work in direct mail.

■ *KEY POINT:* *Sweeteners support our sales message.*

GUARANTEES ARE CRUCIAL TO SUCCESS IN DIRECT MAIL

The brochure should also include a detailed description of our guarantee. Guarantees are crucial because they reduce the prospect's risk. They must be included in every piece of the offering and must be strongly emphasized in the brochure.

■ *KEY POINT:* *The brochure is the place to emphasize the guarantee.*

"Please don't say no. . . . Surely you owe it to yourself and your family to at least try this new money-making program for a 30-day FREE TRIAL—we mean just that. Because if you decide the program does not merit a place in your future plans, simply return it within 30 days and your $10 check will be returned uncashed," is typical of the kind of copy that guarantees the buyer's satisfaction.

It is easy to make the guarantee into a separate visual element, bordering it with a line and perhaps printing it in a different color.

Figure 9.6 is an excellent example of a guarantee from the Cushman Fruit Company, which markets a unique variety of oranges.

Guaranteed Wealth Building Strategies for Small Business

Free Gift for Business Owners Only
($29.95 for anyone else)

Describes 211 of the smartest ways to use your small business to multiply your personal wealth and shelter more money from taxes.

- A way to take $10,000 . . . $20,000 . . . even $30,000 or more out of your business without owing a penny of tax.

- How to "pyramid" your personal wealth and tax savings by owning several small companies.

- How to pay your family lucrative "directors' fees"—tax deductible to your company yet tax-free to them.

- Perhaps the finest tax break available to the small business owner today. (Yet not one business owner in 100 knows how to take advantage of it.)

- Smart way to write off trips with your spouse to foreign countries.

- How to write off an office in your home, even for a part-time venture, and get Uncle Sam to pay for a portion of all your phone, electric, utility, mortgage or rent bills.

- A simple way to make 85% of all the dividends you earn from stocks tax-free.

- 7 steps to turn your successful local business into a nationwide franchise. (It may be the best opportunity you'll ever have to multiply your sales and income hundreds of times over.)

- Best ways business owners can reduce their risk of audit.

- How a single phone call to major credit card companies could save your business an extra $1,000-$2,000 per year.

- How to acquire successful small businesses with no cash down.

- How to raise the capital you need at the lowest rates in America.

- New ways to use accelerated depreciation to multiply your real estate holdings and personal assets.

- Numerous fringe benefits you may be overlooking.

- How to give yourself a raise in earnings with no increase in before-tax profits.

- How to slash the cost of employee fringe benefits.

- How to let Uncle Sam pay for renovating your business property.

```
Dear Business Colleague:

        The list on which I found your name tells me you are a business owner,
or plan to be one soon.

        If this is correct, I'd like you to have a free copy of a new $29.95
manual we've just published.  It's called Guaranteed Wealth Building
Strategies for Small Business.

                    Your Financial "Bill Of Rights"
                         as a Business Owner

        As no book ever published before, this manual illustrates the scores
of ways you can use your small business to...

            * Multiply your personal wealth;

            * Generate thousands of dollars a year tax-free;

                                                        (over please)
```

Figure 9.5 We have to catch ourselves before we realize the book is only a gift. (Courtesy *Small Business Wealth Builder*)

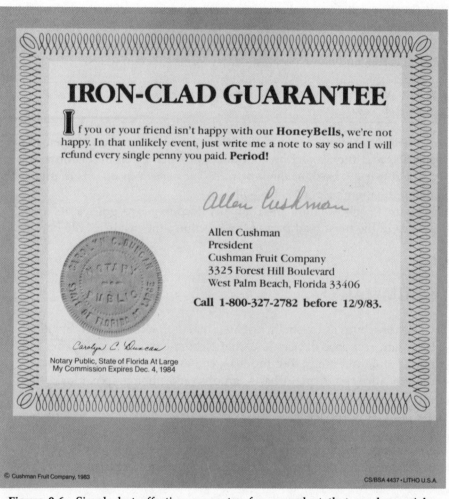

IRON-CLAD GUARANTEE

If you or your friend isn't happy with our **HoneyBells,** we're not happy. In that unlikely event, just write me a note to say so and I will refund every single penny you paid. **Period!**

Allen Cushman

Allen Cushman
President
Cushman Fruit Company
3325 Forest Hill Boulevard
West Palm Beach, Florida 33406

Call 1-800-327-2782 before 12/9/83.

Carolyn C. Duncan
Notary Public, State of Florida At Large
My Commission Expires Dec. 4, 1984

© Cushman Fruit Company, 1983   CS/BSA 4437 • LITHO U.S.A.

Figure 9.6 Simple but effective guarantee for a product that needs special stressing owing to its being perishable. (Courtesy Cushman Fruit Company)

HOW DO WE USE FACILITATORS IN BROCHURES?

Brochures also reemphasize the facilitators we used in the letter and throughout the entire offer: the ease of the decision and how simple it is to respond, with hardly any effort. We offer credit terms or payment by credit cards, and allow purchase order forms for companies.

■ *KEY POINT: Use facilitators in the brochure to make the decision and ordering easy.*

We include anything that will make it easy for prospects to come to a decision and then to act on that decision, such as an order form or a prepaid tear-out card, in the brochure. The easier our offer is to understand, the more responses we will gain.

Figure 9.7 shows how one company encourages responses. Its order form is in the most read part of the brochure, the inside, at the bottom right.

SUMMARY

The brochure is a visually oriented mailing piece that accompanies a letter and response device. It should elaborate on the benefits, description, proof, and method of ordering contained in the letter. However, the brochure can display charts, graphs, and photographs much more extensively than the letter. It can also offer much more information on the product or service.

The main focal point of the brochure is the headline. The headline and subhead lead the reader's eye to major benefits. Headlines let prospects choose to read about the benefits that interest them most.

The Computer Connection for Teachers

"The program certainly succeeds in using the computer to demonstrate the effective use of computers in education. It should be an ideal tool for courses and workshops."

Robert Rude
Professor of Elementary Education
Rhode Island College

CONTENTS

Module 1: Introduction

An introduction to the computer's keyboard and a few interactive exercises quickly give the user a sense of being in control of the machine. This module includes a presentation of some common "myths" about computers in the classroom, and directs the user to modules in the program which clarify those issues.

Module 2: Computer Basics

Fundamental concepts and vocabulary. Key terms, such as input, output, CPU, memory, are defined, as are the most common programming languages and their special purposes.

Module 3: Drill & Practice CAI

A game that teaches the concept of X - Y coordinates in mathematics demonstrates one effective use of the computer's graphics capabilities, and shows teachers how a program can be modified for different classroom needs.

Module 4: Tutorial CAI

Once again, imaginative, colorful graphics, and an interactive format are used—this time to teach a new subject: cell reproduction. The teacher is encouraged to look for the factors that make good use of the computer in a tutorial situation.

Module 5: Simulation CAI

Shows how real world problems can be presented as computer models, allowing the student to manipulate information, gain useful feedback from choices made, and achieve a sense of competence without direct involvement with the actual situation. Demonstrates problem solving with a computer.

Module 6: Computer Managed Instruction

Here the teacher will discover the many ways a computer can ease the burdens of classroom management: testing, giving assignments, keeping records, writing reports. An example of monitoring students of varied abilities in a geography lesson shows how it's done.

Module 7: The Software Supermarket

Examples from yet another curriculum area — reading — provide guidelines for the teacher in selecting software for classroom use from the vast array of available programs. Illustrates examples of good and poor program design. Includes a brief introduction to the process of creating one's own software.

Module 8: A Computer for your Classroom

Interactive case studies illustrate the various strategies for using computers in the classroom. Introduces the teacher to basic management decisions involving scheduling, budgets, availability of software, and individualizing instruction.

The Computer Connection was written and programmed by IDEA — a group of experienced teachers/instructional designers.

INSTRUCTIONAL SOFTWARE, INC.
1278 Massachusetts Avenue · Cambridge, MA 02138 · (617) 492-0386

No-Risk Guarantee

When you receive *The Computer Connection for Teachers*, it's yours to examine for up to fifteen days without obligation. If you decide to keep it, simply return the invoice with payment. If for any reason you decide not to keep the program, simply return all materials along with the unpaid invoice.

The Computer Connection for Teachers includes:
- Two 5¼ inch disks for use with Apple II, II+ or IIe (48K) computers.
- Student/User Manual that includes complete instructions, summaries of the eight program modules, and a list of additional published resources.

Total Cost: $75.00

Includes full-color animated graphics!

It's easy to order.

Simply enter appropriate information on the order form below or call (617) 492-0386. Clip coupon and mail to: **Instructional Software, Inc., 1278 Massachusetts Ave., Cambridge, Mass., 02138.**

Order Form

Instructional Software, Inc. 1278 Massachusetts Avenue, Cambridge, Mass. 02138

☐ Please send me *The Computer Connection for Teachers*. I understand that I am free to review materials for up to 15 days without obligation. Then I will return it or send full payment of $75.00.

Name _____

Dept. _____

Institution _____

Address _____

City _____ State _____ Zip _____

Figure 9.7 Order form on page with benefits. (Courtesy Instructional Software, Inc.)

DESIGNING AND 10
LAYING OUT THE
DIRECT MAIL
BROCHURE

In this chapter we will look at how to use design and layout to reinforce copy in brochures. Copy and design must be better integrated in the brochure than in any other part of the mailing piece.

BROCHURES LET PROSPECTS PICK OUT BENEFITS THAT INTEREST THEM

As we know, our goal is to get our body copy read. Brochures are no exception. Design by itself does not sell. Rather it is used to bring readers' eyes to the copy we want them to read. So we must base the design of our brochures on how people read.

■ *KEY POINT:* **Good design points the reader's eye to copy.**

In our discussion of the stages of readership, we saw that the amount of time people will spend reading is directly related to their interest. We buy increments of reading time by piquing their interest. In the first stage, readers decide whether our product or service is relevant for them. Remember, direct mail does not create interest in a product—it develops and enhances interest and lets prospects skip what they don't want to know.

■ *KEY POINT:* **The brochure allows readers to single out the most interesting benefits.**

HOW PROSPECTS READ DETERMINES DESIGN OF THE BROCHURE

Prospects begin reading by scanning the major headline. This gives them a summary of the offer and a primary benefit in as many as 30 words. If the headline arouses their interest, they move on to subheads that describe other major benefits. From there, they move to *flash heads*—short sales slugs such as "winter sale," "one-time offer," "no-risk guarantee"—and picture captions. Captions are critical to the success of photographs and illustrations in brochures.

■ *KEY POINT: Prospects start reading the brochure by scanning the headline.*

But none of these sell by themselves; they can't persuade anybody to do anything. All they do is get readership from prospects who are already interested in the offer. They get readership for body copy, which should carry the emotional force needed to convince prospects to buy.

■ *CAUTION NOTE: Headlines can't sell by themselves, they only buy readership for body copy.*

After readers scan the strongest visual parts of our brochure, they turn to other graphic material. So we give them charts, tables, diagrams, lists, picture captions, and other materials that let them make a tentative decision to buy our product or service. They scan these, but also take the time to read some of the copy related to these devices.

■ *KEY POINT: Visual materials like graphs and charts encourage a tentative decision.*

BODY COPY CONFIRMS THE DECISION TO BUY

Finally, after racing through all the visual aspects of the brochure, prospects get to our body copy. This is what confirms their decision to buy.

■ *KEY POINT: As in the sales letter, body copy in the brochure confirms the decision to buy.*

Does body copy in the brochure say anything different from what was said in the headlines, captions, and support material? No. All say exactly the same things—but in different words, so prospects don't realize we are repeating ourselves.

■ *KEY POINT: Body copy continues the consistent sales story told in the letter.*

■ *CAUTION NOTE: Don't repeat the sales story in the same words.*

How, then, does this affect the design of our brochure? First, the brochure is not like our letter. Rather than being several pages long, it is usually one single *sales surface* of scannable text that buys readership for the body copy.

■ *KEY POINT: Brochures usually have one primary sales surface.*

But like the letter, the brochure must give prospects enough emotional reasons for them to make decisions. If any part is left out that should be there for reinforcement, all is lost.

■ *KEY POINT: Like the letter, the brochure is long, to back up emotional reasons to buy.*

■ *CAUTION NOTE: Don't leave anything out of the brochure or sales will be lost.*

Because the brochure lets prospects jump around to read about the benefits that interest them, it must be jampacked with every conceivable reason someone would have for buying what is offered. We don't have a second chance; we're not there in person to find out individual needs. So we must say it all in both the letter and the brochure.

■ *KEY POINT: The brochure must be packed with benefits.*

A CLEAN LAYOUT DOESN'T WORK
IN THE BROCHURE

Because brochures are filled with headlines, subheads, photographs, captions, charts, and body copy, they don't allow for what graphic artists call *clean layout*. A clean layout is often used in awareness advertising: the single headline or short message surrounded by white space or other background color. In our brochure not only don't we have room, but a clean layout allows the eye to slide away from the copy.

■ *CAUTION NOTE:*   *Avoid a clean layout in the brochure.*

A clean layout doesn't work in a brochure. What does work is a sufficient amount of persuasive copy arranged to buy increments of readership, so prospects can make their decision one step at a time.

■ *KEY POINT:*   *Rely on visuals and persuasive copy in the brochure to buy more readership.*

CONTROL HOW PROSPECTS READ
THE BROCHURE

As we have seen, our brochure is designed to buy readership. Now let's look at how to put the principles into practice.

■ *KEY POINT:*   *The need to continue readership is essential in designing a brochure.*

We begin by controlling how prospects will read our brochure. The design of the sales letter is set, in part, by the traditional style of personal correspondence that has been in effect for centuries. Chapter 8 described a logical and formal way to present copy in the letter. Although the brochure is more flexible and loosely structured, we must still follow certain principles of layout for it. We must present our sales message so prospects can grasp it as easily as possible. The first principle has to do with how the eyes move when people read; we must present our copy in the natural way readers' eyes follow text, left to right, top to bottom. This is how Western readers' eyes look at a page.

■ *KEY POINT:* **The reader's eyes must follow the design from upper left to bottom right.**

Anytime we want to break this natural eye path, moving from bottom to top or right to left, we must use strong ammunition, such as photographs or bold headlines, combined with specific instructions such as numbers, letters, or arrows, to make up for the change in eye direction.

■ *CAUTION NOTE:* **Strong visuals like photographs are needed to change eye direction.**

It never hurts to tell people exactly what to do. Tell them why they should and how to open, to read, to look at the chart, to fill in the form. Tell them visually and in words. Tell them with numbers and with letters.

■ *CAUTION NOTE:* **People often have to be told what and how to read.**

Figure 10.1*a* shows a simple layout that has a headline at the top, a photograph on the left, and the rest body copy. Many brochures are like this. It is a fairly clean layout. As in many brochure layouts, benefits are presented in the middle of the page and in the bottom section, where prospects are asked for a decision and told how to respond. What is to be avoided is letting benefits deflect prospects from acting on the order form at the bottom.

■ *CAUTION NOTE:* **Benefits in the middle of a layout often deflect prospect from going to the order form at the bottom.**

How do we change this? By breaking up our design and by changing where we put our copy. The layout in Figure 10.1*b* begins like the first layout but we add a small photograph or two near the bottom to draw the eye there. We also place the information on how to order higher up on the page and add another strong benefit, in bolder type, underneath it.

But we want to get readers' eyes back up on the middle area and the

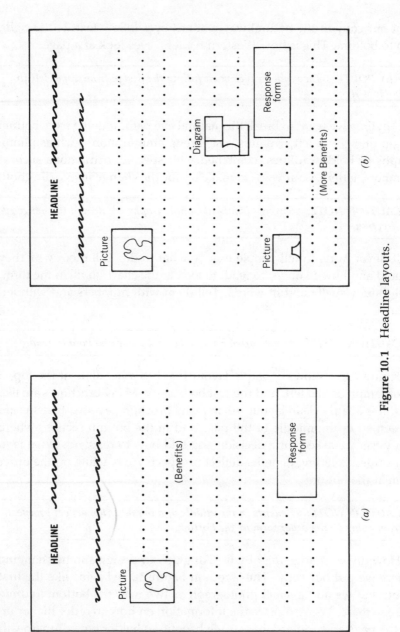

Figure 10.1 Headline layouts.

response information after they have read the bottom of the page. So we use a combination of a photograph and an arrow. We can even ask a reader to go to the middle section.

■ *KEY POINT:* *Put a benefit under the order form and use a picture or arrow to divert the reader back.*

What have we done? We have controlled our readers' eye path by design. We have gotten them to read the parts we want them to read, the parts that will help them make a decision and act on it. We have fulfilled the function of getting the copy read.

BEWARE OF EYE PATH CROSSING AND WHITE SPACE

In creating a brochure layout, we must keep other fundamentals of design in mind. One is to never have an eye path cross itself. We don't want readers' eyes to go back to where they were before. They've already been there and readers don't like to repeat themselves. Our layouts should take this into account.

■ *CAUTION NOTE:* *Never let an eye path cross itself.*

The only exception is in the response vehicle. Readers will go back up into the design if the order form is clearly marked.

Second, never make the eyes jump across an expanse of white space. Remember, white space fails to hold the eye in brochures. But it is also hard to eliminate entirely. Whatever color your "white" space is, make sure it doesn't interfere when you want the eye path to leave one area and go to another. Don't barricade your message with white space.

■ *CAUTION NOTE:* *Avoid white space.*

RULES FOR CONTROLLING THE EYE PATH

Here are the major rules for controlling eye path in laying out a brochure.

1. Start the eye path with a main headline that outlines the offer and a major benefit.
2. Have the eye path leave the headline at a point where the copy continues with major benefits.
3. Join other elements of the layout where you want the eye to travel next.
4. Use photographs or other strong visuals to entice the eye to continue its path to other parts of the text.
5. When you want the eye path to deviate from its natural movement, use visual elements to pull the eye in the correct direction.
6. End the eye path at the copy that tells the readers how to respond.

These rules, although simple, give a framework for the laying out of benefits, description, and support material point by point. They let us set up a sequence as natural to the eye path as possible, so that we can reveal our proposition in the way that suits us best.

BROCHURE COMPONENTS HAVE DIFFERENT POWERS OF ATTRACTION

Before we make our final layout of copy, we must consider another basic principle: The elements we use in the brochure have differing abilities to attract the eye.

The color photograph is the strongest visual element for attracting a reader's eye.

Next are large headlines, black-and-white photographs, and color drawings, which are all about equal in attracting the eye path. Drawings depicting satisfied customers using our product are hard to create, while photographs are definite and clearcut. However, a well-done color drawing can draw the eye as effectively as a black-and-white photograph.

■ *KEY POINT: Photographs strongly influence the eye path.*

Black-and-white drawings are the next level in attraction power. Generally, neither black-and-white nor color drawings are as strong as their equivalents in photography.

Subheads, charts, tables, and graphs rank lower than drawings in their ability to draw the eye. But they are still stronger than body copy, which is the weakest in attraction power.

■ *KEY POINT: Drawings, subheads, and charts influence the eye less than pictures.*

■ *CAUTION NOTE: Body copy has the least attraction power.*

LAYING OUT THE BROCHURE

Now that we know the basic principles of how brochures are read, and understand how to use the tools of design, how do we lay out a brochure? Let's take these principles and create the simplest of brochures—a one-page layout.

We start by dividing the page into five to eight separate and distinct subareas, each making a key point about our offer. In this way we link both copy and design (Figure 10.2). Notice that in each example the headline is the major way the offer is introduced. It is the first part to draw the reader's eye.

■ *KEY POINT: Use the brochure headline to introduce the offer.*

In all three examples in Figure 10.2, the benefit-oriented copy is in the middle, where it is most likely to be read. And following the normal eye path, the visuals, either photographs or drawings, attract the eye to the bottom right, where the response form is located. We use the various attraction powers of headlines and photographs to keep the eye focused on the benefits described in the body copy and moving toward the response form (Figure 10.3).

■ *KEY POINT: Locate benefits in the middle.*

■ *KEY POINT: Photographs and other visuals can focus the eye where most important.*

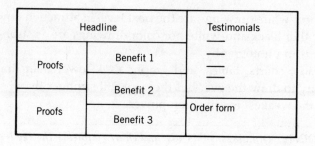

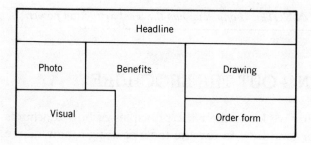

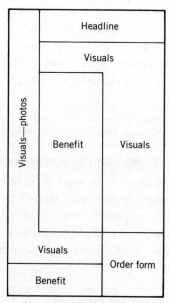

Figure 10.2   Brochure layouts.

Figure 10.3 Excellent example of photographs drawing the eye to copy. Note the order form on the sales surface. (Courtesy *ARTNews*)

WIDE AND TALL FORMATS

Tall layouts usually don't work as well as wide ones, because they present obstacles to the normal eye path. Of the two natural ways the eye moves in reading, left to right and top to bottom, it is easier to get readers to change direction and go from right to left than it is to get them to go back up into copy once they've reached the bottom.

■ *KEY POINT: Wide layouts allow the best eye path.*

Whenever you have a choice, your brochure should be designed the widest way. The only exception to this is again the response vehicle, because people will go back into it for copy.

All layouts have two strong areas of focus that draw the eye. If your brochure is wider than it is tall, one of these areas is slightly above the middle and to the left of center (see Figure 10.4). Since the eye falls to

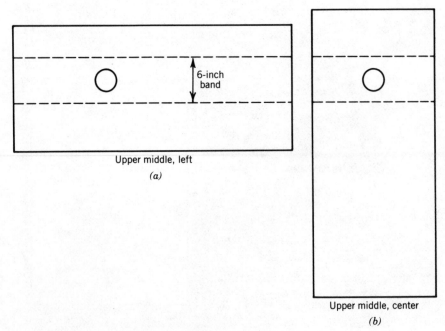

Upper middle, left

(a)

Upper middle, center

(b)

Figure 10.4   Wide (a) and tall (b) layouts.

this area naturally, take advantage of it by putting a major benefit or an important subheadline there.

■ *KEY POINT:* *The eye is drawn to the upper middle left area of the layout.*

Readership is also strongest in a 6-inch-wide band slightly above the middle (Figure 10.5). This is another justification for use of wide rather than tall: You can get more into this area.

■ *KEY POINT:* *Brochure readership is strongest in a 6-inch-wide band just above the middle.*

Even if you place a large dominant spread in this "area of focus," with a big photograph and perhaps even a request for prospects to call, you must organize the information for easy scanning diagonally from top left to bottom right.

■ *KEY POINT:* *Keep copy within the area of focus arranged from top left to bottom right.*

We can overcome the falloff of readership of the space above the area of focus by putting a dramatic easy-to-read headline there.

■ *KEY POINT:* *Compensate for not being in the area of focus by putting a dramatic headline or picture there.*

If the brochure is taller than it is wide, put the response form and some graphics near the bottom, or even put a benefit in a headline there as in Figure 10-5.

READERS FOCUS ON A SINGLE SALES SURFACE

Do we treat a two-page spread as one or two pages? It is always one page. When people open a brochure, they open it to the middle. No matter how many times the brochure is folded, people go to the middle first.

Once the brochure is opened, the middle pages become the "primary

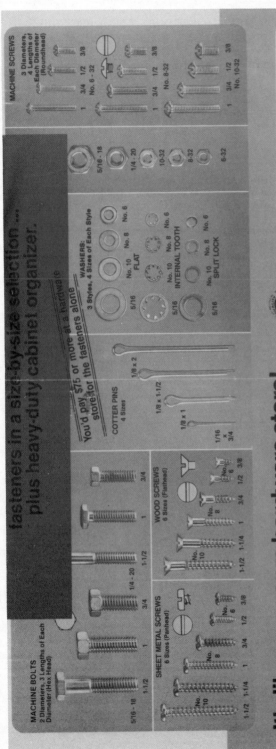

Figure 10.5 An example of a major benefit taking center stage. (Courtesy DRI Industries)

203

side," where you present your proposition in its most scannable and readable form.

■ *KEY POINT:* *No matter how many pages or folds a brochure has, readers open it to the middle.*

Readers also don't look at one side of the page at a time. They scan the whole surface in front of them and see it as a single visual unit. Design must reflect this.

■ *KEY POINT:* *The reader sees the whole surface broadly.*

The pages in Figure 10.6 are designed as one unit. See how much more visual power they have, compared with a design that treats the two pages separately. You double the size of your impact when you treat two pages as one.

■ *KEY POINT:* *Two pages seen as one double the sales impact.*

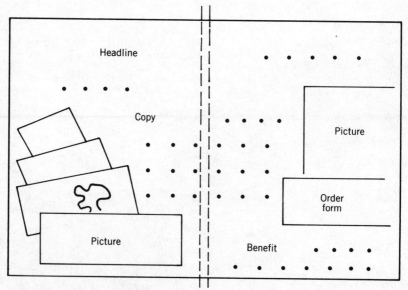

Figure 10.6 Brochure layout.

THE FRONT AND BACK PAGES MUST LEAD TO THE CENTER

The front and back pages of a brochure are not selling surfaces. The front page merely introduces what is inside. Its job is to get the page turned. Because we don't want to give away the whole story on the front, we use this surface to maintain the interest aroused in the sales letter and to announce that the benefits of the product or service are described inside, on the selling surface (Figure 10.7).

■ *KEY POINT: The front page of the brochure should do nothing more than introduce what's inside.*

One common error in designing the brochure cover is to use such an enticing photograph or other visual aid that the page doesn't get turned. If the inside is filled with body copy and has no visuals at all, the brochure's ability to sell is killed. Keep important visuals and copy woven together, so that pictures reinforce reading.

■ *CAUTION NOTE: Avoid too attractive a visual on the cover of the brochure.*

■ *KEY POINT: Save important pictures and charts for the inside sales surface.*

Similarly, the back page of the brochure is not useful for heavy selling. Advertisers often put order forms on the back page, but nothing could be worse from a sales point of view because few readers ever get to the back page.

■ *CAUTION NOTE: Don't put an order form on the back page of the brochure.*

■ *CAUTION NOTE: Few prospects read the back page of the brochure.*

You can put on the back of the brochure extra information that is not essential for the sale (Figure 10.8). If you're selling a book you could present its table of contents (Figure 10.9). If you're selling a household appliance, give its engineering specifications. Once in a while this information is read, but most buyers will not use it to make their decision.

Figure 10.7 Flashy, with color, but not so much as to overwhelm the contents inside. You know just enough about the product to want to turn the page. (Courtesy *Hot CoCo* magazine)

Figure 10.8 Here's a back cover that leads you back to the center sales surface. (Courtesy *ARTNews*)

Nine Reasons Why You Should Own this New Guide to DP Training Courses

Here are nine good reasons why you should keep a copy of the new **Guide to DP Training courses** on your desk. They summarize the massive contents of this remarkable new reference book. You'll use it day after day to answer questions, solve training problems, generate new ideas.

1. **Data Base**
Data Base Fundamentals . . . Data Base Management . . . IMS Data Base Design to Implementation to Debugging to Management to Administration . . . VSAM Programming, Structure, File Design, Performance . . . CICS Command Level Programming, Design, and Debugging . . . Adabas Concepts, Facilities, and Design courses . . . DL/I Programming and Applications . . . How to build and manage an Information Resource Directory among many other DP course offerings.

2. **Programming Languages**
Languages and Operating Systems . . . How languages are used in program design; Advanced Programming Techniques and debugging in Cobol ADA, Assembler, Fortran, JCL, Pascal, PL/I, RPG II, SAS . . . Structured programming Design and Techniques . . . Fundamentals of Operating Systems, Development Levels in systems as MVS, FOCUS, CMS, JES3.

3. **Project Management**
Organizational Needs and System Requirements from fundamentals to productivity to leadership skills to long-range planning . . . Developing the On-line Application . . . Control and Security Considerations for Information Systems . . . Making Human Fac-

tors a Reality in Interactive Systems . . . Problem-Solving Leadership Workshop.

4. **Systems Analysis and Design**
Advanced Structure and Design Techniques . . . Systems Analysis . . . Application Software Design . . . Building On-line Applications . . . Designing Security Controls . . . Screen Design . . . Structured Analysis and Design . . . Structured maintenance . . . Quality Assurance . . . Certificate in Information Science.

5. **Systems Programming**
Programming and Modeling Techniques from Entry Level Programming to Advanced Debugging . . . MVS VSAM for System Programmers . . . RDOS System Programming . . . Structured Programming, Analysis, Design, and Testing . . . Systems Programming . . . Basic Systems Programming . . . MVS/SP1.3 Functional Characteristics . . . VSAM for Systems Programmers.

6. **Data Communications—Telecommunications**
Components, Systems, and Networks from Design, to Management Concepts to Applications . . . Digital PABX, DPPX Applications, Analysis, and Design . . . Telecommunications Concepts to Management to Network Design . . . SNA Formats and Protocols

. . . and there's lots more!
To find the training information you need, simply check the easy to use index and in seconds you'll be able to solve problems . . . answer questions . . . generate creative new ideas.
To order your copy simply mail the postpaid card. This outstanding sourcebook will be yours to examine FREE for 30 days.

7. **User Training**
Courses users can take: DP Fundamentals for End Users . . . DP User Courses . . . Integration of Word Processing and Electronic Data Processing Systems . . . User Documentation . . . Becoming a Word Processing Specialist . . . WP Implementation Workshop . . . WP Management . . . Data Processing using SAS . . . Executive DP Concepts.

8. **Communications Skills**
Communications Skills for DP supervisors, managers and employees . . . Data Processing Communications . . . Improving Managerial Communications . . . Person to Person Communications . . . Active Listening Skills . . . Organizational Communications . . . Business Writing for Data Processing Professionals . . . Writing Strategies for Technical Managers.

9. **Management and Motivation Skills**
Leadership, Productivity, and Supervisory Skills . . . Management and Financial Development Skills . . . Managing and Motivating People . . . Using the Computer as a Management Tool . . . Auditing and Accounting for Non-Financial Managers . . . Financial Information Systems . . . Supervisory Cost Control . . . Developing Business Analysis Skills . . . Situational Leadership . . . Data Processing for the Non-Data Processing Executive . . . Human Relations: Forming Productive Working Relationships . . . Interpersonal Managing Skills . . . Video Instructional Systems . . . Action-Oriented Problem Solving.

ABOUT THE EDITORS . . .

Roger Sullivan, Consulting Editor for **The Guide to DP Training Courses** is Director of the Corporate Resource Center at the Commerical Union Insurance Company and Chairman of the North American Computer Education Council. He is the Senior Editor of "Quest," a newsletter for the data processing educator. He has written over 100 papers on DP education and adult learning. His experience includes 20 years of working in the data processing field. He is currently working on the book **Microshock: Its Effect on the Workplace and Workforce.**

Human Resource Development Press (HRD) has been publishing training and reference books for 10 years. Its staff is composed of experts in publishing, information gathering, and consultants in training.

Figure 10.9 Good use of the back page. It even gives a final selling punch. (Courtesy Human Resource Development Press)

They want to know what the product will do for them, and the inside sales surface tells this.

■ *KEY POINT:* *Use the back page for extra details on the product that are not essential for selling.*

LAYOUT STRATEGIES

Ignore the crease in the center of the page when running a headline across both inside pages. Keep the important material, such as major benefits and what prospects must do, in the center. Also highlight it by keeping it black and white, which gives it the highest degree of contrast. Other material such as testimonials and guarantees, although important, need not be emphasized as much.

■ *KEY POINT:* *Highlight key benefits in the center of the selling surface.*

Whenever possible, wrap copy around the visuals and integrate it into the design (Figure 10.10; also, see Figure 10-3). You get more readership if you use a picture to point toward copy. One technique that promotes readership is to use a photograph of a person pointing. You can cut off the edge of the photograph and show the arm extending beyond the picture frame into the copy.

■ *KEY POINT:* *Wrap copy around graphics.*

To conclude the message on your sales surface, use a summary paragraph, as you did in the letter, and lead the reader to the order form, which should be immediately to the right or below.

■ *KEY POINT:* *Conclude the sales message with a summary paragraph that leads to the order form.*

What goes into the summary paragraph? If you used only four or five benefits in your sales message, repeat them in the summary. "What you will get out of threshing your grass instead of cutting it is. . . ." This makes it seem as if there are more than four or five benefits. You double

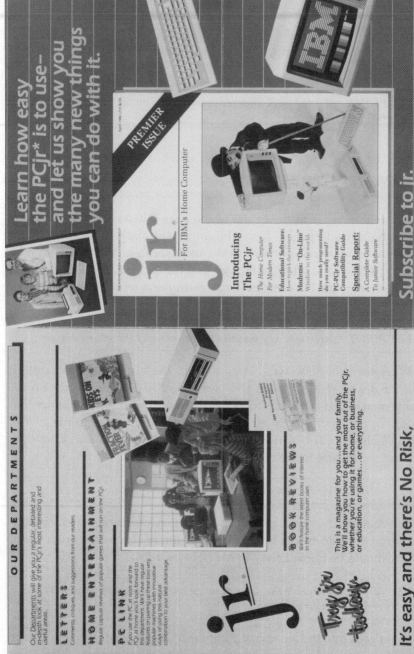

Figure 10.10 A good copy-wrapping example. (Courtesy *PC Jr.* magazine)

up on the impact. If you used more than four or five in your sales message, repeat the ones that are most important.

■ *KEY POINT: Double up on benefits in the summary paragraph by repeating them from the body copy.*

Also place your response form on the selling surface (Figure 10.11). Never separate the do's from the get's—what prospects get from what they give up.

■ *KEY POINT: Place the order form on the selling surface of the brochure.*

■ *CAUTION NOTE: Never separate what prospects get from what they have to give up.*

HEADLINES PROMOTE READERSHIP OF COPY

In addition to following an overall layout strategy, you start the brochure's selling surface with a headline, whose purpose is to promote readership of the other copy. As we saw in the last chapter, headlines should sum up the offer. We also build our other copy around it.

■ *KEY POINT: The purpose of the brochure headline is to promote readership of body copy.*

Place the headline high up on the sales surface. If a photograph is placed above it, the headline will appear to be a caption for the picture. Place photographs in other places to draw the eye to copy. However, do not place them too low; you don't want to draw the eye to the bottom too early, before prospects have read the body copy. If a photograph is at the bottom of the page, readers have little incentive to go back up and read more.

■ *KEY POINT: Place the headline high on the sales surface.*

■ *CAUTION NOTE: Avoid a photograph at the bottom, which stops readers from going back up to read more.*

Figure 10.11 Never separate what the prospect is going to get from what he or she has to give up to get it. (Courtesy Watson-Guptill)

Thus start the sales surface with a headline that holds the right promise for the right person. As we saw in the last chapter, headlines may be 30 or more words long.

■ *KEY POINT:*   *Create headlines that target interested prospects.*

■ *KEY POINT:*   *The headline may be 30 words long or more.*

Much copy, especially in boldface type, can overwhelm the top of the selling surface. What do we do? Carry copy all the way across the page in the first line and in the second line only a third of the way across. Stop with a break in the thought and use an ellipsis (. . .). The rest of the headline is picked up in a prominent, but less bold, typeface further down the page.

■ *KEY POINT:*   *Break a long headline with an ellipsis.*

Stopping the second line a third of the way across lets you end it near where you want prospects to start reading the body copy.

■ *KEY POINT:*   *Pick up body copy no more than one third of the way across the selling surface.*

Headlines should never end at the extreme right side of the page, because the margin stops the eye path. We want prospects to read our other copy. Ending the headline in the first third of the page allows the scanning motion of the natural eye path to continue.

■ *CAUTION NOTE:*   *Never end the headline at the right margin, which inhibits further reading.*

■ *KEY POINT:*   *The remainder of a long headline can be placed in a strong position below.*

Laying out a long headline this way accomplishes several goals. First, it lets us use 30 words or more without overwhelming the top of the brochure. Second, the headline ends where we want prospects to start reading body copy. And third, it brings part of the important headline message down into the rest of the copy to help tie it into our sales story (see Figure 10.12).

In Figure 10.12, the top section of the headline ends just where the

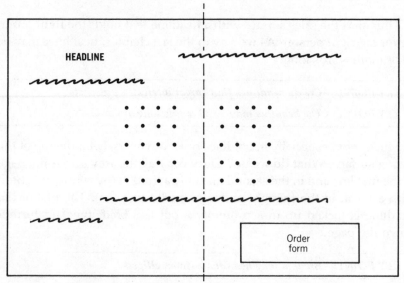

Figure 10.12 Brochure layout with order form.

important benefits are highlighted in the body copy. The headline starts again after the body copy and asks for the order (Figure 10.13).

HOW TO DESIGN PARAGRAPHS

In general, the secret of designing paragraphs is to keep them short, no more than six lines. This is true whether the mailing piece is directed to a home or a business. However, this rule is somewhat flexible because we must also vary the length of our paragraphs. We don't want every paragraph the same length. Thus use longer paragraphs only for variation.

■ *KEY POINT:* *Make most paragraphs no longer than six lines.*

■ *KEY POINT:* *Vary paragraph length.*

We don't organize brochure paragraphs according to idea or meaning, as we learned to do in school. Direct mail, like all advertising, is different. We organize paragraphs so that they will look easy to read. This is true even if we are writing to a sophisticated audience. After all, scientists don't like to read textbooks all the time. When they read direct

Figure 10.13 Headlines lead into and continue after body copy. (Courtesy *In-cider* magazine)

mail, they don't want anything too heavy. So keep paragraphs short and visually easy to read.

■ *KEY POINT:*   *Don't arrange paragraphs according to meaning, but for ease of reading.*

As we saw in the last chapter, we must keep our concepts simple. We must present our copy in as easy-to-grasp a manner as possible.

■ *KEY POINT:*   *Ease of reading is the major design guideline for paragraphs.*

As you did in the letter, indent the first line of each paragraph. This lets prospects know you are not a computer communicating with them.

■ *KEY POINT:*   *Indent the first line of each paragraph.*

You should also keep ragged-right borders, as you did in your letter. If paragraphs are flush right and left, the copy will look awkward to read and prospects may think you're trying to use every inch of space. The look will be too formal and not as interesting. They may not read as much.

■ *CAUTION NOTE:*   *Avoid making copy flush right in the brochure.*

As we have seen, reading is a vertical act. Everybody reads down columns or down the page. We want to assist this act by indenting the start of each paragraph and leaving a *widow*—a single word or part of a line—at the end. Then when readers finish the paragraph, it's easy for their eyes to drop down to the next one, because it begins near where the other ended. This encourages the downward movement of reading.

■ *KEY POINT:*   *Leave "widows" at the end of paragraphs to keep readers reading downward.*

HOW TO MOVE THE READER'S EYE TO THE NEXT COLUMN

When we get to the bottom of a column of copy, we can help readers go to the top of the next column by ending the column in the middle of a word and continuing the word at the top of the next column. Also we try to disguise what the word is, so readers will look for the rest of it in the next column. For example, if we cut "understand" at "under," readers are likely to know the word is "understand." But if we stop at "Un," readers are more likely to start reading the next column to find out what the word is.

■ *KEY POINT: End a column with an incomplete word, finished at the top of the next column.*

Another way to draw the reader's eye to the next column is to put a photograph or other visual diagram near the top. It will draw the eye up.

■ *KEY POINT: A photograph can be used to draw the reader's eye to the top of the next column.*

A third way to draw the eye to another column is to start the column with your guarantee, which can have a fancy, eye-catching border. But keep it easy to read. Don't use extra color or reverse printing.

■ *KEY POINT: Guarantee can move the eye to the top of a column.*
■ *KEY POINT: Make the guarantee easy to read.*

BUY READERSHIP WITH PHOTOGRAPHS SHOWING PEOPLE SIMILAR TO PROSPECTS ENJOYING BENEFITS

Should we illustrate our brochures with photographs that get attention? Absolutely not. We already have our prospects' attention. We don't want to distract them from our sales message. So we use photographs that show people like our prospects enjoying the benefits of our product or service. This draws the interest of readers who are looking for these benefits. And that's what sells.

■ *CAUTION NOTE: Never use photographs that get attention.*
■ *KEY POINT: Photographs should show people enjoying the benefits of the product.*

In your photographs you want to show real people who look like your prospects, who dress the same and are in similar situations. But they must look better, more glamourous. We don't want the people in the brochure to be real; we want them to be "sort of" like real people.

■ *CAUTION NOTE:*   *Photographs should glamorize real people.*

Do we use pictures of our product? Only if they show someone happily using it. We may on occasion use a drawing, especially if we are selling something hard to photograph, like a contact lens or electronic equipment.

■ *CAUTION NOTE:*   *Don't use a picture of the product unless you show someone using it.*

■ *KEY POINT:*   *Drawings can often make technical details simple.*

Generally, photographs offer a more precisely delineated image than do drawings. Photographs are best used to show people in real situations using the product or service (Figure 10.14).

■ *KEY POINT:*   *Photographs are best at showing the product in a real-life situation.*

Photographs are one of our best ways to buy readership. Whether in black and white or in color, photographs convert more lookers to readers than any other part of a brochure.

■ *KEY POINT:*   *Photographs are the strongest tool in the brochure to buy readership.*

PICTURE CAPTIONS SELL THE OFFER

What do we put under the photograph? A caption. It should be at least 100 words long, because each word will be read. Captions do not talk about the picture. They may refer to it, but their real message must relate to our offer.

■ *KEY POINT:*   *Picture captions should be long and relate to the offer.*

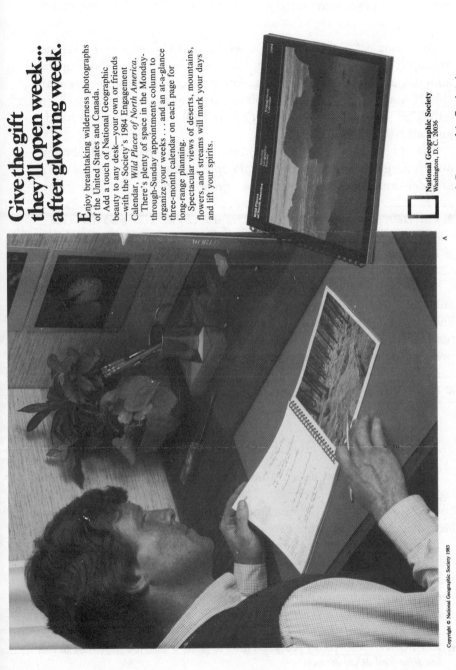

Give the gift they'll open week... after glowing week.

Enjoy breathtaking wilderness photographs of the United States and Canada.

Add a touch of National Geographic beauty to any desk—your own or friends —with the Society's 1984 Engagement Calendar, *Wild Places of North America*.

There's plenty of space in the Monday-through-Sunday appointments column to organize your weeks . . . and an at-a-glance three-month calendar on each page for long-range planning.

Spectacular views of deserts, mountains, flowers, and streams will mark your days and lift your spirits.

National Geographic Society
Washington, D. C. 20036

Figure 10.14 Excellent photographs of a product in use. (Courtesy National Geographic Society)

For example: "In the picture you see Bill using his new Turbo-Whirler to keep his grass threshed . . . and this machine will run continuously for a day and a half on one-half gallon of gasoline, and service is available 24 hours a day . . . our people are so nice to do business with, for only $295 you can have the power of the Turbo-Whirler in your hands, just call 1-800-234-4000 for. . . ."

The offer, benefits, even how to order—that's what we talk about in our captions. Don't waste captions. People always read them. Use them for sales-oriented copy that will move prospects to the next selling step.

■ *CAUTION NOTE:*   *Don't waste caption space by describing what's in the picture.*

■ *KEY POINT:*   *Use picture captions to promote the offer.*

When your prospects finish reading captions, and you want to guarantee that they will continue reading, add another sentence along the lines of "Please read the next paragraph, where you will find two more reasons why you should thresh your grass with a Turbo-Whirler." Tell prospects why they should read more.

■ *KEY POINT:*   *Picture captions can buy more readership.*

TESTING THE SUCCESS OF A LAYOUT

Here's a simple test you can take to find out whether you have designed your brochure correctly. Take masking tape and cover all the body copy. Leave only the headlines, subheads, flash heads, charts, tables, diagrams, and picture captions.

If what's uncovered is all that's needed to make a decision, the brochure is well designed. Readers shouldn't have to read body copy to get the essentials of the offer. They will read body copy to confirm their need for the product, but the offer, benefits, and how to order must be displayed visually.

■ *KEY POINT:*   *Everything prospects need to make a decision should be in the headline and other visuals.*

■ *CAUTION NOTE:*   *The prospect should not have to read body copy to make a decision.*

BROCHURE DESIGN DO'S AND DON'T'S

Do's

Use single sales surface for brochure.

Keep order form on sales surface.

Make headline either 20- or 24-point boldface type.

Start headline high on sales surface.

Split long headline copy with ellipsis.

Connect headline and other visual elements.

Use photographs to buy more readership.

Have photographs show people using product.

Use picture captions only to sell.

Give readers easy-to-read typeface for body copy.

Use 10-, 11-, or 12-point typeset characters.

Use 2-point leading between lines.

Use serif letters.

Indent paragraphs.

Leave widows at ends of paragraphs.

Keep strongest part of message in greatest contrast (black and white).

Use "matte finish" paper or blade coated stock.

Don't's

Don't use front and back pages to sell.

Avoid white space.

Never use picture captions to describe picture.

Don't use 9-point type for body copy.

Don't use italics.

Don't reverse print (white on black) copy.

Don't use a decorative typeface.

Don't use all caps in a headline.

Don't use expanded lettering in body copy or headline.

Don't use condensed lettering.

Don't use extra bold or extra wide typefaces.

Don't "surprint" over photographs.

Don't "reverse out" over photographs.

Don't use shiny paper.

Don't use "woven" paper.

SUMMARY

The main thing to keep in mind when designing brochures is that the reader's eye will scan your copy from upper left to lower right. Following this path is not something you get people to do; it is something they do naturally when they scan.

An effective layout lets you capitalize on this natural movement whenever possible. If you must deviate from the natural eye path, keep the deviation to a minimum and compensate by using numbers and arrows to show readers what they should read next.

Design itself does not transmit much—an image of quality and of style, a perception of worth. Our photographs let us transmit an image of the product and how it is being used. Effective though these visuals are, however, they don't sell. At best they can only draw attention to copy that sells.

GETTING ACTION WITH CREATIVE RESPONSE TECHNIQUES

11

In this chapter we will see how to design and write copy for the response vehicle. We will also explore other techniques to get prospects to act.

PROSPECTS READ THE RESPONSE FORM FIRST

The response device is an essential part of the mailing package. As we found out earlier, prospects read two parts of any direct mail piece first: the postscript at the end of the sales letter and the *response form*. Prospects look at both to see what we're offering, and will continue reading only if what we're offering makes sense for them. Once they go through the rest of our material, they will *re*read the response form to confirm their decision to buy.

■ *KEY POINT: The response form is often read first.*

■ *KEY POINT: The response form is reread to reaffirm the decision to buy.*

Our response device, then, must give prospects a capsule version of the offer. It must also contain a strong request for a response. Because it must do two tasks, the response vehicle has its own rules for copy and design.

■ *KEY POINT: The reponse device must summarize benefits and close strongly.*

There are many different kinds of response vehicles: ''Reservation

223

certificates" often reserve a special magazine offer, "acceptance forms" can reserve financial or insurance offerings, "catalog forms" offer easy ordering, "membership certificates" can offer a membership position, "store redemption forms" can generate walk-in store traffic, and "surveys" can get leads for salespeople, among others. In this chapter we will see how to write and design these and other response devices for maximum effectiveness.

THE RESPONSE DEVICES BEGIN WITH A STATEMENT OF ACCEPTANCE

Just as letters begin with a lead paragraph and brochures begin with a headline, response vehicles begin with a *statement of acceptance*. This statement relates to the offer: It reiterates a major benefit or what the prospect will get. For example, "Yes! I want the old-fashioned quality, value, and savings of The Customers Club. Sign me up . . . ," "Yes! I'm convinced I can profit from keeping up with all the breaking news on computer use in education . . . ," and "Yes! Send a 20-pound box of 36 Cushman HoneyBells to every business friend . . ." are acceptance statements that tell buyers exactly what they are getting and remind them of a benefit.

■ *KEY POINT:* **The acceptance statement summarizes the offer.**

Direct mail specialists affirm that statements of acceptance that mention benefits get 10% to 30% more responses than order forms that only ask for the order. Asking for the order is fine, but it's not enough. The acceptance statement must also stress what prospects will get.

■ *CAUTION NOTE:* **The response form must do more than ask for an order.**
■ *KEY POINT:* **The acceptance statement must stress benefits.**

WHAT GOES INTO WRITING AN ACCEPTANCE STATEMENT?

Acceptance statements should contain several major elements. First, they mention one benefit prospects will get out of having the product or service. This benefit should be one that prospects have already read about in the sales letter and brochure.

Second, acceptance statements should ask for the order. If response vehicles that ask only for the order are wrong, so are those that pile on benefits but fail to ask at all.

Third, they should tell prospects exactly what is offered. Prospects must know what they are getting. So if you're selling a product, give a brief description. If you're raising funds, offering a service, or generating inquiries, name and describe whatever it is and what prospects get for responding.

Fourth, acceptance statements should distinguish your product or service from similar products offered by your competitors.

Fifth, they should mention all the sweeteners and facilitators that go along with the offer. Particularly important are those that relieve risk, such as "30-day money-back guarantee," and those that make it easy to pay, such as "quarterly installments" or "bill me later."

Finally, acceptance statements must tell prospects how to respond. We must tell them how much to pay, whether they can use credit cards or cash, and also what reply card or envelope to use.

In short, acceptance statements should contain benefits, ask for the order, describe what is offered, explain how it is different from the competition, state what extras go with the product, use facilitators to make ordering easy, and show prospects exactly how to respond.

SUCCESSFUL COPY STRATEGIES FOR RESPONSE DEVICES

The following strategies use many of the rules just given for developing the acceptance statement. The strategies are meant to position the product or service in the prospect's mind, and thereby gain higher response.

■ *KEY POINT:* **Strategies for response devices position the product favorably.**

Free Examination, Pay Later. Free copies with the choice of paying later is a common strategy for the response device (Figure 11.1). But you can have collection problems with any offer that does not require cash up front. Direct mailers use this strategy strictly because it reaps more responses than bad debts. If that trend starts to reverse, they go for payment in advance.

Lower Price.   Lower price is the main theme of these response devices (Figure 11.2).

Introductory and Charter Subscriptions.   Similar to "free trial" and "lower price," this response device gives prospects the perception that

Figure 11.1   Free copy-pay later emphasis in this response vehicle. Response devices don't have to be fancy. This is a modest, plainly designed card that emphasizes free examination–pay later principle. It has been formally typeset. (Courtesy *Art & Antiques*)

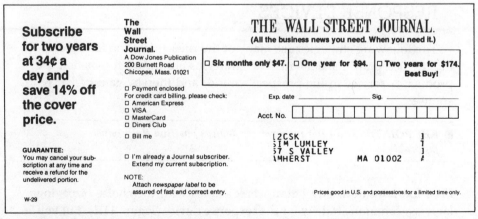

Figure 11.2   Lower price is used as the main theme of this response device. (Courtesy *The Wall Street Journal*)

they are getting something special by getting into something early (Figure 11.3).

Sweeteners. This response device highlights a special to prospects (Figure 11.4).

Special Guarantees. This response device emphasizes a money-back guarantee (Figure 11.5).

Figure 11.3 Finding a new reader who may stay for years is the name of the game for magazines. (Courtesy *Vanity Fair*)

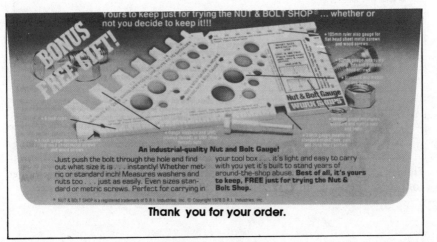

Figure 11.4 A free gauge for ordering nuts and bolts might make the difference for this competitive product. (Courtesy DRI Industries)

Your $1,000 Guarantee

Try **Small Business Wealth Builder** for just 3 months. If during that time it doesn't show you how to make at least an additional $1,000 in profits, or slash at least $1,000 off your tax bill, just let us know. We'll promptly give you a refund of every penny you've paid. And the $29.95 bonus manual, *"Guaranteed Wealth Building Strategies for Small Business,"* will be yours to keep free, our "thank you" for giving the newsletter a fair trial.

©Enterprise Publishing, Inc. MCMLXXXIII

For Your Free $29.95 Manual and No-Risk Subscription, Mail This Today

YES, please mail my free copy of *"Guaranteed Wealth Building Strategies for Small Business."* This free manual, a $29.95 value, features 211 of the smartest ways to use a small business to multiply personal wealth and shelter more income from taxes.

Also enter my Charter Subscription to **Small Business Wealth Builder,** the unique new monthly newsletter for business owners. It will show me how to take full advantage of the many ways I can use my small company to build my personal wealth...generate thousands of dollars a year tax-free...borrow my way to wealth using "OPM" (other people's money)...drive stronger deals with suppliers, lawyers, employees, others...get higher returns on corporate investments ...and more.

I am protected by your $1,000, money-back guarantee described at left. And, even if I decide to cancel my subscription, the $29.95 manual will be mine to keep, just for giving the newsletter a try.

Here's How to Order
Please enter my Charter Subscription for:
☐ One Year (12 issues) $96 (Save $49 off regular rate.)
☐ Two Years (24 issues) $192 (Save $98 off regular rate.)
☐ Check or money order enclosed.
Charge to: ☐ MasterCard ☐ VISA ☐ American Express

Card No.

Card Expires Signature

DR-90W

JIM LUMLEY
5 VALLEY RD
AMHERST, MA 01002

Please make any necessary correction in name and address for shipment

Small Business Wealth Builder™

Mail to: 725 Market Street Wilmington, DE 19801

DW002

Figure 11.5 Special "$1,000 Guarantee" just guarantees money back that mail-order buyer is entitled to anyway. But it's a bold claim that helps sell. (Courtesy *Small Business Wealth Builder*)

A First Edition Invitation for a Friend of Southern Living®

Preview the First Edition of the first adventure book Walter Cronkite has ever written—his first collaboration with seascape artist, Ray Ellis.

Also receive a superb Ellis print—that's yours to keep free whether you keep the book or not.

DETACH THIS RESERVATION CARD ALONG DOTTED LINES, AND MAIL TODAY IN THE ENVELOPE PROVIDED

Southern Living® Gallery presents...

SOUTH BY SOUTHEAST

☐ YES! As soon as it is published in October, send my First Edition of SOUTH BY SOUTHEAST by Walter Cronkite and Ray Ellis, and enclose with it my free Ellis print worth over $10.00. Bill me later in three monthly installments of just $13.32 each, plus postage and handling. I save $10.05 off the regular retail price during this special pre-publication offer. If not delighted, I'll return the book within 30 days at your expense and owe nothing. Either way, the print is mine to keep—free!

4003230 000000305 4002740171
JAMES LUMLEY OH
57 S VALLEY RD
AMHERST MA 01002

SEND NO MONEY NOW:
Mail this card in the postpaid envelope to:

Southern Living® Gallery P.O. Box 2463, Birmingham, Alabama 35201

539E

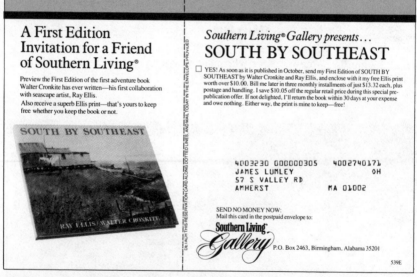

Figure 11.6 Walter Cronkite's endorsement helps this otherwise average coffee-table book. (Courtesy Southern Living Gallery)

Famous Names.   Prospects will often be influenced by a famous name attached to a product, service, or cause. Whether the person is Arnold Palmer, Bill Cosby, or Walter Cronkite, the celebrity's perceived support helps gain responses for otherwise lackluster products (Figure 11.6). Fund raising and political campaigning often need such public recognition in addition to their emotional appeal. The names of Jerry Lewis and Ronald Reagan collect millions from an apathetic public that might not otherwise show its concern for the cause for which Lewis and Reagan were collecting.

Membership Acceptance.   Instead of selling a magazine subscription, sell a membership (Figure 11.7). The magazine becomes the tangible re-

---

SIERRA CLUB MEMBERSHIP ENROLLMENT FORM

Enroll me as the newest Member of the Sierra Club.
I am joining because:
☐ I want to enhance my outdoor pleasures
☐ I want to help protect the environment
☐ I want to do both.
I am enclosing my annual membership
dues in the category I have checked. I
understand my membership benefits
and privileges include the bi-monthly
Sierra magazine, special discounts on
books, and the chance to participate
in local and worldwide outings.

Y678
MR. JIM LUMLEY
57 S. VALLEY ROAD
AMHERST, MA   01002

Enroll me in the following membership category:

	Individual Dues	Joint Dues
Regular	☐ $29	☐ $33
Supporting	☐ $50	☐ $54
Contributing	☐ $100	☐ $104
Life (per person)	☐ $750	
Student or Senior	☐ $15	☐ $19

Dues include subscription to *Sierra* ($3) and regional newsletter ($1).

Telephone number, please _____
                              (area code)   (number)

To help even more, I am enclosing an extra contribution—
over and above my dues—of ☐ $10 ☐ $25 ☐ $50 ☐ $100
☐ Other _____

SIERRA CLUB

P.O. Box 7959
Rincon Annex
San Francisco, CA 94120

Figure 11.7   A well-known organization that uses a magazine to sell its membership. (Courtesy Sierra Club)

ward members get for belonging, while the membership gives prospects the feeling that they belong to a group of like-minded souls. The prospect should consider the subscription as part of a larger "membership." Look at the success of National Geographic.

Consider why it works. Many prospects might balk at spending $15 for a magazine, but they think nothing of paying that much to belong to a group with which they share an affinity. And what do you do to cement the relationship year after year? Give them a fine magazine. They'll think of it as a bonus for belonging.

DESIGN THE RESPONSE DEVICE FIRST

Many direct mail specialists recommend that the response device, whether an order form, reservation certificate, opinion survey, or application, be created first and the other components, such as the sales letter and brochure, be designed around it.

■ *KEY POINT:* **Consider designing the response device first.**

There are two major reasons for designing the response device first. First, because it must be a complete summarized offer, including benefits, proofs, risk relievers, guarantees, and how and what to pay, it can be used as a guideline in creating the other components.

Second, designing the response device first makes referring to it in the letter and brochure easier. In this way the response device can also be the most prominent piece in the mailing package.

Our strategy for designing a response device is to incorporate the order form into the sales letter. For example, it could be at the bottom of the letter.

■ *KEY POINT:* **If designed first, the response device can be used as a guideline and reference.**

Guidelines for Designing the Response Device

Here are some basic considerations for designing the response device:

1. Use a heavy paper stock, heavier than that used for your brochure or sales letter.

2. Make the device large and a different shape from the other parts of the mailing package. Avoid the "envelope-sized" cards everyone else uses. They are too similar in size.

3. Use color either as a background or as a typeface, to draw the eye to major elements within the reply message. A strong color like red or orange will also draw attention to the response device itself.

4. Use a large, bold typeface for the acceptance statement.

5. Use uppercase and lowercase letters in the copy, for ease of reading.

6. Use techniques such as tokens in windows or check-off boxes to encourage involvement. "Preference" choices can work effectively in political and other fund-raising campaigns. For example, a token can confirm a magazine buyer's interest, or a survey form can involve a potential donor in the issues of a cause.

7. Use computer typing or a mailing label to affix the prospect's name and address on the reply form. This makes responding easier, and besides, we all read our own name.

8. Keep the response device's primary sales message exposed. Don't fold it or cover the message up in any way.

Design Strategies for Response Devices

One of the best ways to generate responses is to involve prospects in the process. You might have them pull out a card or apply a token or "gold seal" to their order (Figure 11.8).

■ *KEY POINT: Involve the prospect in responding.*

It's a mystery why some of these techniques work, not that they do in all cases. They are used extensively for offers like magazine subscriptions. They appear to generate responses, but may more often be used to generate lots of less-involved leads by anxious marketers. As we will see in the chapter on "testing," such techniques are of less importance than the dynamics of the offer in making sales.

■ *CAUTION NOTE: Involvement techniques by themselves don't make sales.*

The key to the success of most token-style offers is that the prospect

Figure 11.8 This token even comes glued, just moisten and attach it; everything else is done. This is almost too easy, and that may be a problem when payment is sought; there's little commitment on the part of the buyer. (Courtesy *Omni* magazine)

must do something. The reply form often has the prospect's name and address printed on the card and is designed so it will show through the window envelope containing the mailing package. All prospects need to do is drop the form in the mail. Because this is so easy, their commitment must be tested by involving them in a simple task like affixing a token. Making ordering too easy may mean less commitment on the part of the buyers—it may be difficult to collect at payment time.

■ *CAUTION NOTE:*   *If ordering is too easy, a less committed buyer responds.*

■ *KEY POINT:*   *Involvement gains more committed buyers.*

Another way to involve prospects is to use the response device as an "opinion survey." This technique is often used in fund raising, working best with prospects who already have a strong interest in the cause (Figure 11.9).

You don't have to limit your response form to selling one product at a

Please answer each question. Then detach and return the front copy of Survey/Contribution Reply. Retain back copy for your records.

NATIONAL OPINION SURVEY ON UNION VIOLENCE
Prepared by
The National Right to Work
Legal Defense Foundation, Inc.
8001 Braddock Road
Springfield, Virginia 22160

Please answer each question. Then return your completed Survey in the enclosed return envelope.

SURVEY #		BADT
KEYED TABULATED INT. OK	James Lumley South Valley Bd Amherst, MA 01002	115B

YOUR NAME WILL NOT BE ASSOCIATED WITH YOUR OPINIONS.
ONLY TOTAL SURVEY RESULTS WILL EVER BE RELEASED.

1) Labor Union violence (arson, bombings, vandalism, etc.) is a major cause of property destruction in the United States. Do you think federal and local judges should make labor union officials pay to repair the damage they cause?
   ☐ YES   ☐ NO   ☐ UNDECIDED

2) In most states it is illegal for policemen, firemen, and hospital workers to go on strike because it endangers the public safety. Yet public employee union officials continue to call illegal strikes.
   What kind of criminal penalties do you favor for union officials who try to discipline employees for not participating in an illegal strike?
   ☐ a jail sentence   ☐ a fine   ☐ no penalties   ☐ undecided   Other _____

3) Recently a high ranking U.S. Justice Department official said that Union violence is one of the "most serious criminal problems in the field today."
   Do you think that Union officials would continue to commit acts of violence if they knew they would be prosecuted and sent to jail for their crimes?
   ☐ YES   ☐ NO   ☐ UNDECIDED

4) Under the *U.S. vs Enmons* Supreme Court decision, Union officials can avoid federal prosecution for union related crimes of violence.
   Do you think Union officials should be given any special privileges under the law?
   ☐ YES   ☐ NO   ☐ UNDECIDED

5) Would you be willing to make a contribution to help the Right to Work Foundation with new precedent-setting lawsuits to make Union officials pay for their acts of violence?
   ☐ YES   ☐ NO   ☐ UNDECIDED

Your initials here   For office use only   12345

Contribution Reply

Yes, Mr. Harris, you can count on me to help you expose the *Enmons* decision to the American public—and to help pay for your precedent-setting lawsuits to make Union Bosses legally responsible for their acts of violence.

I'm enclosing my tax-deductible contribution for:

☐ $15   ☐ $25   ☐ $50   ☐ $100   ☐ Other $_____

Please make your check payable to: FROM: BADT
NATIONAL RIGHT TO WORK FOUNDATION   James Lumley
8001 Braddock Road • Springfield, Virginia 22160   South Valley Bd
                                                    Amherst, MA 01002   115B

Your contribution to the National Right to Work Foundation is fully tax-deductible.

Figure 11.9   This fund-raising "contribution reply" form closes for your money by using a survey to make you feel part of a cause. (Courtesy National Right-to-Work Foundation)

time. Use it to encourage prospects to buy more than one of a product, to be given away as gifts. Your design can include space for the names and addresses of the recipients (Figure 11.10).

Perhaps the most common design technique is to make the order form a tear-out card that is part of a larger surface which is used as

Give Them

CUSHMAN HoneyBells

T.M.

for Christmas 🎄

Say ☑ YES! by December 9, 1983...or wait a full year.

☐ **YES!** Send a 20-pound box of **36 or more Cushman HoneyBells** to every business friend I have listed below and bill me later for **only $21.95** per box, plus only **$2** for shipping. (More in some states; see back of this form.) You **GUARANTEE** my satisfaction...and my **friend's** satisfaction, so if **anyone's** unhappy, I'll write and tell you about it. Your response **is guaranteed** to include a cashier's check for every penny I've paid.

☐ **NO!** I'll wait. (Maybe next year. Maybe **not**.)

YOUR NAME & ADDRESS APPEAR BELOW. (Please change as required.)

M4513

```
LORIS PARFUM
REALVEST PROFESSIONAL BUS BOOK
57 SOUTH VALLEY RD - PELHAM
AMHERST MA  01002
```

☐ Bill me.   ☐ Bill my **company.**   Bill my ☐ VISA ☐ MasterCard

Acct. #:_____ Exp. Date:_____/_____ **YOUR** ph. no. (   )_____

YOUR signature _____

TITLE _____

PLEASE PRINT OR TYPE

SEND BOX OF 36 or more HoneyBells TO:

1. NAME _____ TITLE _____
COMPANY _____
ADDRESS _____ APT. _____
CITY _____ STATE _____ ZIP _____
Sign HoneyBell Holiday Card "from _____"

2. NAME _____ TITLE _____
COMPANY _____
ADDRESS _____ APT. _____
CITY _____ STATE _____ ZIP _____
Sign HoneyBell Holiday Card "from _____"

3. NAME _____ TITLE _____
COMPANY _____
ADDRESS _____ APT. _____
CITY _____ STATE _____ ZIP _____
Sign HoneyBell Holiday Card "from _____"

Figure 11.10 Here's one order form that doesn't want just one order, it wants 12! It's a sound marketing strategy—instead of selling one box to one customer, you sell many boxes to one customer who will give them away as gifts. (Courtesy Cushman Fruit Company)

234

selling space (Figure 11.11). The act of tearing off the order card involves prospects in the act of responding.

DESIGNING REPLY ENVELOPES

The envelope prospects are to use to mail the response back to you is also a crucial part of the mailing piece. You must make it easy for your prospects to respond. However, the envelope need not be color coordinated with the rest of the mailing piece. In fact, it is best to make it easily identified as the envelope for the response and payment, if needed.

■ *KEY POINT: Use color and size to identify the reply envelope.*

Return postage must be affixed. Business-reply postage is used most often. But if you want to show unusual concern for your prospects, es-

Figure 11.11   The part of the response vehicle used to order must be torn off and separated from the part selling benefits. (Courtesy *Inc.* magazine)

pecially in raising funds for a cause, you might put genuine, commemorative stamps on your return envelopes. Sometimes this increases response.

■ *KEY POINT:*   *Always affix postage.*

■ *KEY POINT:*   *Consider using real stamps when fund raising.*

You can encourage responses by typing the prospect's name and address in the upper-left "return address" position on the envelope. With modern computer printing techniques, this is now possible.

■ *KEY POINT:*   *Consider putting the prospect's name and address on the reply envelope.*

You can incorporate the response form into the reply envelope when mailing to customers, present subscribers, or donors with whom you are in contact (Figure 11.12). This reduces your cost. The technique is not advised for mailings to new prospects or to casual customers.

■ *KEY POINT:*   *For customer mailings, combine the order form into the envelope.*

■ *CAUTION NOTE:*   *Never use the combined order form and envelope in prospect mailings.*

WHAT DO WE DO WITH PROSPECTS WHO DECIDE TO SAY NO?

If all else fails, canny marketers can make one last attempt to sell prospects who have decided against the offer by using a *response intensifier*. A simulated personal note, this often starts with a printed "handwritten" lead such as, "Still undecided? Please read this brief message. . . ," "Read this only if you've decided *not* to subscribe," or "If you've decided to say NO, please read the letter inside."

■ *KEY POINT:*   *An additional "personal" note can often boost responses.*

This lead prefaces a fuller message, usually on a small folded sheet,

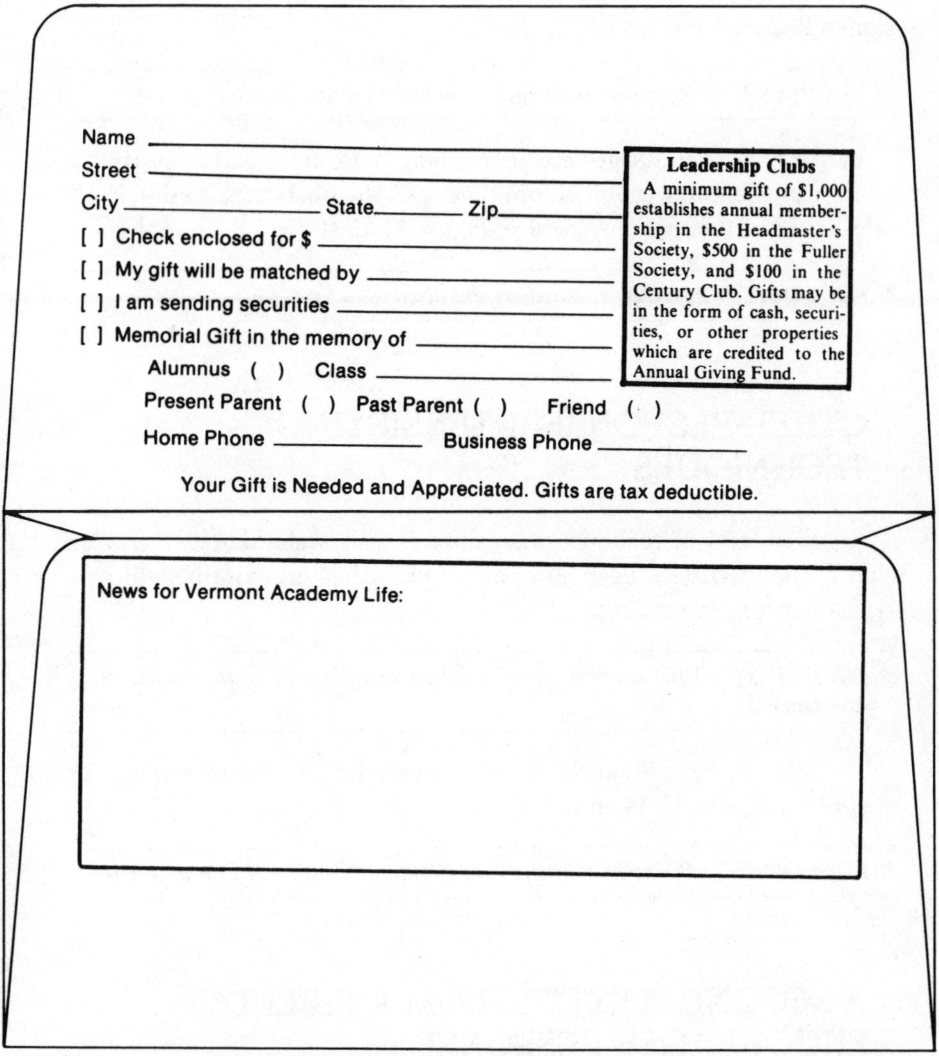

Name _____

Street _____

City _____ State_____ Zip_____

[ ] Check enclosed for $ _____

[ ] My gift will be matched by _____

[ ] I am sending securities _____

[ ] Memorial Gift in the memory of _____

    Alumnus ( ) Class _____

    Present Parent ( ) Past Parent ( ) Friend ( )

    Home Phone _____ Business Phone _____

Leadership Clubs

A minimum gift of $1,000 establishes annual membership in the Headmaster's Society, $500 in the Fuller Society, and $100 in the Century Club. Gifts may be in the form of cash, securities, or other properties which are credited to the Annual Giving Fund.

Your Gift is Needed and Appreciated. Gifts are tax deductible.

News for Vermont Academy Life:

Figure 11.12 This response form is for donors or customers only. It is integrated into the reply envelope. (Courtesy Vermont Academy)

that tells about an additional benefit of buying now or offers a special discount. This letter contains additional selling copy and is often designed like a mini-sales letter.

■ *KEY POINT:*   *"Response intensifiers" are often mini-sales letters.*

In truth, these messages are not actually last-ditch efforts—prospects often read them first, even before they read the postscript on the "real" sales letter or the response device. Figure 11.13 shows an example.

■ *KEY POINT:*   *Response intensifiers are often read first.*

OTHER RESPONSE-INTENSIFYING TECHNIQUES

Another kind of response intensifier is also a simulated note, also with a "handwritten" lead, that offers prospects an extra benefit or a sweetener for responding.

■ *KEY POINT:*   *Other tools to boost response can identify extra benefits or sweeteners.*

The main thing is that both kinds of letters make a strong request for the order (Figures 11.14 and 11.15).

■ *KEY POINT:*   *All response intensifiers should press strongly for a decision.*

A SECOND "LETTER FROM A FRIEND" ENCOURAGES RESPONSE

Another similar sales technique is the *Letter from a Friend.* This seemingly objective, third-party message is usually a short letter in a small format that contains an extra "personal message" from someone unconnected with the seller. It could be from a "reading consultant" who ad-

National Geographic Society

WASHINGTON, D.C.   20036

Dear Friend,

I'd like to remind you that National Geographic's Land of
Liberty six-volume set is yours to examine free. There is
absolutely no purchase obligation.

And...if you are still undecided about this offer, please
read these words of praise from our Society members:

> "Only a few moments ago, I finished reading THE
> REVOLUTIONARY WAR....I am proud to be a member of
> the National Geographic Society and an American."

> "Your book THE CIVIL WAR is indeed history at its best."

> "Thank you for TRAILS WEST. I consider it an out-
> standing publication."

> "I have just finished The Wild Shores: AMERICA'S
> BEGINNINGS. I thoroughly enjoyed reading this
> splendid book. I could not stop!"

> "OUR COUNTRY'S PRESIDENTS is beautiful. We shall
> prize it always."

> "All have been excellent, but INTO THE WILDERNESS
> gets a special rating!"

Considering such enthusiastic response, we're confident that
you'll be pleased with your Land of Liberty six-volume set, as will
those who receive the set from you as a gift.

But do hurry and get your order to us, because the supply is
limited. We've sold more than two million of these books already.
And we're receiving more orders every day. To assure yourself a set,
mail the enclosed Reservation Card without delay.

Sincerely,

Robert L. Breeden

Robert L. Breeden
Vice President
Publications and Educational Media

Figure 11.13 A good salesperson never stops selling. (Courtesy National Geographic Society)

From: **Ralph B. Titus**

For: **The Harvard Business Review**

We're going all out to let you see for yourself how much The REVIEW can contribute to your business thinking. Just return the card in the accompanying invitation and we'll put the current issue in the mail to you. You've got to like it or you don't pay for it -- that's cut and dried.

And if The REVIEW doesn't meet your standards anywhere along the line -- after the first, second, third, fourth, fifth or sixth issue -- you can tell us to cancel your subscription and we will refund your money. <u>Every cent</u>.

Even if you cancel, your gift copy of PATHS TOWARD PERSONAL PROGRESS: LEADERS ARE MADE, NOT BORN is yours to keep. No charge. No questions asked.

That's as plain as I can make this rare offer. There's no "fine print", no "angles", no hidden costs or surprises. You must be satisfied or we lose you and our investment in you as a subscriber.

This unconditional no-risk guarantee applies whether you pay for your subscription or your company does. And two out of three companies <u>do</u> pay because they know that anything that helps an executive do a better job helps the company succeed. Your management, too, can't fail to notice your interest in keeping up with the best business thinking.

Naturally, the subscription price is tax-deductible no matter who pays. So please return the card promptly. Offer of the free Premium with 100% refund guarantee is valid for a limited time only.

I look forward to sending you PATHS TOWARD PERSONAL PROGRESS and starting your REVIEW copies on their way to you.

Sincerely,

Ralph B. Titus

Ralph B. Titus
Circulation Director
The Harvard Business Review

Figure 11.14 This miniletter touches on many of the ingredients included in a full sales letter. (Courtesy *Harvard Business Review*)

You are a valued friend...

and to show our appreciation for all your kind support and interest in 1983, we'd like you to have—and use—this special gift...a certificate worth $5.00 off the price of any book in this mailing when you buy one copy of THE JOY OF WATERCOLOR at the regular price of $23.50.

It's a great way to save money on another copy of THE JOY OF WATERCOLOR or any of the other fine books described in the enclosed brochures!

Simply decide which book you'd like to save $5.00 on, fill in the title, correct order number and your name and address on the certificate. Then include your completed $5.00 certificate with your order for THE JOY OF WATERCOLOR.

But make your selection soon! This special $5.00 certificate will expire on Thursday, December 15, 1983.

So from all of us at Watson-Guptill, we wish you Happy Holidays and a colorful, creative New Year!

Watson-Guptill Holiday Coupon

**worth $5.00 off the price of any book
when included with the purchase of
THE JOY OF WATERCOLOR at the regular price of $23.50**

This certificate expires Thursday, December 15, 1983.

SAVE $5

I would like to use this special coupon toward the purchase of the book I have listed below.

Order #_____

Title_____

Name_____

Address_____

City/State/Zip_____

SAVE $5

DRJS–0370

Figure 11.15 Here's one that sweetens the offer with a gift coupon. (Courtesy Watson-Guptill)

241

From the desk of **Judith M. Hobart**

           As a librarian, I am always on the lookout
           for books — especially books about history —
           that are appealing to children.

Dear Member,

    Anytime you find a history book that's more an adventure story
than a lesson, it's time to cheer! That's why I'm so delighted with
The Story of America. It's a book I'm sure young people will thoroughly enjoy, while learning what made America great!

           In his foreword, Alistair Cooke explains
           that history is a continuous attempt to
           find out what happened, how it happened,
           and why. And that to him, "the main fas-
           cination of history is the fun of playing
           detective."

    In the true spirit of Sherlock Holmes, this new illustrated
children's atlas examines the evidence of America's past. Intriguing
portions of honest-to-goodness diaries and letters add suspense and
capture curiosity. Ballads and true-to-life stories sustain the
interest of young people. And old photographs in combination with
National Geographic's gorgeous illustrations provide a visual treat.

    At a time when just about everybody is worried about the quality
of education, The Story of America will draw young readers right into
a remarkable narrative about their country in the way a textbook
never could! And the time-line wall chart will give them easy-to-
find answers for homework.

    I can't think of a better way to encourage young people's inter-
est in history...and learning. And this book will remind readers —
at an age when it's most important — of their great American heritage!

    The Story of America is everything you could hope for in a
children's book. Why not reserve a copy today — and see for yourself?

           Sincerely,

           Judith M. Hobart

JMH/am   Children's Librarian

Figure 11.16 This miniletter from a children's librarian packs that extra sales
punch needed to get responses. (Courtesy National Geographic Society)

vises parents about benefits of a particular reading program for their children. It could be from one of the writers of the publication being offered. It could even be from someone who presents himself or herself as a colleague of the prospect.

■ *KEY POINT: A short letter from an "objective party" helps boost response.*

What do these miniletters say? Besides highlighting more benefits, of course, they are also testimonials, written in an easy, conversational style by a supposedly objective observer (Figure 11.16).

Their primary goal, however, is to gain a favorable decision from prospects if more ammunition is needed.

■ *KEY POINT: Third-party letters often highlight benefits.*

12

SUCCESS WITH SELF-MAILING BROCHURES AND CARD DECKS

In this chapter we will look into self-mailing brochures and postcard decks.

SELF-MAILERS ARE BROCHURES AND CARD DECKS

A self-mailer is any kind of direct mail piece without a separate envelope that does a selling job by itself.

The two major styles are the self-mailing brochures and the postcard deck. The self-mailing brochure is often folded in half to a final size of 8½ inches by 11 inches or 5½ inches by 8½ inches. Most have four pages; some with more elaborate folds have six or eight pages. Many styles and combinations of page and fold are possible.

The self-mailing brochure does not have an envelope. The name and address of the recipient is affixed, usually with a mailing label, on the outside surface.

Postcard decks are normally postcard size, 3½ inches by 5½ inches, and are often mailed in a clear plastic envelope along with cards offering other products and services.

Self-mailing brochures and postcard decks must both contain complete selling messages.

■ *KEY POINT:* *The sales message of self-mailing brochures and cards must be complete.*

SELF-MAILING BROCHURES DO A COMPLETE SELLING JOB

Though self-mailing brochures resemble brochures that accompany sales letters, there are major differences in how they are created and used.

First, self-mailers must do the job of the sales letter, the letter brochure, and the response device. They must have the intimacy and persuasion power of the letter and the select-for-myself aspect of the brochure. They must also gain decisions from readers and give them an easy way to respond.

■ *KEY POINT: The self-mailing brochure must do the job of the letter, the brochure, and the response device.*

Second, because self-mailers are a single identifiable piece, they are easy to pass around. Therefore they are often sent to prospects who are involved in group decisions. Specifically, self-mailers work well in business mailings, where several people may be involved in making a decision.

■ *KEY POINT: The self-mailer's pass-along capability works well in business.*

SELF-MAILERS WORK WHEN WE CANNOT TARGET THE PROSPECT BY NAME

In business mailings, you may not be able to identify the person or persons who will decide on your product or service. Therefore you want a mailing piece that can be passed from one individual to another until it reaches the right party. Self-mailers fill this requirement because they consist of only one piece and they contain a complete sales message.

■ *KEY POINT: The self-mailer has the best chance of being passed along to the right party.*

We can try to ensure that our self-mailing brochure reaches the person who will make the decision by adding a "routine message" under the mailing label. For example, we could use "ATTENTION: Mailroom Personnel—Please reroute if necessary. . . . This important dated announcement should go to the person in charge of data processing training."

■ *KEY POINT: A "routing" message can help get the self-mailer into the right hands.*

You can also address self-mailers to positions or titles rather than to individuals, in case the occupants have changed job responsibilities or are no longer employed. Although this holds for other types of mailings as well, the self-mailer is recognized by prospects as not being personal mail. For example, you could direct self-mailers to the attention of Circulation Manager, Promotion Manager, or Marketing Manager. Because mailroom workers usually sort enormous quantities of mail daily, it is best to give them clear instructions.

■ *KEY POINT: Self-mailers can be directed to job titles.*

■ *KEY POINT: Make instructions clear for the mailroom staff.*

Self-mailers correct a prevalent problem in business-to-business mail. Mail often gets lost, not just by the Postal Service but within companies. If your specific prospect is no longer in charge of making the decision, or if you don't have a specific prospect, you can lose out with a letter mailing. If the envelope with the sales message inside doesn't get to the right party immediately, it's not likely to be opened or passed on to the correct decision maker. Self-mailers, however, don't require opening because they're already open. Employees have only to expose the main sales surface.

■ *CAUTION NOTE: Letter mailings don't always get passed along.*

Also even if a mailing piece is opened by the right employees, they must often pass it along for the approval of others in the chain of command. It is harder for these people to focus on a package containing a letter, brochure, and response device about something they may not be interested in. This is why self-mailers work well in business: They package the entire sales message and method of responding into one piece.

■ *KEY POINT: The self-mailing brochure makes group decision easier.*

SELF-MAILERS ARE NOT FOR ALL PROSPECTS

If self-mailers are so great, why don't we use them all the time? The reason is, they don't work as well as full mailing pieces for many consumer mailings and even for selling certain products and services to business. Self-mailers don't let you tell your entire story. They also have limited space for presenting benefits to prospects.

■ *CAUTION NOTE: The self-mailer doesn't have enough space to tell the full sales story.*

Self-mailers can incorporate some of the intimacy of a letter, but they are also similar to brochures in that the reader can move around and select what is interesting. The danger is in letting readers jump around, which can work against making the message clear.

■ *CAUTION NOTE: The self-mailer's selection capability can hurt a consistent sales message.*

Still, in many business mailings in which we can't identify prospects and in which decisions may require approval by several people, it's worth it to sacrifice the personal touch of the letter and to use self-mailers to get our message to the right people.

USING PSEUDOLETTERS WITHIN THE SELF-MAILER

We can retain some of the persuasive power of the letter by incorporating a pseudoletter in our self-mailer. Unlike the sales letter discussed in Chapter 7, letters for self-mailers are rarely more than two pages long. They can be used for the first page of the self-mailer to introduce the offer, or can be highlighted on the inside sales surface. The copy follows the same guidelines as those discussed in Chapter 7.

■ *KEY POINT: A letter in a self-mailer keeps the message one to one.*

Figure 12.1 is an example of how a sales letter can be used in a self-mailing brochure.

THE PRIMARY SELLING AREA OF THE SELF-MAILER IS THE EXPOSED INSIDE SURFACE

The major sales surface of the self-mailer is the same as that in the brochure, the inside when the piece is fully opened. We load this full surface with benefits to attract prospects, as we see in Figure 12.2.

■ *KEY POINT: The self-mailer's inside surface is used for selling.*

Dear Executive;

You'll find them all here, ready for you to use. All the creative sales promotion ideas others have used and are using successfully. Proven sales-boosting promotion ideas . . . proven cost-cutting promotion ideas . . . proven profit-producing promotion ideas!

Within your easy reach, the Dartnell SALES PROMOTION HANDBOOK, puts scores of up-to-date, battle-tested plans and ideas for:

— Spearheading your company's sales activities.
— Backing up your dealer's efforts.
— Setting up profitable store displays, industrial exhibits, consumer advertising contests, etc.

— Motivating your Sales Force.
— Introducing new products.
— Revitalizing old sales territories.
— Allocating budgets.
— Writing effective promotion copy.

—plus dozens of programs, hints and shortcuts for developing such business-building activities as: salespeople's manuals, customer service programs, store and home demonstrations, finding and effectively using good prospect mailing lists, measuring your sales promotion results . . . and much, much more.

In addition, you'll learn how some of America's most successful companies promote their goods and services. These are practical, tested sales promotion ideas that took "millions of dollars" to develop and prove. And they're all yours to use as you wish. Here are just a few you'll have instant access to:

— How SKF Industries merchandises its trade advertising.
— How Kodak's inquiry-producing system works.
— Why Motorola uses its "People-Finder" box to test new product introductions.
— Hanes (L'EGGS) new concept values and how to use them.
— How Johnson & Johnson developed its series of sales manuals.
— Why Chevrolet uses its "Mini-Theatre" for dealer training.
— How Johns-Manville organized its industry's sales promotional forces behind the retail dealer.

Best of all, the Dartnell SALES PROMOTION HANDBOOK saves you hours of precious time you would otherwise spend developing sales promotion programs. Precious time you can devote to your other important promotion duties. (If you save only four hours, the handbook has more than paid for itself!) Plus . . . the peace of mind that comes in knowing you are using ideas that have successfully worked for others.

RETURN THE ATTACHED TRIAL CARD
FOR YOUR 15-DAY FREE "LOOK-SEE" COPY

Without cost or obligation, see how the Dartnell SALES PROMOTION HANDBOOK will help you boost sales and profits. Just complete and mail the attached card. Then, within 15 days of its receipt, decide for yourself whether this hefty handbook isn't worth its weight in gold!

If you agree that it is, OK our memo invoice for $53.50. Otherwise, return the book and forget the whole thing. No questions asked.

Return the attached free-examination card today, and use the Dartnell SALES PROMOTION HANDBOOK Free . . . for 15 full days.

Sincerely,

James M. Vesely
James M. Vesely
THE DARTNELL CORPORATION

P.S. To get a better idea of just how BIG a value the Dartnell SALES PROMOTION HANDBOOK is, check the table of contents on the next page.

Figure 12.1 This letter is on the second page of a six-page 2-fold self-mailing brochure. Notice how it includes all the major benefits, summarizes the offer, and shows how to order. It adds one-to-one intimate appeal to an otherwise static brochure. (Courtesy Dartnell Corporation)

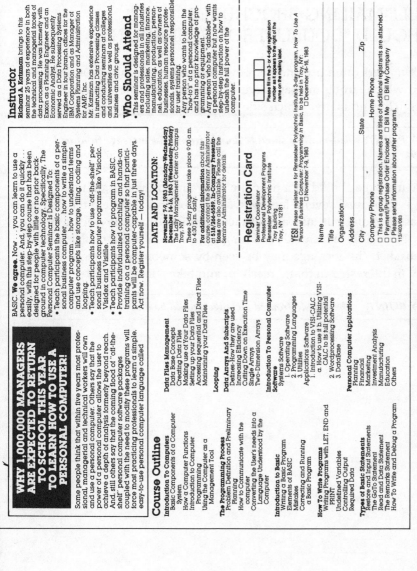

Figure 12.2 The inside of this 5½-inch by 8½-inch brochure has a headline and major benefits running across the top two thirds of the two-page surface. Again the order form is at the bottom right. (Courtesy Rensselaer Polytechnic Institute)

Other surfaces of the self-mailer are used for secondary selling messages (Figure 12.3).

SELF-MAILING BROCHURES SHOULD "DOUBLE FRONT" HEADLINES

Self-mailers often use another powerful technique called *double fronting*, in which strong messages are printed on both the front and back covers. Thus no matter which side is up, the sales message is exposed.

■ *KEY POINT: Self-mailers should "double front" the message front and back.*

The message should be a headline with a major benefit, in type large enough to be read several feet away. This not only will help the mailer get passed along but may also attract attention from unexpected prospects. No matter which side is facing up, or even if the mailer is in a wastebasket, the message may be seen by someone who might think, "Oh, I'm interested in that," reach in, and take a look.

■ *KEY POINT: The double-fronted message should be a bold headline.*

ATTENTION SALES

Now, more than ever before the difference between a good profit and none at all will be the ability of you and your sales people to negotiate and close sales.

You do negotiate . . . whether it is persuading the customer to pay your proposed or list price . . . getting the buyer to increase volume or hold more of your inventory . . . or negotiating changes in specification, price or delivery.

The amount of satisfaction that your customer gets is not the result of the price he pays. Satisfaction to your customer can be the result of good equitable negotiation even if your selling price is high; conversely, continual dissatisfaction can be the result of a poor negotiation even though the Buyer received the best possible price.

This seminar will show you how to leave your customer with more satisfaction regardless of price. We stress how to close sales, avoid deadlocks and at the same time leave the negotiation with a better, **more profitable** long lasting agreement and relationship. We cover strategy and defenses to help sales people resist buyer pressure and win their objectives. We'll show you how the buyer thinks, what tactics he employs and what to do to defend your position.

Even if you have had considerable negotiating experience, you are in for a unique learning and renewal experience. I have designed each part of the program to integrate the hard-hitting preparation and planning sessions, the video and live discussion with their arsenal of tips and techniques. I have also selected an especially dynamic and experienced leader to conduct the seminar. Check us out—you will see why we have won the respect, the following and the references of the highest executives in 150 of America's largest corporations.

Sincerely,

Dr. Chester L. Karrass

P.S. CHECK PAGE 5 for your company's name. A prearranged discount is available to our licensees who are using Effective Negotiating in-house and have each trained from 500 to 3,000 of their sales, purchasing and technical people. Each has been astounded by the high ratings and have documented staggering cost savings.

HOW TO REGISTER FOR THE TWO DAY EFFECTIVE NEGOTIATING* SEMINAR WORKSHOP

Attendance will be limited to personalize individual coverage.

Call now, (213) 453-1806

or mail the enrollment form below at once. SEMINAR TIME: First Day 8:30 registration; Seminar, 8:45 am to 5:30 pm. Second Day, 8:15 am to 4:30 pm.

(These fine reference materials included for each attendee).

FEE INCLUDES:
• Tuition • 11 hour Audio Cassette Series • Give & Take (hard bound book) • The Negotiating Game (hard bound book) • Workbook • Luncheon • Certificate of Completion

FEE: $525 individual fee
$456 for individuals from licensed companies (see details p. 5)
$450 per person for two or more
Fee includes $25.00 registration charge (nonrefundable)

Cancellation of a reservation does not affect registrant's financial liability unless we receive notice seven days before the meeting. SUBSTITUTIONS ANY TIME. Please make your own hotel reservations. A limited number of rooms have been set aside. Please mention that you are with the EFFECTIVE NEGOTIATING* group for special attention.

Mail entire coupon to: INSTITUTE FOR NEGOTIATION RESEARCH, INC. 1625 Stanford Street, Santa Monica, CA 90404 (213) 453-1806

INSTITUTE FOR NEGOTIATION RESEARCH, INC.

The Institute for Negotiation Research, Inc., a non-profit corporation, has been organized to foster research in the field of negotiation, to publish information regularly, to sponsor and conduct conferences and seminars and to provide educational assistance for those who wish to study and conduct experimental research in negotiation relating to industry and government. Write to us if you wish to do research in negotiation—limited funds available.

Figure 12.3 The back panel of this six-page three-fold format is used to add secondary benefits and the method of ordering. (Courtesy Institute for Negotiation Research)

See how double fronting is used in the example in Figure 12.4.

Also each side of the double-fronted cover should tell prospects what to do and how to respond—keeping together the "get's" and the "do's."

■ *CAUTION NOTE:* *Avoid separating "do's" and "get's" on the front and back covers.*

SELF-MAILING BROCHURES CAN HAVE LOTS OF SPLASH, TOO

Self-mailers, like their cousin the letter brochure, can offer lots of color and reasons to buy. Photographs, graphics, and shading can be used extensively to emphasize major benefits.

■ *KEY POINT:* *Lots of colored photographs can make a self-mailer more effective.*

WRITING COPY FOR THE SELF-MAILER

The best messages for self-mailers are brief, succinct ones that tell a basic sales story in less than 200 words, in headlines and major sub-heads that describe the major benefits and summarize the offer. However, the overall copy length for self-mailers can often be quite lengthy.

■ *CAUTION NOTE:* *Keep the sales message of the self-mailer brief.*

Readers will not spend as much time on self-mailers as they will on letter mailings with their multiple parts. As we saw earlier, one basic principle of direct mail is that prospects who are inclined to act favorably on our offer usually need many reasons to confirm their decision. It may not be possible to give readers enough reasons to act in short copy, even if they are inclined to do so. That's the major disadvantage of self-mailers: They don't have space to offer enough reasons for prospects to act.

WANT HANDS-ON TRAINING ON A PERSONAL COMPUTER?

HOW TO USE A PERSONAL BUSINESS COMPUTER: PROGRAMMING IN BASIC

ATTEND OUR 3-DAY SEMINAR

At Last, An Effective "How-To-Do-It" Course Guaranteed To Make You Computer-Capable In Just Three Days!

Now . . . you can successfully learn how to use a personal computer — program in BASIC and achieve a depth of analysis formerly beyond reach. And, you can do it quickly . . . easily with this simple, easy-to-understand course in personal business computers called PROGRAMMING IN BASIC. In this course you learn to program in BASIC — the easy-to-use personal computer language. Step-by-step, you'll learn how to design, write, and test personal computer programs . . . receive an introduction to today's most popular software packages including VISICALC . . . how to modify existing personal software packages to fulfill your specific needs . . . and much, much more. Act now. Register yourself — today!

NOVEMBER 7-9, 1983
DECEMBER 14-16, 1983
TROY, NY

PLEASE NOTE: NO PRIOR KNOWLEDGE OF PROGRAMMING OR EQUIPMENT NECESSARY

Professional Development Programs
Rensselaer Polytechnic Institute

HOW TO USE A PERSONAL BUSINESS COMPUTER: PROGRAMMING IN BASIC

Registration Details

Enrollments are accepted on a first-come, first-served basis.

Phone 518/266-6589 for immediate confirmation of your registration.

Give the 3- or 4-digit registration number as it appears to the right on the mailing label.

SAMPLE **372A**
JOHN SMITH

. . . Or- mail the enclosed registration card. Allow approximately two weeks for your return confirmation. Information regarding the course schedule, starting times and the like will be included.

Course Fee: $545 per person, per course, payable to: Rensselaer Polytechnic Institute

Teams of three individuals from the same organization receive a 10% discount. Additional discounts are available to larger groups; phone the seminar administrator at the above number for details. Note: Fee includes the cost of luncheons and all meeting materials.

Tax Deduction for all expenses of continuing management education (including registration fees, travel, meals and lodging) undertaken to maintain and improve professional skills (Treas. Reg. 1-162-5 Coughlin vs. Commissioner, 203F2d307).

Cancellations made less than three working days prior to the program's start date are subject to a $50 cancellation fee. Refunds will not be granted after class has begun. If, for any reason, the program is cancelled, enrollees will be notified and fees refunded in full. Substitutions may be made at any time, please advise in advance.

Continuing Education Units (CEUs) are awarded to participants in this program. The CEU gives formal recognition to persons continuing their education and keeping up to date in their chosen field or profession.

Hotel Accommodations are, of course, not included in the registration fee. However, if you desire overnight accommodations, please call 518/266-6589 for information.

Note: We use multiple mailing lists to announce our programs, and it is not always possible to cross-check these lists. As a result, you may receive a duplicate of this announcement. Please pass it on to an interested associate.

Qualified students are admitted to RPI and its programs without regard to sex, religion, race, color, marital status, national or ethnic origin, age or handicap.

Non-Profit Org.
U.S. Postage
PAID
Troy, NY
Permit No. 385

Professional Development Programs
Rensselaer Polytechnic Institute
Troy Building
Troy, NY 12181

LD503
MR JIM LUMLEY   220
57 S VALLEY RD PELHAM
AMHERST   MA 01002

LD 503

IMPORTANT DATED MATERIAL.
Please do not delay.

Figure 12.4 Whichever way this brochures falls in the wastebasket, you'll see the title. (Courtesy Rensselaer Polytechnic Institute)

255

■ *CAUTION NOTE:*   *Self-mailers are not usually long enough to carry a sufficient sales message.*

■ *KEY POINT:*   *Give prospects many benefits to stimulate them to act.*

If you need more than 200 words to get your basic message across, you might consider switching to a full letter mailing. But if you stay with the self-mailer, be sure to load it with benefits—the reasons or what's-in-it-for-me's that make people act, seen in many of the examples in this chapter.

■ *CAUTION NOTE:*   *Avoid using a self-mailer if the sales message must be long.*

THE RESPONSE DEVICE IS A KEY PART OF THE SELF-MAILER DESIGN

The self-mailer's response device is a key element in getting decisions from prospects. As we saw in the letter brochure, directions on how to respond, as well as major benefits, must be prominently displayed on the sales surface.

■ *KEY POINT:*   *The response form should be on the sales surface in the self-mailer.*

Instead of incorporating the response form in the sales surface, you can make it a separate, loose insert so that prospects don't have to tear it out.

Separate cards can double responses to free offers, because they make it easy for prospects to act. When prospects open the self-mailer, the insert may fall out, attracting their attention. If they pick it up and see that it offers something of interest, and carries little risk, they are more likely to return it than if they must tear out a reply card.

■ *KEY POINT:*   *A "loose" response form may involve the prospect enough to encourage an order.*

To hold a loose response device, self-mailers must have a third fold that wraps around the insert. Don't use glue or staple it. You don't want to break up the inside sales surface. Also the card won't fall out when prospects open it. And that's what you want it to do.

■ *CAUTION NOTE: Don't attach the reply form to the sales surface of the self-mailer.*

SHOW A SAMPLE OF THE SELF-MAILER TO THE POSTMASTER FOR APPROVAL

Always show a sample of your self-mailer to your postmaster. You want his or her approval that it meets size and other postal regulations, especially if you plan to use a loose insert as a response device.

■ *CAUTION NOTE: Get the postmaster's approval before printing a self-mailer.*

Many postmasters may tell you you can't use a loose insert because it can cause processing problems. Even though mailing regulations are standard for the Postal Service, you have to rely on local postmasters to interpret them. One way to alleviate their fear of a particular piece is to show them some self-mailers that use the same technique. Generally, this is not a problem within most postal areas.

POSTCARD DECKS OFFER MANY PRODUCTS TO MANY PROSPECTS

Postcard decks are a package of postcard size (3½ inches by 5 inches) cards sent to prospects likely to be interested in the products offered. Fifty to a hundred or more cards may be sent in a plastic envelope. Because they are inexpensive to produce, they get your sales message to thousands of people at a low cost per prospect.

■ *KEY POINT: Card decks offer products to many at a low cost.*

If all the products offered are produced by the same company, the card deck may include a short sales letter outlining the benefits of the products (Figure 12.5). Also an order form may be used instead of or in addition to a letter, so that prospects can order a number of products. (Figure 12.6).

■ *KEY POINT: A short letter or sales message should introduce the prospect to the types of products offered.*

CARD DECKS HAVE EASY-TO-UNDERSTAND MESSAGES

The cards themselves have simple messages because there is little space for anything else. They must rely on strong leads like, *"DIRECT RESPONSE REVOLUTION: Because you're in the middle of one, it's smart to have a revolutionary new weapon!,"* or *"Make a big impression with our new $80 typesetting system."*

■ *KEY POINT: Cards in a card deck must rely on a simple but strong message.*

Many cards mention several secondary benefits, capsulized in sub-heads, but the copy is kept to a minimum and graphics or a photograph of the product is used instead (Figure 12.7).

■ *CAUTION NOTE: Although copy is kept to a minimum in a card deck, pictures help gain response.*

The sales message can be printed on both sides of the card or just on one, which leaves the other side free for the return address.

CARD DECKS WORK WELL IN BUSINESS-TO-BUSINESS MAIL

Card decks are often sent to businesses or professionals assumed to be interested in the family of products being advertised. This is the key to success with card decks: Get into one that goes to target prospects

WILEY PROFESSIONAL
BOOKS-BY-MAIL

John Wiley & Sons, Inc. • Somerset, N.J. 08873

Dear Professional:

Here's Wiley's new deck of "Free-Examination Postcards," which allows you to review the new and important books in your field.

In the deck, you'll find cards on over 40 new and classic reference books that will help you save time, work and money.

What's more, you can examine and use any book for 15 days--FREE--without obligation. Here's how:

For the books you want to examine, simply complete the appropriate

(over, please)

postcards and drop them in the mail. We'll ship the books to you promptly.

Examine them . . . actually use them in your work . . for 15 days. Then, either remit the price shown or return them without further obligation.

For an additional saving -- send check or money order now (plus your local sales tax) and Wiley pays postage and handling charges. Same return privileges, full refund guaranteed.

Look through the cards now and make your selections. There's no obligation to buy anything.

Sincerely,

E. A. Connor

E. A. Connor
Wiley Professional
Books-By-Mail

P.S. If your order totals $100 or more, please attach a purchase order to the appropriate postcards or enclose 25% partial payment.

Figure 12.5 A card deck letter helps give the reader a reference point as to what contents are about. (Courtesy John Wiley & Sons)

259

Examine any of these practical books for 15 days—FREE!

When ordering more than one book, we suggest you use this postpaid multi-book order form. It offers you the convenience of receiving one consolidated shipment and a single invoice. You need pay only for the books you keep. All others are returnable in 15 days without further obligation.

If your order totals more than $100, please include payment—plus your local sales tax —or authorized purchase order. Enclose with this form and send to **Van Nostrand**

Reinhold, Mail Order Service, 7625 Empire Drive, Florence, Kentucky 41042. On prepaid orders we pay postage and handling. Money refunded if not fully satisfied.

☐ VISA ☐ MasterCard Please charge my credit card (publisher pays postage and handling). If you return the book(s) at the end of 15 days, charges will be canceled.

Card No._____Exp.__/__

Signature_____

No. Copies	Title	List Price
	Adjusting to an Aging Workforce (21493-6)	$22.50
	Basic for Microcomputers (27843-8)	$21.95
	Bonds as Investments in the Eighties (27532-3)	$24.95
	Business Idea (22163-0)	$14.95
	Business Negotiating Power (23613-1)	$24.95
	Business Planning for the Entrepreneur (28970-7)	$21.95
	Business Planning and Budgeting: An Apple Business Users Guide (930-76462-5)	$14.95 paper
	Business Planning and Budgeting: An Apple Business Users Guide (Disk Edition) (930-76471-4)	$29.95
	Business Planning and Budgeting: An IBM PC Business Users Guide (930-76461-7)	$14.95 paper
	Business Planning and Budgeting: An IBM PC Business Users Guide (Disk Edition) (930-76470-6)	$29.95
	Controlling Financial Performance: An Apple Business Users Guide (930-76458-7)	$14.95 paper
	Controlling Financial Performance: An Apple Business Users Guide (Disk Edition) (930-76469-2)	$29.95
	Controlling Financial Performance: An IBM PC Business Users Guide (930-76457-9)	$14.95 paper
	Controlling Financial Performance: An IBM PC Business Users Guide (Disk Edition) (930-76468-4)	$29.95
	Costing Human Resources (21501-0)	$19.95
	Data Processing Contracts (21034-5)	$44.50
	Directory of Software Publishers (21429-4)	$24.95
	Electronic Mail (21691-2)	$14.95 paper
	Executive Guide to Fitness (29670-3)	$16.95
	Finding, Selecting, Developing, and Retaining Data Processing Professionals through Effective Human Resource Management (26012-1)	$24.95
	Guide to Foreign Investments in United States Real Estate (27215-4)	$34.50
	Handbook of Applied Mathematics, Second Edition (23866-5)	$67.50
	Handbook of Business Planning and Budgeting for Executives with Profit Responsibility (22188-6)	$42.50
	Heyel Management Library (23617-4)	$24.95
	How to Borrow Money (25204-8)	$13.95
	How to Profitably Sell or Buy a Company or Business (23336-1)	$22.50

No. Copies	Title	List Price
	How to Win Government Contracts (23265-9)	$24.95
	IBM Displaywriter Simplified (28044-0)	$32.50
	Industrial Publicity (27781-4)	$19.95
	Letter Perfect (88021-9)	$18.95
	Major Equipment Procurement (20870-7)	$42.50
	Marketing Accounting Services (22003-0)	$24.95
	Matrix Management Systems Handbook (21448-0)	$52.50
	Maximizing Profits in Small and Medium Sized Businesses (21268-2)	$24.95
	100 Greatest Corporate And Industrial Ads (27246-4)	$19.95
	Performance Measures for the Growing Business (22605-5)	$19.95
	Practical Accounting for Small Businesses (28420-9)	$21.95
	Practice of Planning Strategic Administration (21917-2)	$19.95
	Project Management for Executives (25920-4)	$28.50
	Project Management for Small and Medium Sized Businesses (24660-9)	$24.50
	Project Management with CPM and PERT and Precedence Diagramming, Third Edition (25415-6)	$27.50
	Project Selection and Economic Appraisal (21607-6)	$29.95
	Realworld Management Deskbook (28809-3)	$24.95
	Reportpack Simplified (28111-0)	$37.50
	Selecting and Developing Media for Instruction (20976-2)	$21.95
	Statistical Methods for Managers and Administrators (23124-5)	$24.95
	Strategic Analysis for Venture Evaluation (24507-6)	$19.95
	Techniques of Structured Problem Solving (21223-2)	$18.95
	Using the Apple Business Computer (26016-4)	$19.95
	Using the IBM Personal Computer (25815-1)	$19.95
	Using the Osborne Personal Computer (26010-5)	$19.95
	VNR Dictionary of Business and Finance (20949-5)	$18.95
	Word Processing Handbook (22526-1)	$34.50

Please fold and staple or tape.

B C D 9251

Figure 12.6 Here's an order form in case you want to order several books. (Courtesy Van Nostrand Reinhold)

Increase Your Income by 50% or More Using Your Present Skills

SUCCESSFUL CONSULTING FOR ENGINEERS AND DATA PROCESSING PROFESSIONALS

By Steven P. Tomczak

Here is the first no-nonsense, step-by-step guide to consulting for technical professionals. This book introduces every aspect of independent consulting —from starting your own business to identifying prospects and getting new clients.

You'll find vital information on how to find prospects and turn them into clients. There's also important practical advice on such matters as how to determine and structure your fees, tax planning, and more. 352 pp. (1982)

1-86135-9   **$43.95**

■■■■■ FOR *FREE* TRIAL COPY, MAIL THIS CARD TODAY!■■■■■

John Wiley & Sons, Inc., One Wiley Dr., Somerset, N.J. 08873   **Please print**

Please send me this book to use FREE for 15 days. I'll either keep it and send $43.95, plus my local sales tax and a small charge for postage and handling; otherwise, I'll return it within the trial period and owe nothing. (Offer valid in U.S. only.)

Sign:_____
          (Order invalid unless signed.)

Name_____

Firm_____

Street_____

City_____

State/Zip_____

Offer expires 6/30/84   **063   4-0616**

Figure 12.7   Copy and photo kept to a minimum. (Courtesy John Wiley & Sons)

who will not be overwhelmed with products too much like the one you're selling. For example, if you're selling a spike and noise suppressor for computers, you want to be sure the card deck will go to people who own computers, and that none of the other cards offer spike suppressors—at least, none that shows yours to disadvantage.

■ *KEY POINT: The product must be targeted to the audience of the card deck.*

■ *CAUTION NOTE: Avoid card decks with competing products.*

Card decks work well in business-to-business mail because, like self-mailing brochures, they have a high pass-along value.

■ *KEY POINT: Card decks have the high pass-along value required for business-to-business mail.*

They also get good readership because they are often used to bring new and different products to the marketplace and to the attention of prospects who might not otherwise learn about these products.

■ *KEY POINT: Card decks are often used to promote unusual products.*

Card decks are also popular because they make it easy for prospects to scan offers for many products in a few minutes.

■ *KEY POINT: Many cards can be scanned quickly to identify products of interest.*

CARD DECKS SELL UNCOMPLICATED PRODUCTS AND SALES LEADS BEST

Card decks are best for selling familiar products, like books (Figure 12.8) or subscriptions, or products that are low in cost and thought of as accessories, such as office supplies.

■ *KEY POINT: Card decks can sell familiar, low-cost products.*

Impulse items such as miniature book lights, rulers with built-in clocks, or brass-encased humidity indicators may sell to executives and others who may use them as gifts.

■ *KEY POINT: Impulse items sell well in card decks.*

Card decks also work well for offers of free information or catalogs that will lead to a product sale later. Higher cost products, such as office furniture, are best offered by such two-step sales campaigns.

■ *KEY POINT: Use offer of free information or catalog to gain sales leads for a higher cost product.*

STRATEGIES FOR CARD DECKS

It is wise to offer the same product in several different decks. For example, if you are offering a book on saving business taxes, you might

Gain Valuable Leads Through Direct Mail Advertising

HOW TO SELL MORE REAL ESTATE BY USING DIRECT MAIL, 2nd Ed.

By James E. Lumley

You'll find its detailed, 12-point marketing plan one of the most practical guides currently in print. At each stage of your direct mail program, the plan outlines responsibilities, schedules personnel, measures results, and offers procedures, checklists and guidelines.

This edition features a considerable amount of new material. Most important, its content has been tested thoroughly, expanded and confirmed by the experience of countless real estate professionals who have used the first edition. You'll learn how to • set objectives and create a strategy to meet them • establish realistic budgets • write dynamic copy for various DM campaigns • build mailing lists of "hot" prospects • follow up on promising leads • evaluate the results of your mailing.

229 pp. (1982)   1-86163-4   **$37.95**

■■■■■ FOR *FREE* TRIAL COPY, MAIL THIS CARD TODAY! ■■■■■

John Wiley & Sons, Inc.
One Wiley Drive, Somerset, NJ 08873

Please Print

Please send me this book to use FREE for 15 days. I'll either keep it and send $37.95, plus my local sales tax and postage and handling; or, I'll return it within 15 days without further obligation. (Offer valid in U.S. only.)

NAME

FIRM

STREET

"PLACE ADDRESS LABEL HERE"

CITY

X
_____
SIGN HERE: Order invalid unless signed.

STATE   ZIP

Offer Expires 10/31/85   063   5-0683

Figure 12.8 Books are typical of the easy-to-understand offer that works best in a card deck. (Courtesy John Wiley & Sons)

try the same sales message in three or four decks that each go to different segments of the business market. Then you can repeat the best results in other similar markets.

■ *KEY POINT:* **Test the product in several decks.**

If you can, always buy the top position in the deck. People start scanning a deck from the top, just like a deck of playing cards. If they get distracted or bored by what they are seeing, they may never reach your card. And if they do come back to the deck, they will tend to start at the top again, unfortunately for those further down. So try to get as close to the top as possible, even if it costs more.

■ *KEY POINT:* **Always try to buy the top position or near the top of the card deck.**

In short, card decks work well in business-to-business mail where a strong pass-along value is important. Because they are powerful for generating inquiries, you can gain leads or buyers you might not from other types of direct mail. They are a good addition to letter mailings or self-mailing brochures because they let you round out your selling strategy.

ADVANTAGES AND DISADVANTAGES OF CARD DECKS

Advantages

High market penetration
Low production cost
Lost cost per thousand
High number of inquiries
Low cost per lead
Low cost per sale
High return on investment

Disadvantages

Inefficient scatter-shot approach
Many similar products
Little space to build sales story
Work best with low-cost items
Erratic success record

COPY STRATEGY FOR 13
CATALOGS

In the first few chapters we learned that relationship marketers—those who look to a long-term relationship with customers—are the professionals in direct mail. The catalog is their major tool because it lets them offer more than one product to a group of customers with varying needs.

■ *KEY POINT:* *A catalog establishes a long-term relationship.*

THE BASIC PRINCIPLES OF DIRECT MAIL COPY AND STRATEGY ARE TRUE FOR THE CATALOG

Many of the basic principles of direct mail also hold true for the catalog. Whether prospects are reading a brochure or a catalog, they scan headlines and picture captions first. They need to see how benefits affect them in a personal way. They respond only if they perceive that the product will give them more than what they have to give up to get it. They need sweeteners to enhance the sale, and facilitators that make it easy for them to order. All of these devices need to be at work in the catalog, just as they are in letter mailings and self-mailers.

This chapter and the next, on catalog design, will show how best to use these devices in catalogs and the special attributes a superior catalog should have. Because catalogs are primarily visual pieces, much of the work of creating them has to do with design and layout. However, the photographs that show each product are meant to get copy read—the copy that describes the products and asks for the response.

■ *KEY POINT:* *Design supports copy.*

None of the copywriting techniques described earlier should be forgotten when we write catalog copy, but additional principles apply to catalogs.

EACH PRODUCT HAS A COMPLETE DESCRIPTION TO SHOW HOW IT BENEFITS CUSTOMERS

For one thing, each product must have a complete description. Copy must describe not only what the product is, but how it works and how it can benefit the user.

■ *KEY POINT:*   *Catalog copy should show how the product benefits the user.*

The first principle in writing descriptions for catalogs is to tell how customers will use the product. Describe how specific features are of personal benefit. If the product is a cold-weather jacket, tell about the unique down-insulated inner lining that allows the jacket to be worn in subzero temperatures. If it's a kayak, describe how the specially rounded bottom increases stability and ensures safety. *"Our 100% suede-finished Egyptian safari jacket has the world's finest long cotton fiber, woven 340 threads per square inch, a density that keeps you dry and cool at the same time."*

■ *KEY POINT:*   *Catalog description should tell the customer how to use the product.*

Descriptions should also show *who* will use the product. Make sure you do this without limiting the product's range of customers. For example, *"These sport sunglasses offer top-flight protection for boaters, climbers, and drivers,"* or *"The no-nonsense case-hardened blade of this indestructible knife can help hikers, campers, or anyone around the house"* shows broad categories of people who could benefit from using the product. Figure 13.1 shows an example.

■ *KEY POINT:*   *Copy should identify the typical user.*

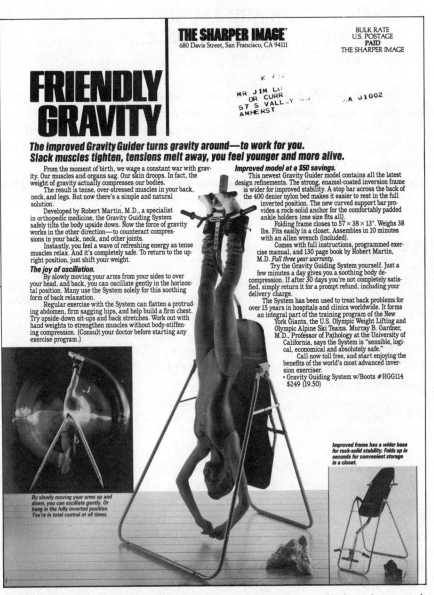

Figure 13.1 See how this prime back page gets right into the broad range of people who could benefit from this product, and how it works. Lots of copy works well in catalog sales. (Courtesy The Sharper Image)

DESCRIPTIONS ARE BACKED BY COMPARISONS, TESTIMONIALS, AND PROOF

Products should also be compared with their competition. You do this by pointing out what features make them superior to other similar products. For example, *"Many sharpeners can put an edge on soft iron, but the Brass Pocket Hone with its pure tungsten-carbide surface microgrooved with diamonds instantly shaves away a dull edge on hardened steel quickly and easily,"* or *"No other battery can match our space-age cell, which gives you bright, even light for up to 18 hours of continuous burn!"* Each positions its product favorably against the competition.

■ *KEY POINT: Compare the product with its competition.*

Descriptions of products should also use testimonials to add credibility. An expert's word, or the credentials of the designer, gives customers a unique perspective on a product and distinguishes it from others. Camping knives are great for this: "This streamlined masterpiece of lightweight design was created by revered knifemaster Blackie Collins," or "The Boker 2000 is testimony to Boker's 146 years of experience producing superb knives."

■ *KEY POINT: Catalog copy should use testimonials to add credibility.*

Descriptions can also include proofs of how well the product performs. For example, *"Our armored binoculars floated over Class IV rapids on the Wachatash River for three miles before we found them unharmed,"* or *"You can mash your rabbit fur hat in a suitcase, you can sit on it, you can wear it in the rain . . . the only thing that will destroy an Akubra fur felt hat is if your dog eats it"* shows the product's durability with facts and humor.

■ *KEY POINT: Copy should show the customer how the product performs.*

Descriptions should, if possible, be accompanied by line drawings or photographs of the product in either black and white or color (Figure 13.2). Photographs normally show the product being used, preferably by a person similar to the customer. More hints on photographs are contained in the next chapter on design.

BUDDHIST COUNTRIES--FISTICUFFS CAN RESULT...

Authentic
FIELD *jacket*

A truly spectacular jacket, exceptionally light-weight for all the warmth it provides. Ours is the original, designed by Uncle Sam to prove the New World has a few good ideas of its own. We changed the color of the sturdy cotton/nylon mountain cloth to practical khaki tan and navy. All else is regulation: four roomy snapshut pockets, two with pint-size bellows extensions; genuine brass heavy-duty zipper; heavy cotton lining plus drawcords at waist and bottom; hideaway hood with rain-shedding neck extension outside the coat; bi-swing expanding back; expansion tucks in outer sleeve seams; sleeve extensions to fold down over gloves when it's really cold. Don't settle for a knock-off, copied by so-called "designers." Have the original U.S. Government issue field jacket, which has more bells and whistles than a military band banging out Sousa. For men and women.

COLOR: **Khaki tan, Navy**
SIZE: **XS S M L XL (runs 1 size large)**
#**3083 Field Jacket $69.**

Figure 13.2 Description compares the "authentic" field jacket with copies. (Courtesy Banana Republic)

EDITORIAL COPY INCREASES
READERSHIP AND INVOLVES THE READER

Readership of copy increases if you add editorial copy—set forth opinions—either adjacent to descriptions or as part of the descriptions themselves.

Editorial copy can make your product appear more relevant to your customers' lives and can add a more interesting dimension to otherwise lackluster products. As with the intimacy of a letter, it even helps build an emotional connection between the product and the reader.

■ *KEY POINT:* *Editorial copy builds a link between the reader and the product.*

Editorial content can also be used to enhance your overall offer, for example, to make your guarantee stronger in the mind of your prospect.

Editorial content in a catalog increases readership because customers read more if the subject interests them. Editorial copy thus draws more attention to your product.

■ *KEY POINT:* *Editorial copy builds readership.*

Editorial content also increases the likelihood that prospects will keep a catalog or pass it on to colleagues or other family members. Your remarks can help customers understand how your products work and how they compare with competing products.

■ *KEY POINT:* *Editorial copy connects the product to people's lives.*

Editorials can reinforce the products' credibility and enhance a customer's good feeling for your company (Figure 13.3).

CONNECT EDITORIAL CONTENT TO PRODUCTS

It is important that editorial content be tied to your products. Your copy should give readers a visual picture of how the products will benefit them (Figure 13.4). In this way, it will help them reach a decision.

■ *KEY POINT:* *Editorial copy should give customers a visual picture of how the product will benefit them.*

Further, editorial copy should not be limited to one section of the catalog but should be spread out among many products. You can show how each product or group of products can fit into your prospects' lives.

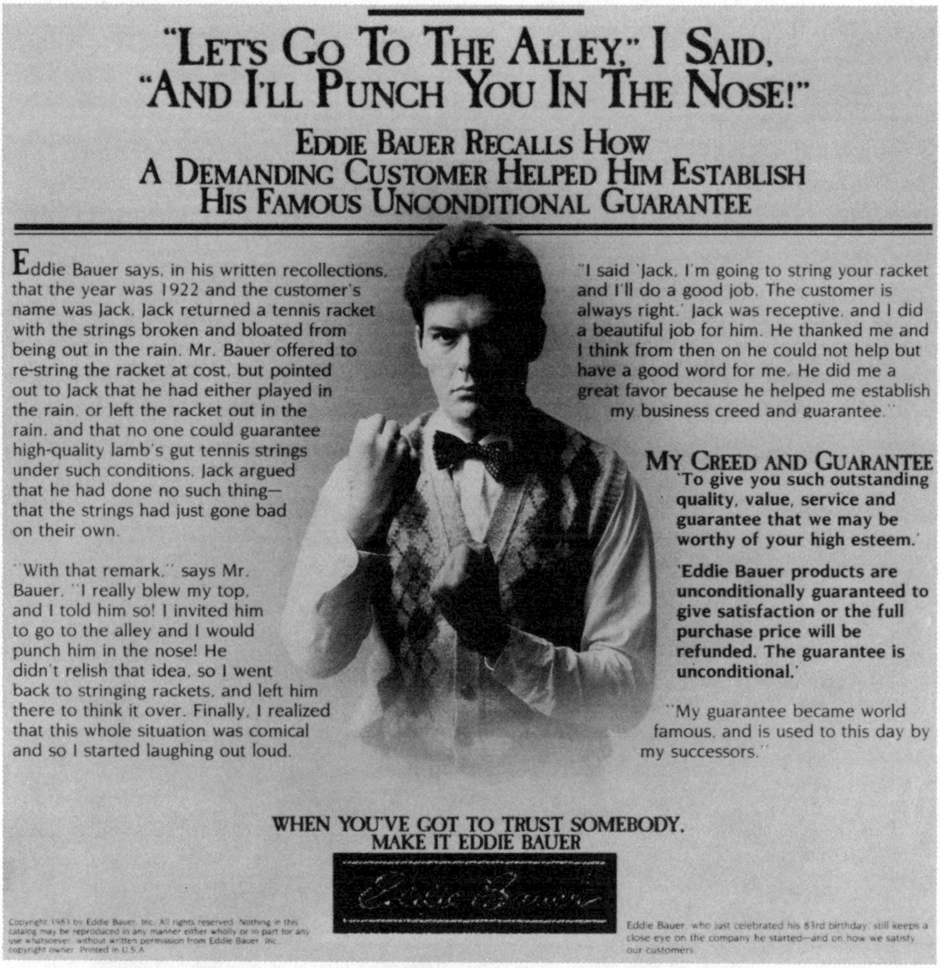

Figure 13.3 Here's how Eddie Bauer uses a story to drive home the guarantee. (Courtesy Eddie Bauer)

GREGORY SNOW CREEK

Every inch of this slim profile touring/expedition pack reflects the quality of design, engineering, and construction found in every Gregory pack. Big enough to hold gear for a week or more. Features include a top loading main compartment with a detachable top pocket over an 11" top extension. The compression sleeping bag compartment is reached through a separate outside zipper for easy access. The stays can easily be removed for use as emergency splints or as emergency self-arrest aids. 2 ice axe loops. 2 outside wand pockets for trail pickets or tent poles. Outside compression straps. **Color:** Silver/black. **Sizes:** Specify torso length—S, M, L, and hip belt size—S, M, L. (See "Fitting your Gregory Pack".)
55-0699 Snow Creek **$209.75**

1. 1" ladder harness adjustment
2. removable custom-fit aluminum stays
3. detachable top pocket
4. 11" top extension
5. conical waist belt
6. slim profile for touring/bushwhacking
7. supporting non slide friction mesh

FITTING YOUR GREGORY PACK

Each Gregory Pack is designed to be custom fitted to an individual wearer for maximum comfort. First, this involves ordering the correct size of pack and hip belt.

Have your partner measure your back from a line across the top of your hip bones, to the point where your neck and shoulders meet. This is your torso length. On the Gregory Snow Creek, the short fits torsos of 15" to 17½", medium 18" to 20½", long 20" and up. Hip belts sizing is: small waists less than 27", medium 27" to 37", large 37" and up.

The second step is the adjustment itself. Each Gregory Pack comes with a complete pack fitting manual, which gives step-by-step instructions. We think you will find this one-time custom fitting process rather enjoyable and it's a good way to get to know your pack.

If you still run into difficulties, we have a pack fitting specialist ready to guide you through the process by phone. Simply call 800-343-9700, between 8:30 am and 5:00 pm weekdays for assistance.

Wayne Gregory
While the world was still discovering external frame packs, Wayne Gregory was working to perfect the more efficient, more versatile, more comfortable internal frame pack. His revolutionary first step was to base his designs on actual human anatomy, not on some boxlike "average" torso. This lead to such innovations as the contoured shoulder straps, hour-glass shaped lumber pad, conically cut hip belt, and custom fitted aluminum alloy stays in a variety of sizes. Since 1977, Wayne Gregory has worked to design the ultimate internal frame packs. That's why his designs are the most sought-after packs in the world.

For more Gregory packs, see pages 46-54. And don't miss the convertible pack/luggage series on page 79.

Figure 13.4 See how some editorial copy on how a product is designed and who designs it helps build confidence in the product. (Courtesy Eastern Mountain Sports)

272

■ *CAUTION NOTE: Don't keep editorial copy in only one area of the catalog.*

■ *KEY POINT: Editorial copy should be spread out among all products.*

■ *KEY POINT: Make sure editorial copy helps customers make decisions.*

CATALOGS ARE OFTEN RETAINED BY CUSTOMERS POSTPONING THE BUYING DECISION

The purpose of a catalog, like any other form of direct mail, is to get a response. The biggest failing of many marketers who use editorial content in their catalog is that they let it get in the way of the decision.

If you do too good a job of making your catalog readable, you may also create a problem: Your prospects may postpone making a decision to buy. They may decide to decide in the future, but that means they may not decide to buy at all. The catalog, like the letter mailing, needs to force a decision now.

■ *CAUTION NOTE: Catalogs encourage customers to postpone ordering.*

Prospects often put catalogs next to the bed for nighttime reading, but they soon get buried under fresh arrivals. Or prospects are interested but decide to wait until payday. The catalog is kept, but the customer puts off deciding to buy.

The nicer the catalog, the glossier, the thicker, the longer it is kept and the longer the decision is put off. So what do we do?

First, because our catalogs are going to customers periodically, we can change some or all of each catalog's offerings. This gives prospects the perception that they must act quickly because the products will be available only in the current catalog.

■ *KEY POINT: Change product offerings in catalogs to get customers to act.*

Second, we can change our prices as of a certain date. We tell our customers the prices in the catalog are good only until that deadline (Figure 13.5).

PRIORITY INTERRUPT

FEEDBACK

This is your space to communicate to all our other customers. It is your opportunity to ask questions or submit solutions. We want the Interrupt to be a dialog among all of us.

Maybe you have seen the recent ad series "Who Uses CompuPro?" being run by CompuPro in numerous magazines. Think of this Feedback Section as being "Who Buys Products from Priority One?" — and the answer is *you*! If you have done something "newsworthy" with products you have purchased from Priority One, we would be more than happy to share your success among our readers (You don't have to reveal any trade secrets, though!).

This is also the place for questions and answers. Maybe you had a problem that you were able to solve, we'll print your solution if you share it with us. Or maybe you have a general problem that you would like answered by our Technical Support Group. This is the place to get that answer.

If you come across an interesting article in a magazine or newspaper, please submit it to us for re-printing. We will contact the publisher for permission to use it, and give you the credit for submitting it.

And what's in it for you — besides getting to see your name in print all over the country? We will send you a special Priority Interrupt gift if we publish what you send us. As with all other publications, anything submitted becomes the property of Priority One Electronics and cannot be returned. We also reserve final editorial rights.

Send Your Materials To:
PRIORITY ONE ELECTRONICS
9161 Deering Avenue • Chatsworth, CA 91311
Attn: Interrupt Editor

HAPPY ANNIVERSARY, IRVINE!

Is it possible that our Irvine System Center Showroom has been open for a year, already? It must be, because February 14 is the One Year Anniversary of our Opening — and you get the presents!

Just present this coupon in either of our retail showrooms and you will be entitled to 10% off our catalog prices!

ANNIVERSARY DISCOUNT COUPON
10% Off All "07" Winter '83/Spring '84 Catalog Prices With This Coupon When You Prepay Your Order (Cash, Check or Credit Card). Must be presented at the time of purchase in our retail locations. Sorry, no telephone sales or mail orders can be accepted, and this coupon is not valid with any other offer. Expires March 31, 1984.

9161 Deering • Chatsworth, CA
(818) 709-5464

18241 McDermott • Irvine, CA
(714) 660-1411

Attention San Francisco Area Customers: Our Booth #1244 (across from CompuPro's Booth) at the West Coast Computer Faire (March 22 - 25) will be a "retail location," so we will honor the above coupon, even if we have to write up a backorder for you!

ORDERING INFORMATION

It is real easy to place an order for product from the PRIORITY INTERRUPT. Simply call directly to one of our courteous and knowledgeable sales representatives and use your MasterCard or VISA as payment. Or mail in your order with an accompanying check or money order. Either way, please tell us you are ordering from the PRIORITY INTERRUPT to qualify for these prices. Because the sale items in the PRIORITY INTERRUPT are priced lower than our catalog prices, all orders must be prepaid.

Include MINIMUM shipping and handling of $3.00 for the first 3 lbs., plus 40¢ for each additional pound. Orders over 50 lbs. are sent motor freight collect. Credit card orders will be charged the appropriate freight. Just in case we have a problem, please include your telephone number.

Prices are valid from February 13 through March 31, 1984; and although we will do our best to maintain them, they are subject to change without notice. Many quantities are limited, so order promptly. Manufacturer's warranties will apply where applicable. We cannot be held responsible for typographical errors.

SALES DEPARTMENT
TOLL FREE ORDER DESK
ORDERS FROM OUTSIDE CA, HI, OR AK, DIAL:

(800) 423-5922

IF YOU'RE CALLING FROM CALIFORNIA, ALASKA, OR HAWAII, DIAL:

(818) 709-5111

Monday thru Friday
8:00 a.m. to 6:00 p.m.

Saturdays:
10:00 a.m. to 5:00 p.m.

Our Sales Representatives will help you place your order and help you choose the shipping method that best suits your needs.

Figure 13.5 Prices are valid for a specific time period in this aggressive newsletter-style catalog. (Courtesy Priority One Electronics)

■ *KEY POINT:* *Change prices at a certain date.*

Third, we can tell customers that our offer is limited because an item is a special purchase and is in limited supply.

■ *KEY POINT:* *Limit the time allowed to order.*

Anything we can do to get customers back into the catalog to order will pay off in increased response. And as these examples show, often people buy because of what they believe they will lose if they don't.

■ *KEY POINT:* *Get customers back into the catalog.*

■ *KEY POINT:* *Make customers feel they are going to lose by not ordering.*

CARRYING AN ITEM TWICE IN THE SAME CATALOG CAN INCREASE SALES

Another technique for increasing catalog sales is to offer the same items twice in the same issue. The product must be a good one, popular with customers. Duplicating items in the catalog lets you genuinely promote them—but it also adds bulk to your catalog. Bulk is helpful if you are just starting out and are not offering many products.

■ *KEY POINT:* *Offering an item twice in the same catalog adds bulk.*

But perhaps the most important reason to carry an item more than once is that it lets you test that product's placement in the catalog. As we will see in Chapter 16 on testing, you should know the dollar amount of revenue generated by every square inch of your catalog.

■ *KEY POINT:* *Carrying an item twice allows you to test its placement in the catalog.*

When we carry the same item twice, we don't use exactly the same picture or copy for it because we don't want readers to feel we are repetitious (the order number is also different). We do use the same price, however. This lets us test which section of the catalog pulls better for that product. Once we know that, we can position the product there in the future for maximum sales.

■ *CAUTION NOTE: In carrying an item twice in the same catalog, don't use the same picture or copy.*

DON'T THINK ABOUT THE PRODUCT, THINK ABOUT SELLING IT!

The key to catalog selling and all other forms of direct mail is to ask yourself what you want your customers to do and then figure out how to get them to do it. Don't think about your products or their features or the gorgeous catalog you're putting together. Don't think about *what* you want to sell. Think about *how* you can sell.

■ *CAUTION NOTE: In creating a catalog, don't think about what to sell or about making a fancy book.*

■ *KEY POINT: In creating a catalog, think about how to sell customers.*

CREATIVE DESIGN FOR CATALOGS 14

Although copy is essential for gaining responses from prospects, design is what carries the message to them. Design is perhaps more crucial for catalogs than for any other mailing piece. In this chapter we will learn how to design catalogs that promote customer response.

THE OBJECT OF THE CATALOG IS NOT A GORGEOUS BOOK, IT'S A RESPONSE

Many marketers make the mistake of thinking they must use a fancy, multipage brochure in full color, one more appropriate for selling African safaris than for, say, the garden tools they are offering. But the purpose of using a catalog is not to put out a gorgeous book. It's to sell a response.

■ *CAUTION NOTE:* **Slick designs by themselves don't get responses.**

It's to turn the prospects into customers, to get them to act. Fancy catalogs work for some products, but they can often work against the sale of a group of products or a product line.

■ *KEY POINT:* **The catalog must get customers to act.**

Only in special circumstances does slickness generate sales, perhaps if you're selling one of those super-duper trips to show where Hemingway camped at Kilimanjaro.

For the rest of us, a fancy catalog is the wrong objective.

■ *CAUTION NOTE:* **Fancy catalogs can work against sales.**

Now that we are clear about wanting to sell something to our customers rather than wanting to tell them what wonderful products we have, we are much farther along than many catalog marketers.

DESIGN OPEN PAGES AS ONE SALES SURFACE

One of the first questions we must decide when designing a catalog is, what is the sales surface? Since we've already discussed sales surfaces in brochures and self-mailers, it is probably clear that the selling surface of any catalog is the full surface of both pages, seen when the catalog is open at any page.

■ *KEY POINT: The catalog sales surface is both pages that show when the catalog is open.*

So we don't design or lay out our copy for one page, but for two, just as we did for the two kinds of brochures. We go for the entire area the eye can see. People treat catalogs like books. They don't bend the pages back as if they were reading a comic book. They open the catalog and scan the two pages as one sales surface.

■ *CAUTION NOTE: Don't design each page in a catalog separately.*

■ *KEY POINT: Design for the surface the eye scans.*

This means that each time readers turn a page, they see another full sales surface as one unit. Design the two pages as one.

■ *CAUTION NOTE: A measure of visual impact is lost when catalog pages are designed separately.*

■ *KEY POINT: People scan things broadly.*

You can tell a good catalog by whether both pages can be seen clearly from a distance as a single visual unit (Figure 14.1).

■ *KEY POINT: A well-designed catalog sales surface is seen as a single unit from a distance.*

USE CATALOG HEADLINES TO BRING ATTENTION TO PRODUCTS

You can use headlines to reinforce the perception of double pages as one sales surface by running them across both pages. This larger surface gives more space where products can be dramatized, helping to bring attention to them. Further, this larger space allows more opportunity for messages asking for the order and encouraging customers to follow through.

■ *KEY POINT:* **Put bold headline across both pages to offer the product.**

Such headlines need not be as long or comprehensive as the headlines in a brochure. They need only identify the type of product that appears on each pair of pages. However, follow the rules set for brochure headlines: Keep them near the top and end them where you want customers to start reading (Figure 14.2).

■ *KEY POINT:* **End the headline where you want the customer to start reading.**

GROUP SIMILAR PRODUCTS TOGETHER

Some marketers spread their products haphazardly throughout the catalog. For example, a camping catalog may offer one kind of tent at the beginning and another at the end. Make it easy on the reader and group similar items. Having to search for particular products irritates customers.

■ *CAUTION NOTE:* **Don't separate similar products in the catalog.**

Catalog marketers also make the mistake of grouping products so they can keep track of them. They ignore how their customers relate to these products. For example, knife sharpeners should not be offered separately from knives in a hunting catalog.

We should keep related products together and let customers know they are related. "All the kitchen tools you need," or "Everything you'll need for tent-camping," are headlines that tie related products together.

Figure 14.1 Two pages as one sales surface. Not all that difficult to do, and it's OK if the pages don't match just right. (Courtesy Early Winters, Ltd.)

Streamlined vest.

(B) Our Silver Lining® **Sleeveless** makes other outdoor vests look and feel chubby. It's your best bet for warmth, ease of movement, *and* a slim, trim profile.

Test it. See how its combination of Silver Lining® radiant barrier and Thinsulate® thermal insulation make this a vest both warmer and slimmer for its weight than ever before possible.

It's the attractive, *streamlined* version of the outdoorsman's classic—with no sacrifice in warmth. So trim you'll be tempted to wear it with your suit jacket.

Test yours and see.

Silver Lining w/ Thinsulate CS150/Taslan outer
Colors: Blue, Khaki
Sizes: See chart at left   Wt.(M): 12 oz.

Silver Lining® Sleeveless, No. 0881—$49.95

Warm, sleek jacket.

(C) When the snow blows and the wind sends shivers down your spine, don our **Jupiter** jacket.

Silver Lining® and Thinsulate® thermal insulation give you warmth that won't bulk you out or weigh you down.

The Jupiter closes with a full-length zipper backed by a draft tube and covered by a storm flap. Recessed nylon knit cuffs and elasticized waist foil cruel winds. Two outside pockets warm hands, inside stash pocket fastens shut.

You needn't look like the Michelin® tire man in order to be warm: Try the Jupiter.

Silver Lining w/ Thinsulate CS 150/Taslan outer
Colors: Blue, Khaki
Sizes: See chart at left   Wt.(M): 24 oz.

Silver Lining® Jupiter, No. 0882 . . . $79.95

High-tech protection.

(D) Forget the cold, the wet, the wind. Our **Ultimo** is your armor against the worst of the elements.

Gore-Tex® Taslan shrugs the nastiest wind and rain. Next is a warming layer of Thinsulate® Then a radiant barrier of Silver Lining, which enhances warmth without adding bulk. Finally, a silky Antron® lining lets the Ultimo glide smoothly on over clothing.

With four outer pockets; two hand-warmer pockets; attached, double-drawcord hood; factory-sealed seams; snap-close storm skirt; adjustable wrists; and underarm zip vents—whew! This is the *ne plus ultra* of outdoor garments.

Colors: Blue, Camouflage
Sizes: See chart at left   Wt.(M): 35 oz.

Silver Lining® Ultimo, No. 1212 . . $195.00

33

281

Micro-magicians.

Two remarkable microcassette recorders. One hidden in a phone, and one that makes history.

World's smallest remote answering machine.

Answering machines are a great convenience, but they can crowd a desk. Or clutter a living room. Now Panasonic has created the world's first *microcassette* answering system. It's no bigger than a book. Measures only 5½ × 7½ × 1⅞".

Records for as long as your caller talks (up to 30 minutes). You can also limit messages to 30 seconds. Or turn off the message tape and leave an announcement only. Your outgoing messages can be any length up to 15 minutes. Automatically switches to a second back-up announcement (i.e. "Please call back later") when message tape is full.

Two ounce remote key lets you playback, repeat or rewind from any phone in the world. Key measures 3 × 2".

Press the *2-Way* button to record an important phone call (has FCC required beeper). Or press Dictate and record memos through the built-in condenser microphone. Rugged brushed chrome and ABS casing. Plugs into AC outlet. Easy soft-touch controls, call-counter

LED and locking Quick Erase. One year limited warranty. Call now to own the world's smallest, most unobtrusive answering system.
Panasonic Microcassette Answerer #PA162 $299 (4.50).

Now call-recording is as easy as lifting the phone.

Recorder Phone™ is a unique dual-volume telephone/speakerphone with a built-in microcassette deck. Tapes telephone conversations with the push of a button. Also records dictation directly through its condenser microphone.

Now keep exact records of important calls, or take down lengthy information for later transcription. You can even playback a tape over the phone. Features one-button record, stop, play and rewind controls.

For hand-held use, lift the receiver to get a dialtone. Or push the Hook button to use as a hands-free speakerphone.

Has Pulse dialing and Automatic Redial. Red LED light and FCC-required beeper indicate call recording. Comes with one microcassette and 90 day warranty. Takes two AA batteries (not included). 8" tall with 2½ × 4" base. 12' cord. Own the newest, most convenient call-recording phone—and get hands-free speakerphone convenience as well.

Recorder Phone #RP128 $119 (3.50).

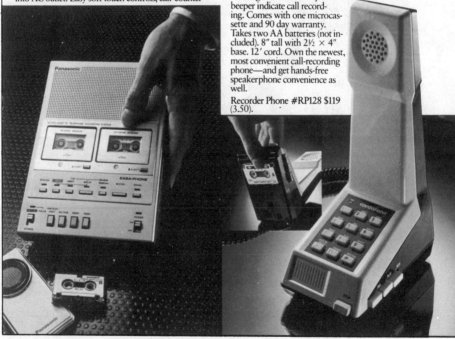

Figure 14.2 Notice this subhead ends where the reader is to start reading copy. (Courtesy The Sharper Image)

■ *KEY POINT:* *Keep related products together in the catalog.*

You can offer as many similar products as you wish, but they should be visually identified as belonging together (Figure 14.3).

However, if you have an item unrelated to the others, separate it visually with a subhead; or use a full color photograph for the more visually related items and black-and-white for what needs to be kept separate.

■ *CAUTION NOTE:* *Keep unrelated items separated visually.*

GUIDE HOW PEOPLE READ

The same eye-path rules described in Chapter 10 apply to catalogs. Whenever you try to make a reader's eyes move in an unnatural direction, you should reinforce the direction with numbers, letters, or arrows. Tell the reader, "Look at the stainless-steel double boiler on the next page." Giving people directions for what to do applies to reading of the materials as well as ordering.

■ *KEY POINT:* *When the eye path is unnatural, give people directions.*

You should give directions on how to read the catalog every step of the way. "Read below," "look for the order form on page 114," a message at the front of the catalog telling where to find outstanding products—these help prospects. Don't rely on them finding their own way to products by chance.

■ *CAUTION NOTE:* *Don't gamble that people will find the right product—guide them.*

FOLLOW THE READER'S NATURAL EYE PATH ON THE SALES SURFACE

Other rules about brochure design also apply here. For example, don't let an eye path cross itself. Keep the eye moving left to right and top to bottom.

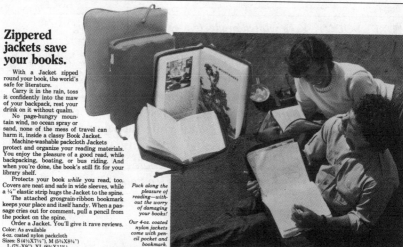

Figure 14.3 Four related items separated visually. (Courtesy Early Winters, Ltd.)

■ *CAUTION NOTE: Avoid having the eye path cross itself.*

Also don't expect readers to jump across an expanse of white space. More than 2 inches or 3 inches of white space causes the eye to slide away.

■ *CAUTION NOTE: Avoid white space.*

Keep layouts wider than they are long. This is more natural in the catalog, however, because you are designing two pages as one sales surface.

■ *CAUTION NOTE: Wide layouts work better than tall ones.*

As in the brochure, the strongest area of eye focus is slightly above the middle of the page and to the left. Use it for a major product.

■ *KEY POINT: Feature a major product in the upper middle left, where the eye falls.*

Black-and-white or colored photographs of individual products are the major eye-catching device used in catalogs. Line drawings are also effective. Photographs and drawings control the eye and bring readership to the copy associated with them (Figure 14.4).

Sometimes customers can be mesmerized by photographs, especially if the photographs are very good and are not supported by interesting copy. Photographs must be tied in with product descriptions and should ideally show the product being used by a person.

■ *KEY POINT: Product photographs should show usage and tie in with the description.*

USE A TOLL-FREE TELEPHONE NUMBER TO GAIN SALES

In too many catalogs, pages and pages of merchandise are offered but the order form is buried in the selling pages. Such catalogs offer a lot of product information but make it hard for customers to order. It's not practical to put an order form on every page, but a telephone number lets us tell readers how to get what they want.

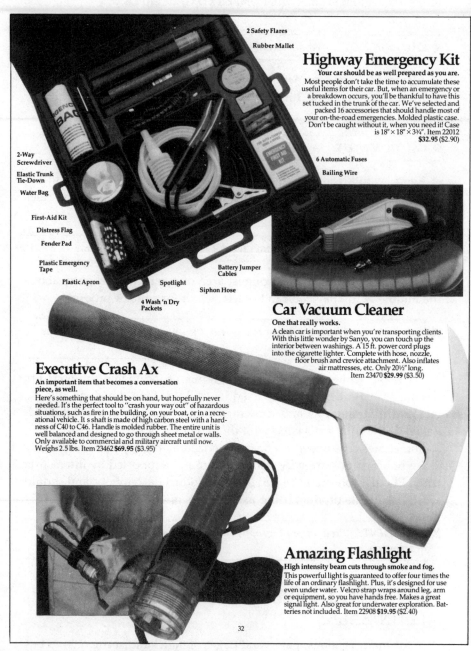

2 Safety Flares

Rubber Mallet

Highway Emergency Kit
Your car should be as well prepared as you are.
Most people don't take the time to accumulate these useful items for their car. But, when an emergency or a breakdown occurs, you'll be thankful to have this set tucked in the trunk of the car. We've selected and packed 16 accessories that should handle most of your on-the-road emergencies. Molded plastic case. Don't be caught without it, when you need it! Case is 18" × 18" × 3¾". Item 22012
$32.95 ($2.90)

2-Way Screwdriver

Elastic Trunk Tie-Down

Water Bag

First-Aid Kit

Distress Flag

Fender Pad

Plastic Emergency Tape

Plastic Apron

Spotlight

4 Wash 'n Dry Packets

6 Automatic Fuses

Bailing Wire

Battery Jumper Cables

Siphon Hose

Car Vacuum Cleaner
One that really works.
A clean car is important when you're transporting clients. With this little wonder by Sanyo, you can touch up the interior between washings. A 15 ft. power cord plugs into the cigarette lighter. Complete with hose, nozzle, floor brush and crevice attachment. Also inflates air mattresses, etc. Only 20½" long.
Item 23470 **$29.99** ($3.50)

Executive Crash Ax
An important item that becomes a conversation piece, as well.
Here's something that should be on hand, but hopefully never needed. It's the perfect tool to "crash your way out" of hazardous situations, such as fire in the building, on your boat, or in a recreational vehicle. It s shaft is made of high carbon steel with a hardness of C40 to C46. Handle is molded rubber. The entire unit is well balanced and designed to go through sheet metal or walls. Only available to commercial and military aircraft until now. Weighs 2.5 lbs. Item 23462 **$69.95** ($3.95)

Amazing Flashlight
High intensity beam cuts through smoke and fog.
This powerful light is guaranteed to offer four times the life of an ordinary flashlight. Plus, it's designed for use even under water. Velcro strap wraps around leg, arm or equipment, so you have hands free. Makes a great signal light. Also great for underwater exploration. Batteries not included. Item 22908 **$19.95** ($2.40)

32

Figure 14.4 See how the eye path is controlled in this placement of pictures— left to right, top to bottom. The pictures and copy are wrapped around each other; white space is minimized. (Courtesy The Sharper Image)

■ *CAUTION NOTE:* *Don't limit ways customers can order.*

A telephone number, in fact, is crucial in catalog sales, because it's the best way to make ordering easy for customers.

■ *KEY POINT:* *The ability to order by toll-free telephone is essential for catalog sales.*

You should put a toll-free number on every double-page spread of the catalog. Also operators who are skilled in selling should take customers' calls. Operators should not just take orders. They should know the merchandise well enough that they can point out accessory items to increase the product's usefulness or even alternative purchases that might be of more use. The idea is to build orders, not just take them.

■ *KEY POINT:* *Have a trained salesperson take telephone orders.*

■ *KEY POINT:* *Use the telephone to increase order size.*

In the catalog, tell readers why they should phone in their orders. Tell them they'll get faster service and can use their credit cards. Tell them their order will be shipped out the same day.

You can tell them to whom they will be talking; this will relieve their uneasiness about giving credit card information. Tell them you won't charge the item to their card until they receive it. You can also offer them something free if they order by phone.

■ *KEY POINT:* *Give customers reasons for using the telephone.*

If you sell the telephone step on every double-page section, your catalog will be better than 9 out of 10. Remember your goal is to get a response.

■ *KEY POINT:* *Use telephone ordering to give a response step on every page.*

USE THE FRONT COVER TO SELL PRODUCTS

Another basic design principle for catalogs is to use prime space for your best and most popular merchandise.

■ *KEY POINT: Use prime catalog space to sell prime products.*

Take the front cover as an example. It is a prime selling surface, but marketers waste it on idealized images which they hope will give the catalog a touch of class.

■ *CAUTION NOTE: Avoid a generalized theme for the front cover.*

Why not sell something on the front cover? It's the most prominent place in the catalog, so why waste it on a picture of yourself? Instead, use a picture of one of your main products with a brief description, and refer to the page inside where readers can get more information. You can also repeat the product offer inside. For example, if you sell office furniture, put a picture of a popular desk on the front cover and tell the reader why it might be perfect for them. That's selling. Figure 14.5 shows an example.

■ *KEY POINT: Use the front cover to sell products.*

You can always tell that a catalog's producers are ego tripping if the cover has a sexy woman or man, a clean layout, or a fantasy design. All are unrelated to the product. And what does this ego mania gain? If prospects don't relate the cover to the products being offered, they're unlikely to open the catalog, especially if they're unfamiliar with the company. Remember, people don't read advertising to be entertained.

■ *KEY POINT: A popular item on the cover will help get the catalog opened.*
■ *CAUTION NOTE: Customers don't read catalogs to be entertained.*

So, Joe Sugarman (JS&A) and Richard Thalheimer (Sharper Image), be warned. Your sexy, ego-soothing covers may work for a while, but to maintain customers over a longer period of time you need to go for the response.

SELL ON THE BACK AND INSIDE COVERS, TOO

What applies to the front also works for the back. Use an actual photograph of a product and a description, and tell readers how they can get it.

Figure 14.5 This L. L. Bean cover is all business. It gets you right into thinking about products—and that's what it's all about. (Courtesy L. L. Bean)

■ *KEY POINT: Use the back catalog cover to sell.*

■ *CAUTION NOTE: Never leave the back page blank.*

The back cover also contains the label, and many customers look at the label to confirm that the catalog is for them before they even open it. In that sense, the back cover is even more important than the front cover. So put your company name on both covers. Make it prominent and use boldface type so that people can see it from a distance.

■ *KEY POINT: "Double front" the company name on the back of the catalog as well as on the front.*

The inside front and back covers are also prime sales surfaces.

■ *KEY POINT: Sell products on the inside front and back covers.*

One mistake many catalog marketers make is to put the table of contents on the inside front cover and the order form on the inside back cover. Nothing could be worse from a selling point of view.

■ *CAUTION NOTE: Avoid wasting prime space by putting catalog contents and the order form inside the covers.*

If you have been using these pages for letters, indexes, or order forms, consider moving them into the catalog so you can use these pages for selling.

■ *KEY POINT: Put nonselling material several pages into the catalog.*

The two-page center spread is also prime space, because a stapled catalog will normally fall open at the center spread. It's one of the most-read pages and is an important place to display major products (Figure 14.6).

■ *KEY POINT: Take advantage of the prime selling space of the center fold.*

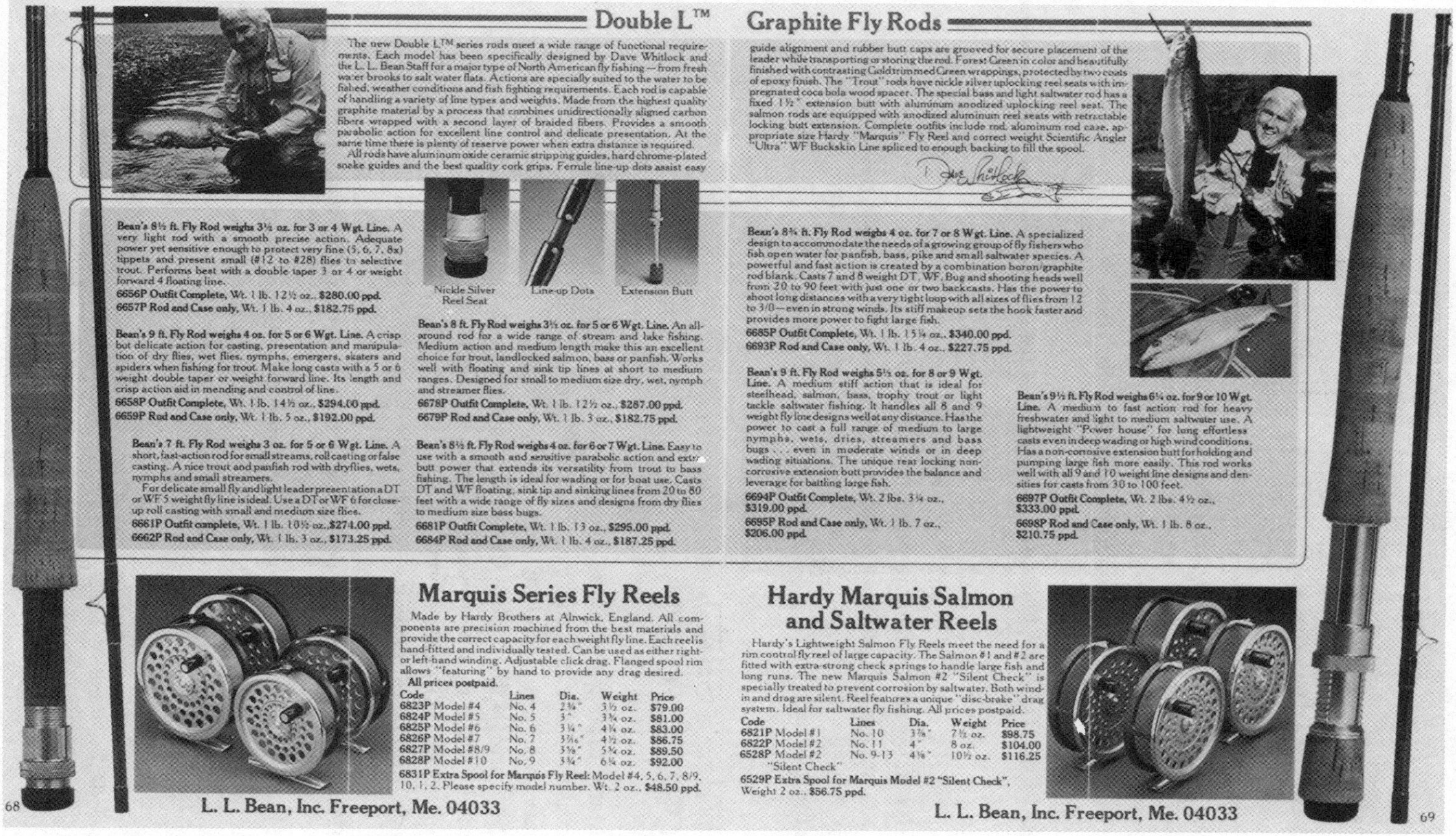

Figure 14.6 Great centerfold by L. L. Bean, a full surface designed as one. Editorial content and testimonial, too. (Courtesy L. L. Bean)

WHERE SHALL WE PUT THE TABLE OF CONTENTS?

You can do two things with a table of contents: either eliminate it altogether or work it into your catalog creatively. If you don't have a table of contents, readers may be more likely to thumb through the entire catalog. This makes sense, particularly if you group your products so readers don't get frustrated looking for what they want (Figure 14.7).

■ *KEY POINT: Work the table of contents into the catalog.*

If you think you need a table of contents, consider stringing it through the catalog. Put the As on the first inside right-hand page and the Bs on the next left-hand page, and continue this through the catalog. To use such a table of contents, readers must leaf through the catalog. This strategy involves them and may be a better solution than omitting the index entirely.

WHERE SHALL WE PLACE THE ORDER FORM?

Many catalog designers want to put the order form at the center, because binding it in there makes catalog production easier. They try to justify this on the grounds that people should be made to focus on the order form. Obviously, the order form must be included, but it shouldn't take up one of your prime selling spaces.

Overrule the designer—it's your catalog. Make the design fit your needs, not the other way around.

■ *CAUTION NOTE: Don't put the order form in prime selling space.*

However, the placement of the order form is important in that we don't want it to hinder prime selling space. For example, we don't want to waste the back inside cover's valuable selling space. We must find a place that is unlikely to gain attention on its own.

Figure 14.7 *(Opposite)*   Better than a table of contents are short subheads identifying each group of products. (Courtesy Eastern Mountain Sports)

EMS TABERNAC 2 and 4-Person
Moderate 4-Season Use.
Total Weight: 2-person, 7 lbs. 8 oz.;
4-person, 10 lbs. 4 oz.

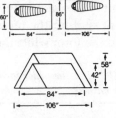

Simple, functional, free-standing protection. Both versions feature big entrances at each end with no-see-um screening and coated storm flap. Domed ceiling gives greater head room. Self standing A-frame with shock-corded aluminum poles. Bound interior seams are reinforced at all stress points. Interior net pockets. Optional vestibules add gear storage space.

58-1116 2-person Tabernac **$145.75**
58-1108 4-person Tabernac **$209.75**
58-6487 2-person Vestibule **$35.75**
58-6495 4-person Vestibule **$45.75**

EMS ARCADIA 2 and 4-Person
Moderate 4-Season Use.
Total Weight: 2-person, 7 lbs. 11 oz.;
4-person, 10 lbs. 5 oz.

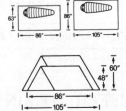

Freestanding A-frame tents with added headroom provided by a center hoop design. Shock-corded aluminum pole system. Full rainfly. No-see-um netted entrance with storm flap. Tub style floor of 1.9 oz. coated ripstop. Reinforced at all stress points. Full rear window with netting. Fly extension shelters window and door for rough weather ventilation capabilities. Optional vestibules add gear storage space.

58-1280 2-person Arcadia **$179.75**
58-1298 4-person Arcadia **$239.75**
58-6503 2-person Vestibule **$39.75**
58-6511 4-person Vestibule **$49.75**

EMS FULL MOON II
Moderate 4-Season Use.
Total Weight: 6 lbs. 9.5 oz.

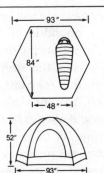

Freestanding dome tent design with plenty of headroom. Shock corded aluminum poles in pole sleeve suspension system. Hooded fly shelters both door and window for adequate storm ventilation. No-see-um netting and storm flap on both door and big back window. Tub style floor. Extra guy-out rings on fly for added wind stability. All seams double lap-felled for strength, reinforced at all stress points. Packs to 7" × 30".

58-1306 Full Moon II **$189.75**

NORTHFACE VE 23
Moderate 4-Season Use.
Total Weight: 7 lbs. 12 oz.

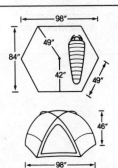

Geodesic design with shock-corded aluminum poles produces extremely windstable, elegant design. Contour fitted fly. Two large netted windows with storm flaps for adequate ventilation. Double door with netting and storm flap. Fly forms door hood for added rain protection. Three identical poles allow fast set up, even in wind. Meticulous construction throughout. Packs to 8" × 28".

58-3146 VE 23 **$276.75**

The two areas readers are most likely to skip are a third of the way from the front of the catalog and a third of the way from the back. Either is an excellent spot for the order form, because readers will look at the space around the form while they fill it out.

■ *KEY POINT: Put the order form one-third of the way from the back or the front of the catalog.*

You might consider putting an order form in both spots. This is easy from a production standpoint if the catalog is stapled in the center. By placing the order form in otherwise "dead" spaces, you turn these spaces into additional prime selling spaces.

■ *KEY POINT: The pages around the order form become prime selling space.*

USE DIFFERENT KINDS OF RESPONSE DEVICES

Another strategy is to use several different types of response devices. Onc could be a bound-in insert, typical of many stapled catalogs, in which the binding splits the order form and attached envelope. Another could be a loose insert that drops out when the catalog is opened (Figure 14.8). Although this may annoy customers, it draws attention to the need to respond. You could also add another order form on a perforated page, which would always be there in case the others got lost.

Consider using all three response devices; in combination they increase responses, because they remind customers of why they are reading your catalog—to buy something.

■ *KEY POINT: A combination of response devices encourages the customer to buy.*

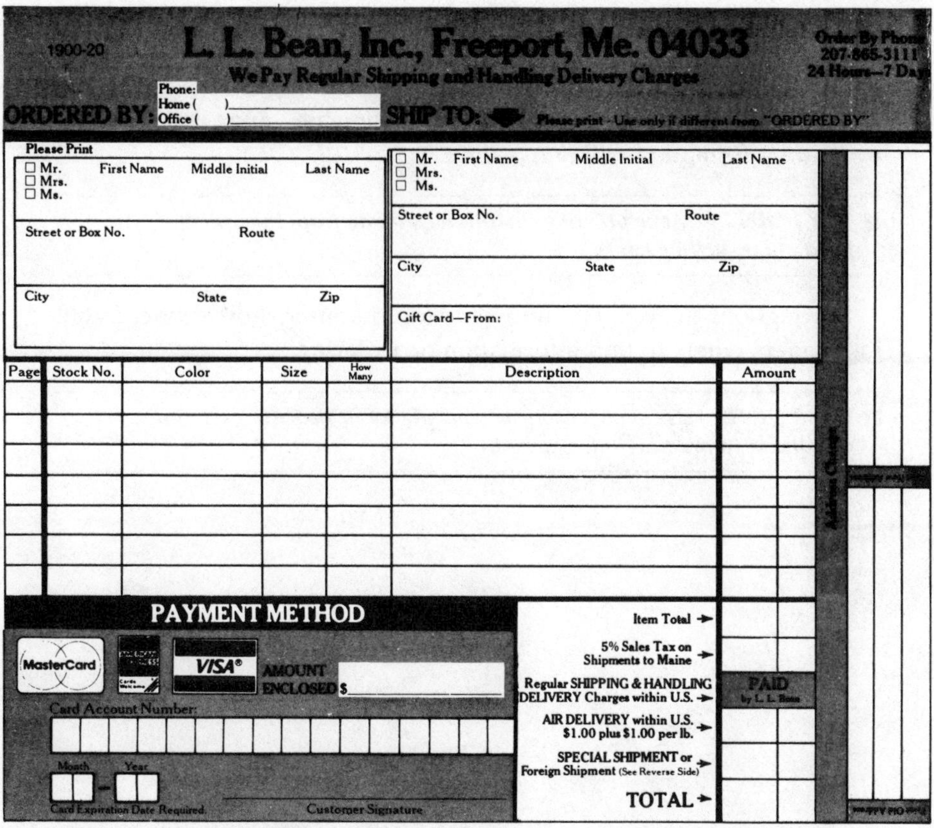

1900-20 L. L. Bean, Inc., Freeport, Me. 04033

We Pay Regular Shipping and Handling Delivery Charges

Order By Phone 207-865-3111 24 Hours—7 Days

ORDERED BY: Phone: Home ( ) Office ( )

SHIP TO: Please print - Use only if different from "ORDERED BY"

Please Print

☐ Mr. ☐ Mrs. ☐ Ms. First Name Middle Initial Last Name

Street or Box No. Route

City State Zip

☐ Mr. ☐ Mrs. ☐ Ms. First Name Middle Initial Last Name

Street or Box No. Route

City State Zip

Gift Card—From:

Page	Stock No.	Color	Size	How Many	Description	Amount

PAYMENT METHOD

MasterCard VISA AMOUNT ENCLOSED $

Card Account Number:

Month Year

Card Expiration Date Required. Customer Signature

Item Total →

5% Sales Tax on Shipments to Maine →

Regular SHIPPING & HANDLING DELIVERY Charges within U.S. → PAID by L. L. Bean

AIR DELIVERY within U.S. $1.00 plus $1.00 per lb. →

SPECIAL SHIPMENT or Foreign Shipment (See Reverse Side) →

TOTAL →

Address Change

Figure 14.8 Example of L. L. Bean order form bound into a stapled catalog and used as a "loose" insert. (Courtesy L. L. Bean)

WHAT SHALL WE PUT ON THE ORDER FORM?

You can use much of the space on the response form to show products customers might buy on impulse after they have decided what they want.

■ ***KEY POINT:** Use extra space on the order form to load up on more products for sale.*

You need instructions for ordering, but these don't have to be on or next to the form. They need only be nearby. Place them a page away or in the farthest column of the opposite page, so the space immediately around the form is free for selling more products. Guide readers to the ordering information with a headline.

■ *KEY POINT: Move ordering instructions away from the order form to create more selling space.*

Throughout the catalog you will want to scatter short subheads telling readers where to find information on ordering.

■ *KEY POINT: Use subheads at various places in the catalog to direct customers to ordering information.*

FINDING AND 15
SELECTING
PRODUCTIVE MAILING
LISTS

In this chapter we will explore the characteristics of quality mailing lists and how to select them.

TARGETING THE PRODUCT TO
THE RIGHT PROSPECTS

The success of direct mail as a way to sell products and services, raise funds, and gain sales leads is well established. Postal workers deliver at least one direct mail piece for a subscription, donation, insurance product, or service to American mailboxes every weekday of the year.

The reason for the phenomenal growth in direct mail is simple: It works! Direct mail is effective—it gets through to the *right people*, with the *right message*, at the *right time*.

In this chapter we will learn who the right people are and how you can find them by selecting mailing lists that meet your exact requirements.

■ *KEY POINT:* *Direct mail must target the right people.*

Today's computer technology lets us target in on our best prospects as never before. We can select prospects by many categories—where they live, where they work, what they do, even their likes and dislikes.

297

We can plan our marketing strategy far more accurately than ever before, and in many cases we can predict what our profits will be.

■ *KEY POINT: Computer technology permits knowing many details about people.*

LIST SELECTION IS THE KEY TO SUCCESSFUL DIRECT MAIL SELLING

Up to now this book has focused on how copy and design can be used to gain sales. Now let's turn to the real key to direct mail selling, mailing lists and how to acquire them.

No matter how outstanding our copy and design are, if our mailing piece goes to the wrong people we might as well send them our money, too—we're not going to make it. The reverse is also true. Less interested prospects with a preexisting interest in what we offer will make us money.

■ *CAUTION NOTE: Well-done mailing pieces fail if sent to the wrong prospects.*

■ *KEY POINT: Even an average mailing piece works with prospects who are already interested.*

Selecting the right lists and using them wisely are the keys to success in direct mail selling. This is where the computer makes a difference. Most of what we've talked about so far—what to say to prospects and how to present our sales message—is derived from long-established data and experience. What is really new in the field of direct mail is use of the computer to qualify people on lists.

■ *KEY POINT: The most important task in direct mail is mailing list selection.*

■ *KEY POINT: One of the major new technologies in direct mail is computer help in making lists.*

Using the computer in list selection will be discussed in detail later in this chapter. It is the computer that has helped cause the recent explosion in direct mail.

COMPILED LISTS GROUP ALL POSSIBLE PROSPECTS

There are two different kinds of lists: *compiled lists* and *responder lists*. Each is created and used differently. Compiled lists are names and addresses generated from available public or private sources of information, such as organization rosters, automobile registrations, telephone company listings, and census bureau records.

■ *KEY POINT:* *Compiled lists group people from many sources.*

Compiled lists can be *demographic*, that is, they tell us statistics and characteristics such as age, salary, postal zip code, and so on. Lists can also tell us how large companies are, how many employees they have, and what their sales are.

■ *KEY POINT:* *Compiled lists give us basic information on people.*

Compiled lists can even tell us to which industry group a company belongs if it uses the Standard Industrial Code (SIC), a uniform numbering system that helps us locate areas of marketing interest. This system guides us to companies classified by specific category and also alerts us to prospects in related fields.

■ *KEY POINT:* *Compiled lists group business into similar industries.*

WHAT CHARACTERIZES A COMPILED LIST?

The people on a compiled list are not necessarily buyers. They are simply association members, telephone owners, car owners, and so on. They haven't proven themselves as mail-order buyers. We can't know whether they've ever used the mail to buy anything.

■ *CAUTION NOTE: People on compiled lists haven't proven themselves as responders.*

In fact, we may get a compiled list that appears to be outstanding because its demographics indicate that the names are likely prospects. When we send out our mailing, however, we get a 1% response rate. What happened?

Part of the problem is that a compiled list contains names of many people who are not oriented to direct mail at all.

■ *CAUTION NOTE: Many on the compiled list won't respond to direct mail offers.*

The names on most compiled lists break down into three groups. The first group will not respond to direct mail at all because they don't like it. The second will respond occasionally. The rest respond to direct mail on a regular basis. This is the group we want.

■ *CAUTION NOTE: The people on compiled lists break down into no's, possibles, and yes'es.*

Wouldn't it be wonderful if we could mail only to those who are used to buying by mail? We could save a lot of money if we didn't bother soliciting those who won't respond anyway. In a sense, we can do just this.

RESPONDER LISTS ARE MADE UP OF PEOPLE WHO HAVE ACTED ON PREVIOUS OFFERS

Responder lists name people who have responded to direct mail offers. These are the names we want.

■ *KEY POINT: People on responder lists have proven they will act.*

Responder lists also tend to be *psychographic*, that is, they tell us something about why people buy. It is this quality that makes these lists so valuable to us.

■ *KEY POINT:*   *Responder lists tell us something about why people buy.*

The problem with responder lists is that they are shorter and harder to get than compiled lists. The good thing is that we can have more success with them and can gain longer lasting, repeat customers.

■ *CAUTION NOTE:*   *Responder lists are small and not always easy to get.*

Responder lists cost more than compiled lists. But they usually work so well that we can still make money from them. Because they are lists of people who, by and large, trust direct mail as a means of doing business, they are the first lists we should look for when planning a direct mail campaign.

■ *KEY POINT:*   *If available, responder lists are often worth the extra cost.*

LISTS OF CONSUMERS OFFER A VARIETY OF SELECTION CRITERIA

Lists fall into one of three general categories: consumer, professional, and business.

Consumer lists are often compiled from names and addresses of home owners or renters, telephone directories, motor vehicle registrations, voter lists, and so on. Names may also come from credit card and consumer companies, special events such as home shows, or sporting events.

■ *KEY POINT:*   *Names of consumers can be compiled from general lists.*

Lists of consumers who are also responders typically are generated from magazine and newspaper subscriptions, other mail-order companies, or donor lists.

■ *KEY POINT:*   *Consumers can also be on responder lists.*

You can often select consumer lists by state, city, and zip code. Zip codes tell us whether our prospects are from urban, suburban, or rural areas. This is important when we are trying to establish our influence in a particular geographic area.

■ *KEY POINT:*   *Consumers can be selected by city, suburban, or rural location.*

Income level is only one type of demographic data often available from government sources such as the census statistics. Other census information includes whether the dwelling is owned or rented, the number of years of education, and the age of the head of the household. Often local planning and development boards also have income, employment, and household information.

■ *KEY POINT:*   *Income, home ownership, and education are known about most consumers.*

Consumer lists typically allow selection by sex, marital status, and job title. In some mail campaigns such as fund raising, where the emotional content of the appeal is important, you should address prospects as "Mr.," "Mrs.," or "Ms." before their full name.

■ *KEY POINT:*   *Sex, marital status, and job title are often known about consumers.*

Other information usually available for responder lists of consumers includes how recently they bought or donated and how much was spent or donated.

■ *KEY POINT:*   *When the consumer bought and how much was spent are available in responder lists.*

LISTS ALSO INCLUDE PROFESSIONALS WHO PURSUE INDIVIDUAL OCCUPATIONS

Professional lists include people in high-status individual, noncorporate occupations, such as doctors, lawyers, and accountants. They are gained from various professional organizations. Responder lists of professionals are often gained from subscription to professional publications.

■ *KEY POINT:* *Professional lists comprise those who pursue individual occupations.*

Since these people are listed as individuals, they can be selected according to many of the criteria available for consumer lists—location, sex, and marital status as well as date and amount of most recent purchase for responder lists.

■ *KEY POINT:* *Selection criteria for professional lists are similar to those for consumer lists.*

In addition, many professional lists of doctors, accountants, engineers, teachers, and others are broken down by specialty. Lists can even include quasiprofessionals such as insurance and real estate people and semi-blue-collar categories like construction supervisors.

■ *KEY POINT:* *Professional lists are sometimes broken down by specialties.*

Except for lists of subscribers to professional journals, most occupational lists are compiled. A responder list, if available, will usually gain more responses than a compiled list of the same population.

■ *KEY POINT:* *Professionals who are responders can generate above-average sales.*

MANY SUCCESSFUL LISTS CONTAIN BUSINESSES AND ORGANIZATIONS

The third category of lists is businesses, organizations, and institutions involved in operating for profit or not for profit. Such lists are compiled by the government, Dun & Bradstreet, and many other private companies that keep track of business and organizational operations. In addition, there are many compiled lists of executives who work within companies.

■ *KEY POINT:*   *Most business lists are compiled.*

Business lists can also be made up of responders. Subscribers, inquirers, donors, buyers of mail-order products, and business trade members all can be found on business responder lists.

■ *KEY POINT:*   *Some lists are available of businesses that respond.*

Most business lists can be selected by geographic area, SIC codes, and net worth.

OVERALL CATEGORIES OF CONSUMER, PROFESSIONAL, AND BUSINESS LISTS

Figure 15.1 is a relatively short list of broad categories that point to thousands of specialized compiled and responder lists of consumers, professionals, and businesses.

THREE IMPORTANT QUALIFICATIONS OF LISTS: RECENCY, FREQUENCY, AND AMOUNT

We must learn three things about any list we are considering using: recency, frequency, and amount.

Recency refers to how often the names and addresses on a list are updated. The average American moves every 4½ years. This means that 22% of a consumer list will be out of date in just one year. And about half of a general United States list would change in just over two years.

■ *KEY POINT:*   *"Recency" of a list refers to how often the names and addresses on it are updated.*

People in some geographic areas, however, are less mobile than in others: Vermonters don't move as often as southern Californians.

As many as 30% of the executive workforce can change jobs in a year.

ACCOUNTANTS..........	ECOLOGISTS............	OIL, PETROLEUM........
ADOPTION AGENCIES....	ECONOMISTS............	PENSION PLAN MGRS.....
ADVERTISING INDUSTRY..	EDUCATION.............	PERFORM. ARTS CENTERS
AGRICULTURE	ELECTRICAL MFRS.......	PERSONNEL EXECUTIVES.
AGRICULTURAL ASSNS....	EMPLOYMENT AGENCIES.	PHARMACOLOGISTS .....
A/C CONTRACTORS......	ENERGY EXECUTIVES....	PHOTOGRAPHERS ....
AIRCRAFT OWNERS/PILOTS	ENGINEERS	PHYSICIANS ....
AIRLINES & AIRPORTS....	ENTERTAINMENT........	PHYSICISTS.............
ALUMNI ASSOCIATIONS..	ENVIRONMENTAL........	PHYSICAL THERAPISTS...
AMERICAN HOUSEHOLDS.	EXECUTIVES	PILOTS.................
AMERICAN LEGION POSTS	FACTORY MANAGERS....	PLANNING EXECUTIVES..
AMUSEMENT PARKS.....	FARMERS..............	PLASTICS ENGINEERS....
ANIMAL HOSPITALS......	FARM SUPPLIES/EQUIP...	PRESIDENTS CORPS......
APPAREL MFRS..........	FINANCIAL EXECS........	PRINTERS ....
APPAREL WHOLESALERS.	FIN. INSTITUTIONS.......	PSYCHIATRISTS ....
APPAREL RETAILERS....	FORENSIC TECHS./MD's...	PTA'S ....
ARCHITECTS............	FORESTERS	PUBLICATIONS ....
ART MUSEUMS	FORTUNE CO. EXECS.....	PUBLIC RELATIONS CO'S..
ASSNS. NAT'L HQS.......	FOUNDATIONS	PURCHASING EXECS......
ATTORNEYS	FRATERNAL SOCIETIES...	RADIO BROADCASTING...
AUDIO-VISUAL EXECS...	FUEL OIL DEALERS......	REAL ESTATE...........
AUTOMOTIVE..........	FUND-RAISING ORGS.....	REC. FACILITIES........
AVIATION...............	FUNERAL DIRECTOR⌐....	RELIGIOUS ORGS........
BANKS	FURNITURE 30,	RESEARCH ENGINEERS...
BEAUTY SHOPS.........	GARDEN SUPPLY STORES	RESORTS ....
BIOLOGISTS	GAS STATIONS..........	RESTAURANTS ....
BOOKKEEPING SERVICES.	GIFT SHOPS............	RETAILERS ....
BOOK STORES.........	GIFT BUYERS-CORP......	SALES MANAGERS ....
BOY SCOUT COUNCILS...	GOLF/COUNTRY CLUBS...	SALES PROMO SERVICES.
BUILDERS-CONTRACTORS	GOVERNMENT...........	S & L ASSOCIATIONS.....
BUSINESS SERVICES.....	HIGH SCHOOLS.........	SCHOOLS ....
CAREER WOMEN.........	HOSPITALS	SCIENTISTS.............
CHAIN STORES HQS......	HOTELS & MOTELS......	SECURITY ANALYSTS....
CHAMBER COMMERCE DIRS	IMPORT COMPANY EXECS.	SERVICE BUSINESSES....
CHAMBER COMM. MBRS...	INDUST. EXECUTIVES....	SHOPPING CENTERS.....
CHILD DEVEL. PROS......	INSURANCE	SKI RESORTS...........
CHIROPRACTORS........	INTERIOR DECORATORS..	SOCIAL SERVICE ORGS.
CHURCHES	INTERNATIONAL CORPS..	SOCIOLOGISTS ....
CHURCH SOCIETIES......	INVESTMENT PROSPECTS.	SPEECH & HEARING......
CIVIC CENTERS..........	JEWISH ORGANIZATIONS.	STATE OFFICIALS........
CIVIL ENGINEERS........	JOBBERS/WHOLESALERS.	STOCK BROKERAGE CO'S.
CLERGYMEN	LABORATORIES	STOCKHOLDERS.........
CLOTHING STORES......	LABOR UNIONS.........	STORES................
CLUBS & ORGANIZATIONS	LANDSCAPE ARCHITECTS.	SUMMER CAMPS.........
COACHES-H.S. & COLL....	LAW FIRMS.............	TAX PREP. SERVICES.....
COLLEGES & UNIV........	LEGISLATORS	TEACHERS ....
COMMODITY BROKERS...	LIBRARIES	TEXTILE MILLS..........
COMMODITY INVESTORS..	LUMBER EXECUTIVES....	TV BROADCASTING......
COMMUNICATIONS IND....	LUMBER-RETAIL	TENNIS INSTALLATIONS..
COMPUTER EXECUTIVES..	MACHINERY MFRS........	THEATRES ....
CONTRACTORS..........	MAGAZINES.............	TRADE ASSO. HQS.......
CONSULTANTS	MAIL ORDER FIRMS......	TRADE SHOW XBTRS.....
CONSUMER ORGS........	MANUFACTURING CO'S...	TRAFFIC EXECUTIVES....
CONVENTION SPONSORS.	MFR'S AGENTS.......17,	TRAINING DIRECTORS....
CORPORATE PLANNERS..	MARKET. ASSOC. MBRS..	TRAVEL AGENCIES.......
CORPORATION EXECS....	MARKET RESEARCH CO'S.	TRAVEL PROSPECTS.....
COUNTRY CLUBS........	MARRIAGE COUNSELORS.	TRUCKING COMPANIES...
CREDIT UNIONS.........	MEDICAL DOCTORS......	URBAN AFFAIRS EXECS...
DATA PROCESS EXECS...	MEDICAL FACILITIES.....	UTILITIES..............
DAY CARE FACILITIES....	METALWORKING EXECS...	VETERANS GROUPS......
DEFENSE CONTRACTORS.	MILITARY POSTS........	VETERINARIANS........
DENTISTS	MOVIE THEATERS........	WATER WORKS ENGRS...
DEPARTMENT STORES...	MUSEUMS	WEALTHY INDIVIDUALS..
DISTRIBUTION EXECS.....	NEWSPAPERS	WHOLESALE TRADE.....
DISTRIBUTORS-WHSL.....	NURSERY/GREENHOUSES	WHO'S PROMINENT.....
DOCTORS	NURSING HOMES........	WOMEN................

Figure 15.1 Here are a few of the general categories that summarize the thousands of specific lists.

If a business list has not been updated in the past 6 months, 15% of it is out of date.

Frequency means how frequently the people on the list have made purchases or donated. People who have bought only once in the last three years are not as good prospects as people who buy several times a year.

■ *KEY POINT:* *"Frequency" of a list means how often people on it have purchased.*

Amount refers to how much was spent on each purchase. Again, persons who bought one item for $20 are not as desirable from our standpoint as people who bought several products at $75 each.

■ *KEY POINT:* *"Amount" in relation to a list means the average amount of each purchase made by the people on it.*

Recency, frequency, and amount are often referred to as R-F-A; they must be considered when purchasing any list.

■ *CAUTION NOTE:* *The "R-F-A" formula must be considered in the purchase of any list.*

We want to reach those with money who are most in need. So prospects who have made frequent purchases and who spend significant amounts can be assumed to be good candidates for our sales message.

SPECIALIZED LISTS ARE PRESEGMENTED BY UNIQUE QUALIFICATIONS

Most lists detail many different qualifications for the individuals, professionals, businesses, and organizations on them. For example, certain lists have information on every kind of educational institution, from nursery schools to universities (Figure 15.2). And lists can usually be segmented by grade, subject, enrollment, function, title, city, state, and other qualifications.

■ *KEY POINT:* *Specialized lists have many unique qualifications.*

NURSERY SCHOOLS&DAY CARE CTRS 37,554

State	#	State	#	State	#	State	#	State	#
MA	838	MD	674	KY	522	IL	1499	ID	178
RI	85	VA	739	OH	1284	MO	791	UT	171
NH	193	WV	124	IN	628	KS	404	AZ	494
ME	108	NC	1380	MI	1003	NE	219	NM	235
VT	80	SC	810	IA	370	LA	1072	NV	123
CT	578	GA	1327	WI	613	AR	398	CA	4487
NJ	1237	FL	2429	MN	468	OK	765	HI	211
NY	1724	AL	799	SD	86	TX	3510	OR	555
PA	1107	TN	791	ND	59	CO	600	WA	618
DE	133	MS	540	MT	118	WY	99	AK	87
DC	191								

ELEMENTARY SCHOOLS 52,682

State	#	State	#	State	#	State	#	State	#
MA	955	MD	800	KY	907	IL	2893	ID	358
RI	182	VA	1189	OH	2406	MO	1351	UT	.327
NH	328	WV	798	IN	1335	KS	956	AZ	587
ME	520	NC	1385	MI	2098	NE	1247	NM	393
VT	289	SC	720	IA	1013	LA	1051	NV	186
CT	652	GA	1232	WI	1336	AR	669	CA	4574
NJ	1348	FL	1244	MN	992	OK	1086	HI	169
NY	2399	AL	956	SD	396	TX	3262	OR	812
PA	2236	TN	1120	ND	359	CO	77,1	WA	1061
DE	111	MS	590	MT	494	WY	243	AK	162
DC	134								

SCHOOLS-ELEMENTARY-CATHOLIC . 8,000
SCHOOLS-HIGH-CATHOLIC 1,473

SCHOOLS-JUNIOR HIGHS 9,440

State	#	State	#	State	#	State	#	State	#
MA	224	MD	163	KY	134	IL	416	ID	72
RI	30	VA	210	OH	489	MO	213	UT	62
NH	36	WV	314	IN	259	KS	159	AZ	97
ME	74	NC	296	MI	453	NE	66	NM	94
VT	14	SC	156	IA	178	LA	187	NV	36
CT	130	GA	208	WI	203	AR	123	CA	781
NJ	222	FL	304	MN	146	OK	224	HI	24
NY	489	AL	112	SD	31	TX	812	OR	145
PA	416	TN	168	ND	15	CO	177	WA	226
DE	22	MS	86	MT	56	WY	37	AK	10
DC	27								

SCHOOLS-SENIOR HIGHS 18,635

State	#	State	#	State	#	State	#	State	#
MA	461	MD	193	KY	304	IL	719	ID	128
RI	54	VA	388	OH	834	MO	564	UT	89
NH	98	WV	204	IN	347	KS	369	AZ	152
ME	164	NC	448	MI	575	NE	297	NM	132
VT	74	SC	346	IA	499	LA	503	NV	52
CT	182	GA	339	WI	408	AR	393	CA	974
NJ	990	FL	566	MN	83	OK	440	HI	54
NY	1577	AL	563	SD	214	TX	1189	OR	239
PA	504	TN	384	ND	266	CO	195	WA	375
DE	52	MS	317	MT	170	WY	49	AK	88
DC	30								

SCHOOLS-PRIVATE 11,592

State	#	State	#	State	#	State	#	State	#
MA	396	MD	226	KY	112	IL	506	ID	38
RI	37	VA	383	OH	176	MO	206	UT	8
NH	77	WV	40	IN	261	KS	62	AZ	273
ME	115	NC	224	MI	493	NE	89	NM	91
VT	43	SC	373	IA	100	LA	209	NV	4
CT	156	GA	375	WI	446	AR	55	CA	1646
NJ	260	FL	674	MN	240	OK	42	HI	90
NY	698	AL	213	SD	81	TX	387	OR	186
PA	553	TN	202	ND	20	CO	139	WA	194
DE	60	MS	130	MT	46	WY	40	AK	23
DC	65								

SCHOOLS-VOCATIONAL&SPECIALIZED .. 10,398

State	#	State	#	State	#	State	#	State	#
MA	137	MD	210	KY	208	IL	58	ID	52
RI	14	VA	264	OH	550	MO	210	UT	102
NH	18	WV	72	IN	278	KS	70	AZ	278
ME	18	NC	247	MI	367	NE	113	NM	110
VT	10	SC	120	IA	148	LA	309	NV	71
CT	70	GA	326	WI	213	AR	213	CA	1820
NJ	468	FL	742	MN	226	OK	149	HI	82
NY	180	AL	266	SD	34	TX	441	OR	63
PA	244	TN	273	ND	42	CO	306	WA	103
DE	7	MS	108´	MT	41	WY	24	AK	7
DC	58								

SCHOOLS-EXCEPTIONAL CHILDREN 3,600

PUBLIC SCHOOL ADMINISTRATORS-HOME ADDRESS............ 10,948

State	#	State	#	State	#	State	#	State	#
MA	193	MD	120	KY	178	IL	638	ID	67
RI	24	VA	233	OH	729	MO	299	UT	56
NH	25	WV	95	IN	313	KS	139	AZ	112
ME	47	NC	183	MI	530	NE	139	NM	81
VT	29	SC	160	IA	216	LA	121	NV	14
CT	232	GA	203	WI	333	AR	124	CA	719
NJ	415	FL	217	MN	262	OK	129	HI	18
NY	853	AL	106	SD	73	TX	818	OR	184
PA	643	TN	182	ND	43	CO	135	WA	169
DE	59	MS	165	MT	51	WY	40	AK	18
DC	16								

SCHOOL DISTRICT SUPERINTENDENTS 11,544

State	#	State	#	State	#	State	#	State	#
MA	235	MD	48	KY	184	IL	619	ID	110
RI	33	VA	146	OH	547	MO	462	UT	56
NH	39	WV	62	IN	254	KS	273	AZ	107
ME	131	NC	109	MI	564	NE	373	NM	77
VT	59	SC	125	IA	426	LA	78	NV	20
CT	101	GA	188	WI	357	AR	410	CA	475
NJ	165	FL	80	MN	434	OK	546	HI	8
NY	485	AL	170	SD	195	TX	889	OR	136
PA	396	TN	136	ND	296	CO	182	WA	241
DE	42	MS	215	MT	153	WY	55	AK	42
DC	10								

STATE SCHOOL SUPERINTENDENTS   749
COUNTY SCHOOL SUPERINTENDENTS   1,442
MUNICIPAL SCHL SUPERINTENDENTS   9,116

2-YEAR COLLEGES................ 1,281
4-YEAR COLLEGES................ 1,885
COLLEGES FOR MEN.............. 61
COLLEGES FOR WOMEN 100
COLLEGES-CO-ED................ 3,010

COLLEGE PRESIDENTS 3,169

State	#	State	#	State	#	State	#	State	#
MA	112	MD	52	KY	52	IL	161	ID	11
RI	12	VA	69	OH	140	MO	86	UT	13
NH	26	WV	28	IN	71	KS	55	AZ	28
ME	34	NC	125	MI	95	NE	34	NM	20
VT	22	SC	58	IA	64	LA	31	NV	8
CT	52	GA	70	WI	76	AR	30	CA	272
NJ	61	FL	74	MN	70	OK	44	HI	13
NY	227	AL	58	SD	22	TX	156	OR	47
PA	204	TN	73	ND	14	CO	42	WA	47
DE	8	MS	46	MT	13	WY	8	AK	15
DC	22								

Figure 15.2 A typical educational market list.

If you want to sell expensive whole-life insurance policies to well-to-do business executives, you could get a list of *Fortune 500* company executives (Figure 15.3).

You can also mail to every household in any town, neighborhood, or county in the United States. You can select by income range, by sex, by private home or multiple-family dwelling, by ethnicity, or any combination of these. There are lists that will let you mail to all the households you desire.

■ *KEY POINT: Some lists permit you to target as many or as few households as you want.*

BIG COMPANY EXECS.

EXECUTIVES OF FIRMS WITH SALES
OF $1,000,000 AND OVER

CHAIRMEN	22,328
SENIOR VICE-PRESIDENTS	17,490
EXECUTIVE VICE-PRESIDENTS	16,140
MISC. VICE-PRESIDENTS	122,757
CORP. SECRETARIES	43,194
TREASURERS	40,521
CONTROLLERS/AUDITORS	19,003
LEGAL COUNSEL	2,336
PURCHASING DIRECTORS	7,452
PERSONNEL MANAGERS	2,246
ADVERTISING MANAGERS	3,360
MARKETING MANAGERS	4,967
SALES MANAGERS	12,138
INTERNATIONAL MGMT EXECS	1,230
R&D/TECHNICAL MGMT EXECS	3,611
SUPTS./SUPERVISORS/PLANT MANAGEMENT EXECS	5,537

PRESIDENTS OF COMPANIES WITH SALES
OF $1,000,000 AND OVER   78,318

MA	2017	MD	1023	KY	1231	IL	5320	ID	391
RI	329	VA	1545	OH	3901	MO	2161	UT	668
NH	317	WV	684	IN	2192	KS	1484	AZ	569
ME	311	NC	1873	MI	2960	NE	1015	NM	389
VT	162	SC	904	IA	1726	LA	1382	NV	181
CT	1130	GA	1619	WI	2170	AR	894	CA	5822
NJ	2115	FL	2635	MN	2167	OK	1622	HI	266
NY	5065	AL	1078	SD	447	TX	5690	OR	836
PA	3718	TN	1526	ND	516	CO	1197	WA	1115
DE	163	MS	750	MT	431	WY	223	AK	116
DC	272								

FIRMS WITH SALES $1,000,000 TO $10,000,000	41,382
FIRMS WITH SALES $10 MILLION TO $25 MILLION	13,488
FIRMS WITH SALES $25 MILLION TO $75 MILLION	11,726
FIRMS WITH SALES $75 MILLION TO $200 MILLION	4,937
FIRMS WITH SALES $200 MILLION TO $500 MILLION	2,793
FIRMS WITH SALES $500 MILLION TO $ ONE BILLION	2,894
FIRMS WITH SALES ONE BILLION AND OVER	1,088

FORTUNE COMPANY EXECS-SEE
BELOW

PRESIDENTS	2,206
RESEARCH	640
SECRETARY	2,070
TREASURER	1,971
SENIOR VICE PRESIDENT	2,705
EXECUTIVE VICE PRESIDENT	1,744

Figure 15.3   This big-company executive list is typical of well-heeled business types.

Suppose you want to market a product to new home owners. You can rent a list, compiled on a regular basis, that identifies middle- and upper-class home owners throughout the United States from public records. You can even identify home owners who qualify for certain levels of mortgages.

Also new home owners are excellent prospects for a wide range of consumer offers.

■ *KEY POINT:* *New home owners are often good prospects for a variety of offers.*

You may wish to mail to certain age groups. Some lists have hundreds of thousands of names by exact age in all 50 states. These lists permit a degree of penetration into market areas that was impossible before the computer.

■ *KEY POINT:* *Many consumer lists categorize people by age.*

Most products and services need to be targeted to narrow prospect groups. For example, because attorneys and pilots have high disposable incomes, they are often good prospects for expensive consumer products (Figures 15.4 and 15.5).

■ *KEY POINT:* *Product mailings are often targeted to high-income groups.*

Or you may wish to target investors. Most list brokers maintain substantial and detailed lists of affluent Americans.

■ *KEY POINT:* *Investors are often sent many offers.*

Here are three typical investor lists:

American Investors Association. 338,000 members and inquirers. These individuals are involved in all kinds of financial investments. Median income is $38,500. Minimum net worth is $500,000.

Investors Exchange. 5,756,480 names compiled from 38 separate investor mail-order files. Income is $42,000 plus. Minimum net worth is $500,000.

ATTORNEYS IN PRIVATE PRACTICE-MASTER FILE 238,781

MA	6018	MD	4241	KY	3315	IL	10661	ID	909
RI	929	VA	4533	OH	11343	MO	5248	UT	1416
NH	877	WV	1200	IN	4351	KS	2367	AZ	3088
ME	1122	NC	4112	MI	7344	NE	1334	NM	1364
VT	279	SC	2188	IA	2184	LA	5423	NV	997
CT	4322	GA	5890	WI	5259	AR	1449	CA	32998
NJ	8263	FL	12986	MN	4430	OK	3399	HI	822
NY	18320	AL	2432	SD	609	TX	13653	OR	3241
PA	10601	TN	3940	ND	359	CO	4564	WA	3865
DE	542	MS	2255	MT	884	WY	480	AK	710
DC	5613								

SR PARTNERS-LEADING LAW FIRMS 29,809

MA	557	MD	474	KY	499	IL	1154	ID	133
RI	111	VA	774	OH	1179	MO	675	UT	137
NH	118	WV	219	IN	599	KS	400	AZ	364
ME	154	NC	860	MI	818	NE	280	NM	182
VT	104	SC	367	IA	414	LA	599	NV	149
CT	543	GA	702	WI	422	AR	309	CA	3015
NJ	1016	FL	1751	MN	483	OK	645	HI	73
NY	2282	AL	428	SD	114	TX	1873	OR	351
PA	1140	TN	579	ND	83	CO	625	WA	469
DE	71	MS	357	MT	122	WY	105	AK	82
DC	797								

LAW FIRMS-TO 5 PARTNERS....... 21,737
LAW FIRMS-6-10 PARTNERS 5,065
LAW FIRMS-11-20 PARTNERS 1,473
LAW FIRMS-21 PLUS PARTNERS.... 1,220

CORPORATE COUNSEL-MASTER FILE 39,674

MA	1110	MD	487	KY	506	IL	3056	ID	102
RI	95	VA	581	OH	2080	MO	1118	UT	139
NH	136	WV	242	IN	720	KS	483	AZ	231
ME	97	NC	624	MI	1449	NE	376	NM	89
VT	39	SC	207	IA	490	LA	475	NV	63
CT	1477	GA	685	WI	809	AR	258	CA	3388
NJ	1529	FL	836	MN	1078	OK	589	HI	80
NY	4941	AL	385	SD	73	TX	3138	OR	255
PA	2118	TN	576	ND	89	CO	599	WA	423
DE	274	MS	199	MT	105	WY	162	AK	42
DC	555								

CRIMINAL JUSTICE/DEFENSE LAWYERS.................. 18,913
GOVERNMENT CONTRACT LAWYERS 1,860
GOVERNMENT RELATIONS LAWYERS 1,006

ATTORNEYS-HOME ADDRESS 59,473

MA	1594	MD	42	KY	1599	IL	1313	ID	322
RI	503	VA	1931	OH	2982	MO	908	UT	
NH	100	WV	487	IN	1676	KS	910	AZ	548
ME	1	NC	1036	MI	2409	NE	494	NM	620
VT	1	SC	782	IA	973	LA	2703	NV	15
CT	1	GA	1171	WI	1419	AR	578	CA	4764
NJ	576	FL	3525	MN	2478	OK	800	HI	290
NY	1983	AL	1186	SD	147	TX	6235	OR	903
PA	1145	TN	899	ND	239	CO	2021	WA	2275
DE	97	MS	772	MT	300	WY	170	AK	217
DC	1								

INSURANCE/NEGLIGENCE LAWYERS 14,686
INTERNATIONAL LAWYERS 893
LABOR REL/ARBITRATION LAWYERS 2,416
PERSONNEL LABOR LAWYERS 1,391

LEGAL FIRMS & PRIVATE LAW OFFICES 125,484

MA	3985	MD	2298	KY	1649	IL	6386	ID	484
RI	439	VA	2556	OH	5333	MO	2061	UT	532
NH	424	WV	678	IN	2100	KS	1211	AZ	1559
ME	578	NC	2123	MI	3753	NE	667	NM	627
VT	206	SC	1160	IA	1158	LA	2412	NV	475
CT	2076	GA	2924	WI	2281	AR	883	CA	16932
NJ	4761	FL	6082	MN	1853	OK	1754	HI	407
NY	13154	AL	1287	SD	303	TX	7711	OR	1285
PA	5681	TN	1961	ND	232	CO	1943	WA	1540
DE	226	MS	1276	MT	460	WY	279	AK	324
DC	2964								

MARITIME LAWYERS 1,125
PATENT ATTORNEYS............. 2,270
ATTYS IN PRESTIGIOUS POSITIONS 4,750

ATTYS-PTNRS LEADING LAW FIRMS 65,148

PR	110	DC	2053	KY	978	IL	3004	ID	305
MA	1325	MD	1085	OH	2731	MO	1504	UT	319
RI	271	VA	1521	IN	1456	KS	905	AZ	687
NH	283	WV	387	MI	2095	NE	678	NM	312
ME	357	NC	1794	IA	1109	LA	1253	NV	291
VT	186	SC	759	WI	1101	AR	534	CA	5891
CT	1233	GA	1589	MN	1287	OK	1146	HI	217
NJ	2045	FL	3501	SD	252	TX	3513	OR	780
NY	5341	AL	905	ND	197	CO	1149	WA	1200
PA	2731	TN	1306	MT	287	WY	185	AK	158
DE	145	MS	697							

REAL ESTATE LAWYERS 18,026

MA	393	MD	328	KY	290	IL	650	ID	84
RI	62	VA	510	OH	759	MO	375	UT	79
NH	86	WV	157	IN	324	KS	246	AZ	199
ME	114	NC	636	MI	487	NE	177	NM	121
VT	91	SC	260	IA	207	LA	359	NV	92
CT	421	GA	447	WI	258	AR	207	CA	1384
NJ	820	FL	1151	MN	278	OK	426	HI	48
NY	1421	AL	296	SD	66	TX	1002	OR	189
PA	721	TN	322	ND	59	CO	437	WA	289
DE	42	MS	243	MT	78	WY	61	AK	32
DC	122								

SECURITIES & FINANCIAL LAWYERS 2,209
TAX LAWYERS 6,918
TRADEMARK LAWYERS........... 1,208

TRIAL & CRIMINAL LAWYERS 35,337

MA	799	MD	584	KY	493	IL	1746	ID	226
RI	176	VA	828	OH	1531	MO	799	UT	180
NH	234	WV	279	IN	781	KS	415	AZ	622
ME	236	NC	562	MI	2405	NE	303	NM	1
VT	105	SC	458	IA	469	LA	975	NV	420
CT	711	GA	975	WI	570	AR	350	CA	2438
NJ	677	FL	2597	MN	689	OK	430	HI	266
NY	1317	AL	668	SD	178	TX	1747	OR	420
PA	1480	TN	673	ND	126	CO	659	WA	815
DE	124	MS	680	MT	224	WY	124	AK	210
DC	431								

TRUST/ESTATE/PROBATE LAWYERS 19,674

Figure 15.4 Typical collection of lists available from brokers on a rental basis.

AVIATION INDUSTRY EXECUTIVES ..	26,559
MAJOR AIRCRAFT MFG EXECUTIVES	3,482
AIR COMPONENT MFG EXECUTIVES	6,763
HELICOPTER MFG EXECUTIVES	161
AIRCRAFT LEASE/FINAN/SALES EXECS	405
AIR DISTRIB&SUPPLY EXECS	2,095
AIR MAINT/OVERHAUL/MODIF EXECS	1,670
AIR TAXI&COMMERCIAL OPER EXECS	3,683
US TERMINAL AIRPORT EXECS.....	676
US NON-TERMINAL AIRPORT EXECS	1,506
AIR COMMUTER&MAIL EXECUTIVES	475
U.S. AIR TRANSPORT EXECS.......	1,726
FOREIGN AIR CARRIER EXECS	811
AIR FREIGHT FORWARDER EXECS ..	533
AIR CONSULTANTS&SPECIAL SVCES	1,150

PILOTS-MASTER FILE **563,073**

MA	8402	MD	6247	KY	4153	IL	23288	ID	4107
RI	1144	VA	11433	OH	19383	MO	11057	UT	4212
NH	3155	WV	2024	IN	10140	KS	10332	AZ	11404
ME	2614	NC	9478	MI	16546	NE	5751	NM	4681
VT	1156	SC	4897	IA	8324	LA	8026	NV	4549
CT	6919	GA	12823	WI	9928	AR	4919	CA	95209
NJ	11278	FL	35118	MN	13462	OK	10802	HI	3594
NY	20132	AL	7534	SD	2545	TX	44332	OR	9979
PA	14903	TN	8523	ND	2809	CO	13271	WA	17931
DE	1363	MS	4280	MT	3892	WY	2147	AK	7691
DC	1186								

PILOTS-AIR TRANSPORT **66,553**

MA	924	MD	595	KY	297	IL	2784	ID	302
RI	108	VA	1458	OH	1540	MO	1341	UT	371
NH	760	WV	195	IN	647	KS	807	AZ	1237
ME	205	NC	969	MI	1218	NE	252	NM	350
VT	105	SC	471	IA	340	LA	922	NV	908
CT	1710	GA	2799	WI	755	AR	384	CA	10603
NJ	1898	FL	5759	MN	1439	OK	838	HI	654
NY	1948	AL	482	SD	91	TX	7660	OR	545
PA	1787	TN	1269	ND	84	CO	2385	WA	2533
DE	194	MS	311	MT	218	WY	146	AK	846
DC	109								

PILOTS-COMMERCIAL **170,238**

MA	2276	MD	1932	KY	1308	IL	6085	ID	1232
RI	340	VA	4564	OH	5312	MO	3154	UT	1253
NH	960	WV	584	IN	2692	KS	2844	AZ	3662
ME	848	NC	3000	MI	4095	NE	1609	NM	1549
VT	358	SC	1716	IA	1975	LA	3215	NV	1315
CT	1923	GA	4201	WI	2418	AR	1776	CA	27479
NJ	3209	FL	11739	MN	3474	OK	3276	HI	1404
NY	5865	AL	3074	SD	758	TX	14556	OR	2737
PA	4205	TN	2627	ND	941	CO	4026	WA	5783
DE	390	MS	1743	MT	1087	WY	625	AK	2604
DC	440								

PILOTS-PRIVATE **302,550**

MA	5037	MD	3590	KY	2421	IL	13971	ID	2494
RI	664	VA	4995	OH	12178	MO	6355	UT	2461
NH	1313	WV	1176	IN	6542	KS	6505	AZ	6234
ME	1486	NC	5148	MI	10916	NE	3802	NM	2611

Figure 15.5 Pilots often have above-average incomes.

Proven Investors. This list comprises 407,000 names, selectable by income and amount invested. 285,000 persons have an income in excess of $65,000 per year.

As you can see, the right list lets you reach almost every potential customer for your product or service. You can mail to upper-income people in the Minneapolis suburbs or apartment dwellers in Phoenix, to the well-heeled in Baltimore, or to female heads of households anywhere.

USE THE STATE PERCENT CHART SELECTOR

In cases where no state count is given for a particular category in a list, you can use the "State Percent Chart Selector (Figure 15.6).

The first number on this chart gives the zip code range for each state. The second number is a percentage of the total for the country for population, manufacturing, and sales in the state.

To use the Selector Chart, simply multiply the total quantity of names on any list and divide this number by 100. You will then have an estimate of the number of names available in any state you wish to target.

GET LISTS BY EITHER RENTAL OR EXCHANGE

We can get the lists of others in two ways. The first and most common is to rent them from a list broker or from a company that makes its list available to other companies.

■ *KEY POINT: Most lists are rented from list brokers.*

List brokering is a very competitive field. Most brokers have selections of many lists and must update names, addresses, and counts continually to stay competitive.

■ *KEY POINT: List brokers can provide many valuable services.*

State Percentages

	State	Zip Code Ranges	Population	Manufacturing	Retail Sales
PR	Puerto Rico	000-009	.01	.01	.01
VI	Virgin Islands		.01	.01	.01
MA	Massachusetts	010-027	2.77	3.60	2.70
RI	Rhode Island	028-029	.47	.81	.45
NH	New Hampshire	030-038	.35	.40	.36
ME	Maine	039-049	.48	.45	.45
VT	Vermont	050-059	.22	.22	.22
CT	Connecticut	060-069	1.49	1.86	1.59
NJ	New Jersey	070-089	3.54	4.63	3.57
NY	New York	100-149	8.91	12.24	8.12
PA	Pennsylvania	150-196	5.74	6.08	5.20
DE	Delaware	197-199	.27	.16	.32
DC	Dis. of Col.	200-203	.37	.18	.56
MD	Maryland	206-219	1.93	1.17	1.95
VA	Virginia	220-246	2.28	1.26	2.19
WV	West Virginia	247-268	.84	.48	.70
NC	North Carolina	270-289	2.50	2.34	2.24
SC	South Carolina	290-299	1.28	.93	1.06
GA	Georgia	300-319	2.27	1.19	2.20
FL	Florida	320-339	3.40	3.01	4.47
AL	Alabama	350-369	1.69	1.25	1.33
TN	Tennessee	370-385	1.94	1.61	1.90
MS	Mississippi	386-397	1.10	.77	.82
KY	Kentucky	400-427	1.58	.97	1.35
OH	Ohio	430-458	5.23	5.19	5.14
IN	Indiana	460-479	2.55	2.30	2.65
MI	Michigan	480-499	4.38	4.61	4.47
IA	Iowa	500-528	1.38	1.15	1.65
WI	Wisconsin	530-549	2.15	2.38	2.14
MN	Minnesota	550-567	1.86	1.84	1.84
SD	South Dakota	570-577	.32	.21	.31
ND	North Dakota	580-588	.30	.16	.31
MT	Montana	590-599	.34	.26	.35
IL	Illinois	600-629	5.45	6.33	5.72
MO	Missouri	630-658	2.31	2.11	2.41
KS	Kansas	660-679	1.11	1.03	1.23
NE	Nebraska	680-693	.73	.81	.76
LA	Louisana	700-714	1.80	1.11	1.42
AR	Arkansas	716-729	.95	.80	.84
OK	Oklahoma	730-749	1.26	1.10	1.16
TX	Texas	750-799	5.56	5.12	5.73
CO	Colorado	800-816	1.10	.98	1.29
WY	Wyoming	820-831	.10	.12	.15
ID	Idaho	833-838	.35	.31	.42
UT	Utah	840-847	.52	.47	.51
AZ	Arizona	850-864	.88	.64	.99
NM	New Mexico	870-884	.50	.28	.51
NV	Nevada	890-898	.24	.14	.33
CA	California	900-961	9.87	11.24	10.33
HI	Hawaii	967-968	.39	.29	.36
OR	Oregon	970-979	1.04	1.30	1.17
WA	Washington	980-994	1.68	1.50	1.76
AK	Alaska	995-999	.15	.09	1.13

Figure 15.6 State percent chart selector.

However, list brokers make their money on the basis of how many names you order from them: the more names, the more money. Therefore you must temper their advice with your own judgment, because they may overestimate how many names you need to buy.

■ *CAUTION NOTE: Beware of being oversold names by list brokers.*

Also list brokers cannot be experts in every field. Their primary interest is in selling you the names they have available. If you are doubtful about a broker's recommendations, seek independent advice.

■ *CAUTION NOTE: List brokers are not experts, and you must often seek independent advice.*

You can also get lists by renting them from competing organizations or companies. The practice of renting lists to competing businesses is becoming more common. Most companies will not rent their lists to firms that are selling the same product or service, but some have found that their own response rate goes up when their customers receive solicitations from similar but noncompeting products.

■ *KEY POINT: Sometimes you can rent a list from a competing company.*

A third way to obtain prospect lists is by exchanging lists with other competing or noncompeting companies.

■ *KEY POINT: Consider exchanging prospect lists.*

You may not be able to get the customer list of your nearest competitor—after all, why would either of you want to exchange these privileged names and addresses?

■ *KEY POINT: With caution you might exchange your list with competitors.*

But companies that can work off of each other's products can obtain lucrative results. Suppose you are selling a personalized book plate. You might benefit from exchanging customer lists with a book-by-mail company. And it in turn might profit from your list. Since you are selling a complementary rather than a competing product, exchanging your lists is unlikely to decrease sales for either company.

■ *KEY POINT: Exchange of lists works well with companies selling related but different products.*

The exchanging of lists means saving the cost of rental.

Most owners of lists protect them from theft by "seeding" them with names and addresses of staff members or relatives. In this way unauthorized use can be detected.

■ *CAUTION NOTE: Rented or exchanged lists are protected against unauthorized use.*

Occasionally owners of lists will let you match your lists with theirs. This gives you more reliable information and increases the chances that your present mailing program will succeed.

■ *KEY POINT: Some list owners even let you update your existing lists.*

BASIC TESTING: 16
PREDICTING PROFITS

In this chapter we will learn the basic principles of testing: what is to test, what makes a valid test, what resources are available, and how to measure profit.

Much of this chapter on basic testing refers to acquiring new customers. In the next chapter we will further develop the testing principles learned here.

DIRECT MAIL RESULTS CAN BE MEASURED

One of the primary advantages of direct mail is that we can count its results. In fact, no other advertising medium can be quantified as precisely as direct mail.

When a solicitation goes out in the mail and a response comes back, we can judge the success of the campaign. Both the responders and the dollars can be counted.

■ *KEY POINT:* *In direct mail, responses can be counted.*

One of the worst things we can do in direct mail is to make decisions on hunches. Being able to count responders removes the temptation to rely on hunches.

■ *CAUTION NOTE:* *Never make decisions on hunches.*

Testing takes the gamble out of direct mail. We can use what works to plan future campaigns.

We measure the effectiveness of our mail by matching certain criteria,

317

such as the names we solicit or the sweeteners we offer to the number of responses we gain. This then lets us make the most profitable decisions.

HOW OFTEN DO WE TEST?

If you learn nothing else from this book, you should realize that every time you do a mailing you should test something. If you don't you've wasted an opportunity to learn something about the prospects who respond to your offer.

■ *KEY POINT:*   *Test every time you mail.*

Direct mail is unique among marketing methods in that we can learn something about our approach to prospects every time we mail. We are constantly refining our process, trying to learn something that will help · us make it better.

WHAT ARE SOME OF THE THINGS WE TEST?

One of the most important things we can test are lists themselves. By testing the lists we have rented or gotten by exchange from other companies, we learn which lists have the most prospects willing to respond to our offer.

■ *KEY POINT:*   *Test names on prospect lists.*

We can also test the offers we make to prospects. The offers include price, payment terms, sweeteners or no sweeteners, a discount or no discount, and facilitators, such as a set amount for shipping and handling charges.

■ *KEY POINT:*   *Tests of offers compare prices, terms, and sweeteners.*

Location or geography tests are common. Certain regions of the country respond better to certain offers. We can test the names in one state from one list, then the names from another state from another list. We also can add a test on price when we mail to different regions.

■ *KEY POINT:* *Location tests measure the responsivity of regions.*

One popular test is to measure responses to personalized mail versus form letters. Many mailers attempt to personalize their direct mail. Some computer programs or ink-spraying machines can produce solicitations that list a prospect's name several times within a letter. They can even repeat our address. This technique is more expensive, but tests have proved it works.

■ *KEY POINT:* *Personalized versus form letters is a common test.*

We can test copy length: three pages versus one page, for example. For a valid test of length, the copy must stay the same.

■ *KEY POINT:* *Test the best page length.*

Postage tests are easy to do. Here we might measure third-class bulk-rate mail against first-class presorted mail with a regular or a commemorative stamp. Nonprofit organizations are often surprised when they find a first-class stamp significantly improves response.

■ *KEY POINT:* *Testing can show if stamps or indicia work best.*

We can also test different versions of our package—fancy versus plain, two-color versus four-color, bond paper versus newsprint. One element is varied at a time so we know what really makes the difference.

■ *KEY POINT:* *Version testing measures the effectiveness of color and paper quality.*

We can also test various components of what we mail to prospects. This is called a package test. It means, for example, sending a brochure to one group while sending all the components to another group. We need not test letters here, though, because the letter is the most read piece in any direct mail package. Eliminating it in a test would be a waste of time.

■ *KEY POINT:*   *Package tests measure which components work best.*

We can also test miscellaneous features: over-sized order forms versus small order forms, fold-up order forms versus tear-off order forms, no. 9 envelopes versus no. 10 envelopes, 6-inch by 9-inch pointed flaps versus rounded flaps.

■ *KEY POINT:*   *Tests of order forms and envelopes yield valuable information.*

The important thing to remember about testing is that a valid test tries to find differences between single elements. Except for occasional tests like changing price in different geographic areas, we don't test items from the same general group. For example, we don't test one brochure against another brochure, one group of pictures against another group of pictures, or different versions of copy. We test major differences like two-color versus four-color, two significant differences in quality of paper, or a real stamp versus indicia.

■ *CAUTION NOTE:*   *Only test differences of major, single elements.*

We can split lists if we wish to test more than one thing at a time, but we never test more than one thing at a time on each part of the list.

HOW MANY RESPONSES MAKE A VALID TEST?

Before we do any mailing, we need to know how many pieces we must mail to get valid results. The answer depends a great deal on what we're testing and how big our market is. But there is a certain number of pieces that is practical to send out to gain the minimal number of responses we need to make an intelligent decision.

We must get at least 20 responses for a test to be valid.

■ *CAUTION NOTE:*   *Always mail to enough prospects to gain at least 20 responses.*

So if we sell a magazine subscription and most of your competitors boast a 2% return, we can tentatively assume 2% as our goal, with the provision that we build in a margin of one half of the anticipated rate.

■ *KEY POINT:* *Double the anticipated response rate to ensure minimal response.*

How does this work? Since we want at least 20 responses, what is the minimum number of pieces we must send out? Twenty responses is 2% of 1000 pieces, but to ensure that we get this amount (in case our response rate turns out to be only half our anticipated rate), we must send 2000 pieces.

The following chart shows how many mailing pieces we must send out, based on the percent response anticipated, for us to receive a minimum number of 20 responses.

Anticipated Response Percent	Number of Pieces to Mail Out
8.0	500
7.0	571
6.0	667
5.0	800
4.5	889
4.0	1,000
3.5	1,143
3.0	1,333
2.5	1,600
2.0	2,000
1.5	2,667
1.0	4,000
0.5	8,000
0.2	20,000
0.1	40,000

This chart helps us get response levels that are statistically significant.

As an example of how this formula works, consider this simple test of letter formats mailed to every other name on the same list. One letter is sent with a real stamp on the outside envelope. The other is sent with indicia on the envelope. Everything else about the solicitations is the same.

You feel from experience you can expect a 2.5% return. Now to ensure that you will get the minimum 20 responses back from each mailing you double the potential responses to 40. On the chart this calculation is done for you. 2.5% anticipated response means you should send out 1600 mailing pieces. If you are right about getting the 2.5% return you will get back 40 returns, but the purpose has been to ensure that you will have gotten back at least 20 in case you only get back half of what you expected.

Using this doubling technique twenty responses is 5% of 1600 pieces sent out. So you mail out 1600 pieces to guarantee 20 or more responses. This will give you a valid test on which to gauge which letter brings the best results.

BALANCING EXPECTATIONS AND RESOURCES

In direct mail, testing means more than determining the minimum number of solicitations needed to make a valid test. To fully solicit the entire universe of prospects and to get maximum yield from the mailing, we need to take into account the money we want to make from our solicitation and the number of names we have to solicit.

■ *KEY POINT: Testing shows us how many names must be solicited to yield a profit.*

We also need to know our financial break-even point. We need to know whether spending another 10¢ on each piece will gain us a higher yield of orders from prospects. Testing gives us some of the answers.

■ *KEY POINT: Testing shows us how much money to spend.*

In a sense, testing tries to give us a formula for balancing *goals* and *resources*. In our mailing we want to balance what we have the least of—resources (money)—against what we're trying to achieve—goals (sales).

■ *KEY POINT: Testing balances expectations and resources.*

Goals can include dollars, sales leads, product inquiries, applications—the specific things we are trying to get from your mailing.

Resources include the money it costs to do the mailing, prospect names, sales and staff time, and the product or service we offer.

THE MOST IMPORTANT RESOURCES ARE MONEY AND PROSPECT NAMES

Money is an essential but finite resource in direct mail. It is used for the initial mailing, and the money made from that mailing is reinvested in succeeding campaigns.

■ *CAUTION NOTE:*   **Money is a finite resource.**

We only spend a certain amount for the first campaign and hope to get back orders and dollars we can reinvest in other mailings. When do we reach the break-even point? Testing can tell us.

■ *KEY POINT:*   **Testing shows when to reinvest.**

Another important resource is the list of names, also a finite resource. As we saw in the last chapter, lists are the key part to direct mail success. We must target the right prospects and know how many there are. But we must realize there is always a limit on the number of prospects interested in our product or service.

■ *CAUTION NOTE:*   **Prospect names can often be a scarce resource.**

You probably know the market for your product. You may sell in a fixed geographic area, for example, cleaning products for local homes. Or maybe you sell an inventory system especially designed for the nation's 11,232 motorcycle dealers. But you assume, naively, that the world is your market.

However, the truth is that there is a limited number of customers for any product or service. Demand is finite.

■ *CAUTION NOTE:*   **A limited number of prospects exists for any product.**

TIME AND THE PRODUCT ARE ALSO NEEDED RESOURCES

Time is another resource. How much time do our office and sales employees have? Do they have the time it takes to get a mailing operation started, write copy, get it produced, check inventory, and fill orders? We must put time limits on what we can accomplish.

■ *CAUTION NOTE: Sales and staff times are limited resources.*

If we are generating leads, the time our sales force needs to follow them up must be taken into account. Salespeople aren't always efficient in following up on leads, particularly if leads are numerous. They tend to wait longer than they should to call prospects. So we don't want to generate more leads than our sales force can follow up within a reasonable length of time. We don't want the largest possible number of responses if our sales force can't follow up all of them. We want only enough leads that we can follow up in a short time.

■ *CAUTION NOTE: Generate no more sales leads than can be followed up in a short time.*

Our last major resource is how much product or service we have available. The last thing we want to do in direct mail is to take a long time to fill an order. The law says we must mail out orders within 30 days or suffer the embarrassment of offering prospects their money back. So we want to have what we're selling in stock. We don't want to generate more responses than we can fill in a reasonable time.

■ *CAUTION NOTE: Always have enough products in stock to fill orders quickly.*

Example of Balancing Expectations and Resources

Perhaps the biggest danger in selling by direct mail (also true for other kinds of selling) is spending more resources than we can expect to get back from customers. Let's translate the concept of balancing expectations with resources into an actual example.

■ *CAUTION NOTE: Never spend more money for direct mail than the value of the customer relationship.*

The test that follows compares two letter mailings. A is a form letter mailed with an imprinted indicia on the outside envelope. B is a personalized letter sent with a real stamp. Both mailings contain the same

	Letter "A" (Form/Indicia)	Letter "B" (Personal/Stamp)
Cost/1000 pieces		
List rental	$ 35.00	$ 35.00
Production	190.00	240.00
Postage	90.00	200.00
Folding, inserting	60.00	60.00
Total	$375.00	$535.00
Responses/1000 pieces	20	25
Response rate	2.0%	2.5%
Cost/response	$18.75	$21.40
Average order size	$80.00	$80.00
Cost of product as percent of price	35.0%	35.0%
Overhead as percent of price	15.0%	15.0%
Percent remaining for reinvestment and profit (RRP)	50.0%	50.0%
RRP order	$40.00	$40.00
Profit/order	$21.25	$18.60
Profit/1000 names solicited	$425.00	$465.00
Profit/total (budget) dollars expended	1.13 ($425/$375)	$0.87 ($465/$535)

copy, brochure, and response device. Each is mailed at the same time to every other name on a prospect list.

The offer is made by a nonrelationship marketer for a single product without any expectation that other products will be offered in the future. All the profit will come from this one-time sale.

The list rental costs were the same for mailing A (form indicia letter) and B (personalized stamped letter). The production costs differed because a costlier computerized typing machine typed each personalized letter individually. The extra labor of stamping each envelope was also taken into account. The postage costs were naturally much higher for the stamped letters. Folding and inserting costs were the same for each.

The cost per thousand on the form letter was $375, on the personalized letter $535. The number of responses to mailing A was 20, yielding a 2.0% response rate. Mailing B brought in 25 sales, for a response rate of 2.5%.

At first glance it looks as if the higher response rate for the personalized letter shows it to be a better mailing piece.

But now we relate the total cost per thousand to the number of responses to each mailing. In mailing A we see that each of the 20 responses has cost $8.75 ($375/20). In mailing B each of the 25 responses has cost $21.40 ($535/25).

Now it appears that the personalized letter costs us more money per response than the form letter does.

Each buyer ordered $80 worth of products. The company's cost for each product is 35% of the retail price. Overhead for salaries, rent, and other is another 15%. So at this point, 50% of the revenue is going to pay the costs, leaving the remaining 50% for profit and reinvestment into future mailings. Another way of looking at this figure is, any amount we spend to sell cuts into our profit.

The company received $40.00 above costs for each order in both the A and B mailings. It can either pocket that money or use it to sell more product.

When we subtract the cost of what it took to get each order from this $40.00, we get $21.25 ($40.00 − $21.40) for mailing B. These amounts, then, are the profit for each order.

We now see that the cost per response is lower and the profit per order is higher for the form letter. However, if we relate the profit to number of responses, we get a different picture. In mailing A, the total profit on the 20 responses was $21.25 × 20 or $425.00; in mailing B, 25 responses × $18.60 each earned $465. Mailing B, then, is better when we look at the profits per each 1000 names solicited.

So if we had chosen the cost-per-response ratio of mailing A, we would have been wrong.

To clarify, in mailing A we get $1.13 in profit for every $1.00 we spend; in mailing B we get only $0.87 for every dollar we spend. In mailing B, however, the personalized stamped letter has given a higher response rate. Therefore we get more profit from our preliminary test.

This test is incomplete. It does not tell us which piece will bring us more profits if our resources are limited.

INTERPRETING TEST RESULTS WHEN DOLLARS ARE LIMITED

All marketers have limited resources. We must define our limits before we can ask ourselves which one of the two mailing pieces just described we should use.

Let's look at two different "real-life" scenarios using the preliminary test results. In the first example, we have budgeted a set amount and therefore money is a scarce resource.

Scenario 1: Budget Dollars Are Least Available Resource

Available prospect names	100,000	100,000
Budgeted amount	$8,000	$8,000
Largest possible mailing with current budget	$8,000/$375 × 1,000 = 21,333	$8,000/$535 × 1000 = 14,953
Actual mailing	21,000	15,000
Gross Profit	21,000 × $425/ 1,000 = $8,925	15,000 × $465/ 1,000 = $6,975

In this first scenario, money is the least available resource. Company management has decided that profits from the mailing will not be reinvested in further mailings because there is only one opportunity this season to solicit prospects. Only $8,000 is budgeted for this one-time offer. There are 100,000 prospect names, but only $8,000 is available for solicitation.

For form letter mailing A, on the basis of test results we know that for each $8,000 we can solicit 21,333 ($8000 divided by $375 cost per thousand), or 21,000 prospects, rounded off. Since our scarcest resource is money, we cannot reach our full universe of 100,000 names.

In mailing B, our $8000 will reach fewer names, only 14,953 ($8000 divided by $535 cost per thousand) or about 15,000, because it costs us more to solicit each prospect.

Which mailing, A or B, will make us more money? If we multiply the 21,000 prospects we actually mail to in mailing A times our dollar profit per thousand of $425, we will make $8925 gross profit for our original $8000 investment.

In mailing B, if we multiply our dollar profit per thousand of $465 by 15, we find we will make a gross profit of $6975—$1950 less than the profit from mailing A!

What have we found? On the basis of our test results, we can predict exactly how much money we will get back from the form-letter and the personalized letter mailing. If budget dollars are our least available resource, mailing A is the one to choose.

INTERPRETING TEST RESULTS WHEN PROSPECT NAMES ARE SCARCE

Let's now look at another possible mailing in which budget dollars are not a consideration. We can keep reinvesting our marketing money to reach available prospects. We don't have a product that is sold seasonally. In this new scenario, however, prospects are a finite group; they are our least available resource.

In scenario 2 (on the following page) we have as much money as we need to reach prospects, as much as $55,000 to mail to our entire prospect universe of 100,000 names. If we had more names we could mail to them also. But in this example, prospect names are our scarcest resource.

In mailing A, $55,000 divided by our $375.00 cost per thousand pieces can reach 146,670, or more prospects than we have available. In mailing B, $55,000 divided by our $535.00 cost per thousand pieces reaches

Scenario 2: Prospect Names Are Least Available Resource

Available prospect names	100,000	100,000
Budgeted amount	$55,000	$55,000
Largest possible mailing with increased budget	$55,000/$375× 1,000 = 146,670	$55,000/$535× 1,000 = 102,810
Actual mailing	100,000	100,000
Gross Profit	100,000 × $425/ 1,000 = $42,500	100,000 × $465/ 1,000 = $46,500

somewhat fewer prospects, but at 102,810 these are also more than the number of names we have available.

Thus in both cases we can mail to all 100,000 names. The only difference is that we get a different response rate and different profit for each mailing.

For the form letter used in mailing A, we get $42,500 (100,000 × $425 profit per thousand) gross profit. And for the personalized letter used in mailing B, we get $46,500 (100,000 × $465 profit per thousand) gross profit—$4000 more! Why? Because we got more responses for mailing B, which allowed us a higher overall profit for each thousand prospects solicited.

What does this mean to us? In this scenario, in which we can keep our money reinvested in gaining new buyers, mailing B is the overwhelming winner. In other words, when names are our least available resource, the more expensive mailing—personalized letters with real stamps on the envelopes—will produce more profit.

In retrospect, if we had used "cost per response" or "response rate" we would have been wrong.

■ *CAUTION NOTE:* *"Cost per response" and "response rate" are often inaccurate indicators.*

What we have learned is that if we test, we can predict what profits we will get back from our mailings.

■ *KEY POINT:* *Testing lets us predict what our profits can be.*

TESTING SHOWS HOW MUCH TO SPEND TO GET BUYERS

In this chapter we will see how to use test results to determine how much money we can spend to solicit prospects and still make a profit.

TESTING MEASURES THE LEVEL OF PREEXISTING INTEREST

We said in Chapter 1 that prospects must already have a need for our product or service before they will act on our offer. Testing lets us measure that level of preexisting interest, or demand.

■ *KEY POINT:* **Testing measures preexisting interest.**

Imagine a hypothetical group of prospects we have never solicited before. We offer them a new product. Some of them order enthusiastically because they are already interested in it. Perhaps they've heard about it before and have just been waiting for a chance to own it.

■ *KEY POINT:* **Some buyers anticipate the product.**

These ready buyers are the easiest people to get responses from because they have the highest level of preexisting interest. We don't need to bribe them with sweeteners. They don't need a fancy four-color mailing package to stimulate their interest. They would probably order if our sales message were printed on brown wrapping paper, because our offer hits them just right.

FINDING OUT WHAT EACH BUYER COSTS

To learn what preexisting interest means in terms of what each buyer costs us, let's look back at the example in the previous chapter.

We had two letter mailings: Letter A was a form letter with indicia on the envelope and letter B was a "personalized" letter with a standard postage stamp. Each mailing went to 1000 prospects, every other name on the same list. All other details of the mailings were the same.

Mailing A cost $375 to send out, mailing B $535. Responses numbered 20 from mailing A and 25 from mailing B. Dividing the number of responses to each mailing into the production costs, we found the cost per response was $18.75 in mailing A and $21.40 in mailing B.

Summary

	Mailing A	Mailing B
Cost/1000 pieces	$375.00	535.00
Responses/1000 pieces	20.0	25.0
Cost/response	$18.75	$21.40
Dollars remaining for reinvestment and profit (after overhead and production cost)	$40.00	$40.00

These are average costs, however, not the cost for gaining each response.

As we know, some buyers are easier to gain than others, because they will buy without much encouragement. The average cost of gaining all 20 responses in mailing A was $18.75. But those buyers who already had some preexisting interest for our product didn't cost as much as the average. They cost somewhat less, perhaps $12, $14, or $16 each.

■ *CAUTION NOTE:* **The preliminary test only shows the average buyer cost.**

Conversely, some buyers cost us more than the average—$20, $22, or $24 each.

We may not know exact figures, but we know some buyers cost less than the average and some cost more.

THE COST OF BUYERS IS PROPORTIONAL TO THE EXTENT OF THEIR INTEREST

The amount any buyer costs us is directly proportional to the degree of preexisting interest he or she has.

■ *KEY POINT: The cost of buyers is proportional to the amount of preexisting interest they have.*

What this means is, the more money we spend the more we increase our ability to gain responses. If we use sweeteners, extra color, personalized letters, and real stamps, we get more readers and more responses. This makes sense, but there's a catch. We are also paying more for each response.

■ *CAUTION NOTE: Each additional buyer costs more.*

■ *KEY POINT: Some buyers need little encouragement to act.*

We know much of this through common sense. But testing tells us with far more certainty exactly what our buyers cost. For example, in mailing B we paid $21.40 for each order. We also got five more orders in mailing B than in mailing A. Does that mean we paid $21.40 for each of those additional orders? Of course not. If we look at our overall cost difference, we see we paid $375 in mailing A and $535 in mailing B. The difference is $160. We paid $160 for five additional buyers. Therefore each one of those five cost us an average of $32 each, not $21.40. Finding out this difference was the reason we tested.

■ *KEY POINT: Testing gives an approximation of what each buyer costs.*

Now we can get a much better idea of what our buyers cost. The cost for each of the additional five buyers we got in mailing B was approximately $28, $30, $32, $34, and $36. This is the extra $160 we spend for a personalized letter with a stamp on the envelope to obtain five more buyers. It got these extra five marginally interested prospects to pay more attention to our mailing piece and converted them.

■ *KEY POINT: Testing shows you what you spent to gain marginally interested buyers.*

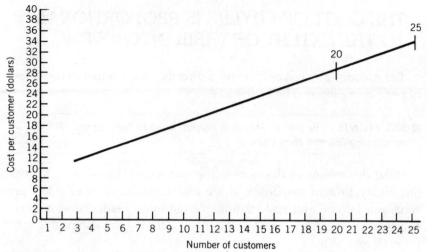

Figure 17.1 Test mailing buyer cost comparison. The difference between 20 and 25 permits us to plot our approximate cost per customer.

We can plot the approximate cost of our additional buyers on a chart (Figure 17.1) As we can see, some didn't need the enticement of a personalized letter and probably would have bought if the offer had been written on a napkin.

HOW MUCH MORE CAN WE SPEND TO GET A NEW BUYER?

Let's look at another consideration. How much more should we spend to get a new buyer? If we had to pay $38 to get one additional buyer, would it be worth it? Yes, because our profit after we pay for the manufacture of our product and our overhead is $40. We have this $40 to reinvest in additional mailings and profit.

In other words, we sell our product for $80 and after product and overhead costs we have $40 to use to gain buyers. We can spend up to $40 to gain buyers profitably (Figure 17.2). And since in our example the company is selling a product to a one-time buyer, we can disregard the possibility of future business.

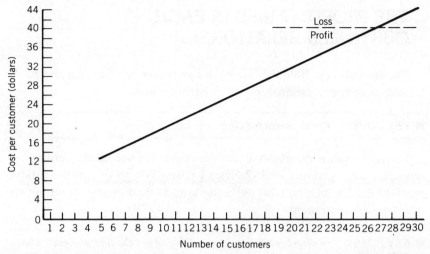

Figure 17.2 Test mailing buyer cost comparison. Customers can cost more than the amount of dollars remaining for reinvestment and profit.

■ *KEY POINT: You can profitably spend on direct mail up to the margin for reinvestment and profit.*

So if another buyer cost us $38, we would still make a $2 profit on the sale. We are spending more money to get this buyer. He or she has cost us more than any of the others.

■ *CAUTION NOTE: The last buyer costs the most.*

When do we stop spending money to get another buyer? When we reach the $40. If we wish to retain customers for a long period, however, as we will see in the next chapter, we may have to spend more than we make to get them initially. But for a one-time sale, we cannot spend more money soliciting additional buyers than we make. We can spend up to the amount remaining for reinvestment and profit.

■ *CAUTION NOTE: In nonrelationship marketing, you cannot spend more than your margin for profit.*

THE PROFIT VARIES IN EACH CUSTOMER RELATIONSHIP

These examples show that we have a varying degree of cost and profit in each customer relationship and in each response.

■ *KEY POINT: Profit varies for each buyer.*

For us to solicit profitably every prospect, we use all the money we have left after product and overhead costs. We go on until we have reach of the last person who needs bells and whistles and on whom we don't make any money.

■ *KEY POINT: In direct mail, you keep selling to get the last prospect who will give you a profit.*

Do we learn precisely who this person is by evaluating our test results? No. But we do know the direction we should go to solicit our full range of prospects. For example, in neither our A or B test mailings did we solicit our entire prospect universe. Our additional cost per response was in the $32 range, less than the $40 we have available. Therefore we did not take up all the potential demand we could and still make a profit.

■ *KEY POINT: Testing shows what you need to do to solicit all prospects.*

This amount remaining from the $40 means we can spend even more than we did in mailing B to get buyers. We can add a sweetener or color to the brochure, or even an additional offer or extra page. The test, then, also shows us which direction we should take to fully reach all potential prospects on a profitable basis.

WHEN WE KNOW WE HAVE SPENT TOO MUCH

Here's another example using our A, B test results. Let's suppose that in mailing B it turned out that several of our buyers cost us $42, $44, and $46 each, each over our margin for reinvestment of $40. This would tell us we have obtained more buyers than we are profiting from. We have started giving away our product.

■ *CAUTION NOTE: Testing can tell you when to stop spending money.*

What do we do? We need an alternative to our form and personalized letters. We want to get mailing A up to a profitable full solicitation but without it costing us as much as mailing B. We might drop the first-class postage stamp, or not personalize the letter in mailing B. In short, we want to reach the limit of what we can do to solicit our full prospect universe profitably.

■ *KEY POINT: Testing shows the limit of profitable spending.*

What if both mailings cost us more than our $40 margin for reinvestment and profit, not in average costs but in terms of direction? Obviously we would spend less. We might send only a form letter, or drop the four-page brochure and substitute a single testimonial page.

NEVER SPEND MORE THAN WHAT WILL GIVE A PROFIT

What's the biggest danger in mailing? It's spending more than we get back in profit. This happens because there is resistance in our prospect universe to our offer. The demand is not there, given what we have to spend to get a response.

■ *CAUTION NOTE: The danger in mailing is spending more than you get back.*

Testing shows that we must never spend more to get a response than the amount of the profit we will make. If we find we are spending too much, we must radically change our offer, either what we sell, its terms, or the people to whom we present it.

■ *CAUTION NOTE: If the cost of mailing is prohibitive, the product or prospects must be changed radically.*

As we have seen, preexisting demand is essential. We cannot sell anything to anybody in direct mail who doesn't already want it.

As we've seen in these tests, it's a question of degree. Some people are more preinterested than others. Prospects who are keenly interested we can get cheaply. For them we don't need all the extras, the sweeteners, the free gifts, the fancy color to bribe them to read and respond. They already want what we've got. They've been waiting for a chance to buy it. To get them to respond we spend far less than our average cost.

■ *KEY POINT: Testing shows the degree of each buyer's interest.*

And of course for other prospects, we must go to the upper limit of profitability to gain their business.

TESTING SHOWS HOW TO PURSUE THE FULL UNIVERSE OF PROSPECTS

The kind of testing explained here shows us what our financial strategy must be for pursuing all those in our prospect universe. As we saw, we spend more dollars sending a "personalized" letter to gain five more buyers. We knew we couldn't have gotten them by spending less. And in this case they were worth it, because they didn't exceed the limit of the $40 we had to solicit prospects and still make money.

■ *KEY POINT: Testing helps us plan financial strategy.*

These two tests don't show us other information we might want. For example, they don't analyze the buyers we gained from the form-letter mailing. For this we would have to run a third test. However, for most products and services we don't need as much selling power as is in the nominally persuasive form letter.

TESTING SHOWS THE PROPER DIRECTION OF EXPENDITURES

The dollars we spend to get a response are related to the resistance level: the degree of demand.

If we want to fully capture demand, including that of marginally interested prospects, in a one-time mailing, we must spend enough to give us a response rate that will give the last, hardest-to-get, most expensive person. Although these tests cannot identify that person precisely, they can show us the direction our expenditures should take.

■ *CAUTION NOTE: Test only what it takes to get the last profitable prospect.*

■ *KEY POINT: Tests show where money should be spent.*

Testing and lists are what direct mail is all about. Lists, as we saw in Chapter 15, locate the probable customers for our product or service. Tests tell us how to fully solicit them without underspending or overspending.

■ *KEY POINT: Tests and lists are the secret of direct mail success.*

DETERMINING THE 18
PRESENT WORTH OF
FUTURE CUSTOMERS

The most profitable relationships with customers are those that occur over a period of time. In this chapter we will see how we can predict how many customers will continue to do business with us each year and how to measure their worth to us.

FUTURE DOLLARS DETERMINE
TODAY'S PRESENT WORTH

Our best customers are those who buy from us over an extended period of time. To find out their present worth to us, we need to know their future value. When beginning our relationship with them, we need to look at the dollars they will give us in the future and to discount those dollars into today's terms. This tells us what we can afford to spend on them.

■ *KEY POINT:* *The present worth of customers is determined by their future value.*

In the examples in the last two chapters, we looked at one transaction in which it was easy to measure worth because we used today's expenditures and today's revenues. However, when we try to evaluate a customer relationship that will last two, four, or six years, we're talking about future revenues that will be worth less primarily due to inflation, but for which we must spend today's dollars.

■ *CAUTION NOTE:* *Future dollars are worth less than those received today.*

We must translate this future value into present value to know what to spend today.

LONG-TERM RELATIONSHIPS MEAN MORE CUSTOMERS AND GREATER PROFITS

To test the value of relationships with long-term customers, we measure the profits we expect over the lifetime of the relationships.

■ *KEY POINT:*   *Testing can measure profits over the long term.*

You might ask why we should bother with the complex task of evaluating future profits. Why not use the same tests as in our previous example, which lead us to act profitably now? Why not find out what gives the highest profits now and just continue these strategies for the long term?

We can do this, and many do. But it may be a shortsighted policy that overlooks the advantages we could gain if we broadened our market scope.

■ *CAUTION NOTE:*   *Many short-sighted marketers insist on profit in the initial mailing.*

First, if we resolicit only those who bought in our first mailing, we may leave out customers who might buy at another time. If we incur a slight loss in an initial mailing, we may end up with many more customers who will buy from us in the future, and give us high profits then.

■ *KEY POINT:*   *A loss on the initial mailing may bring in future customers.*

Second, if we can reuse our prospect lists and turn prospects into customers, we conserve one of our scarcest resources—prospect names.

■ *KEY POINT:*   *If we are successful in turning prospects into customers we conserve prospect names.*

ONE-TIME SALES WASTE PRECIOUS RESOURCES

The real way to make money in direct mail is through multiple, repeat sales. It costs us so much money to get customers in the first place that we just throw this money away if we take one profit and run. We gain far more than immediate profit by reselling our customers time and again.

■ *CAUTION NOTE:*   *Big money in direct mail is not made through one-time sales.*

A nonrelationship marketer who seeks profit from a onetime sale still has expended significant resources to acquire customers. Why waste these resources? The biggest profits come from future relationships with customers you have already acquired; you have already spent scarce resources to get them.

■ *CAUTION NOTE:*   *A single-transaction sales strategy wastes precious resources.*

HOW TO DETERMINE THE NUMBER OF CUSTOMERS RETAINED

The first step in establishing the present worth of the future customer is to estimate how many of the customers gained in an acquisition mailing will stay with us, and for how long. In other words, we must know how many customers we lose, and how quickly.

This would be easy to determine if we already had a customer base and could plot which customers dropped off and when. This is called a *loss rate* and refers to customer losses over time.

■ *KEY POINT:*   *Finding the customer loss rate is the first step in computing future value.*

If we plotted these losses on a graph we could see that many custom-

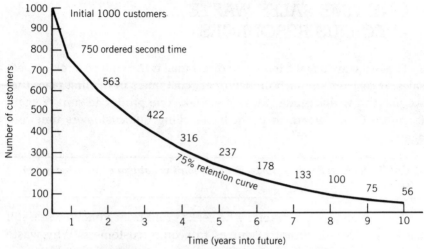

Figure 18.1   Seventy-five percent retention curve.

ers stayed with us for years. The number that remains each year is called the *retention rate*. On a graph it gives us a retention curve.

■ *KEY POINT:*   **The retention rate is the number of customers we hold each year.**

For example, if a particular mailing program's loss rate is 25%, its retention rate is 75%. In other words, we retain 75% of each year's customers the following year.

If we gained 1000 customers from an acquisition mailing, only 750 would buy from us during the following year if our retention rate is 75%. The graph shown in Figure 18.1 presents this concept visually.

The rate at which we lose customers must be diligently examined. Only through experience can we accurately compute our retention rate.

■ *CAUTION NOTE:*   **Accuracy in computing retention rates can only come through experience.**

Figure 18.2 shows some other common retention curves.

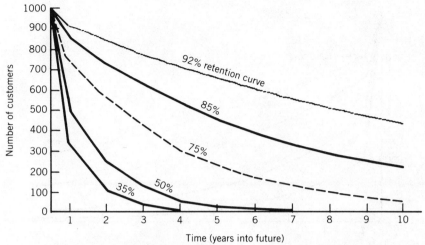

Figure 18.2 Constant-rate retention curves.

THE BIGGEST DROP IN CUSTOMERS OFTEN OCCURS THE FIRST YEAR

Retention rates do not remain the same year after year. Often more customers drop off the first year than in the years that follow. Customers may not have been sure about what they were ordering, or their perception of its value changes. In the next chapter we will look at ways to keep customers. But for now it is important to realize that customers will drop off no matter what the product or service, and most of them will do so the first year.

■ *CAUTION NOTE: The number of customers often drops off rapidly the first year.*

For example, 35% of customers may not buy again the first year, while only 20% of the remaining 65% will drop off each year thereafter. This retention rate is stated as "65%/80%."

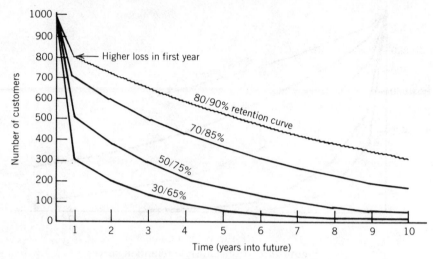

Figure 18.3   Drop-off first year retention curves.

Figure 18.3 shows examples of retention curves in which the dropoff rate is higher the first year.

DIFFERENT KINDS OF OFFERS HAVE DIFFERENT RETENTION RATES

Different mailing campaigns generate different retention rates. If you already have a body of customers, you can plot the drop-off rate in a graph similar to those in Figure 18.3. However, if you don't have a customer base, you can only estimate what you think will happen until you have tested enough customers over time to learn what your true retention rate is.

■ *CAUTION NOTE: Retention rates vary, depending on the type of offer.*

The general experiences mailers have had can guide you in your first estimates.

Retention Rate	Type of Product or Service	Drop off Rate
95% or 85%	Life insurance, home and apartment insurance, college alumni donations, in-house products such as "intercompany" paperwork to established institutions	20% to 30% in first year, includes established fund-raising drives, professional memberships
80% to 60%	Consumer bank services, consumer goods, community fund raising	35% to 45% in first year, includes many magazine subscribers, clothing offers, sporting goods, consumer mail-order products
50% to 35%	Products such as fruit packs for holiday promotions	50% to 70%, includes specialty item catalogs and specialized mail-order products, for which only accessories can be sold later

Some of these figures seem obvious. The drop-off rate for products or services will be lower than for luxuries. A home owners insurance policy is more likely to retain customers than an annual membership in a vacation club.

■ *KEY POINT: The experience of others can help you determine your retention rate.*

These estimates cannot substitute for knowing exactly how your customers, or your immediate competitors' customers, perform. If you have your own customers or access to the experience of your competitors, use it rather than making a rough estimate.

HOW LONG CAN WE EXPECT
TO KEEP CUSTOMERS?

The retention curves shown indicate that most of our original customers have disappeared by a certain time, which varies in each curve. For example, in a 75% curve (Fig. 18.1), most of the original 1000 customers are gone after 10 years. In a 50% curve, most are gone after five years. We will lose most of our original customers in four years if we retain only 35% of them each year.

However, if we retain 92% or 85% of our original 1000 customers each year, we will still have more than 400 or 200 left, respectively, after 10 years.

For retention curves in which the first-year drop-off rate is high, we lose our remaining customers slightly sooner. For example, if we retain 80% of them the first year and 90% thereafter, we still have more than 300 of our original group after 10 years.

But again, these are only estimates. You need your own established base of customers to determine exactly how long any particular offer will retain customers.

■ *CAUTION NOTE:*   *Customer longevity depends on your ability to hold customers.*

Without a testing program like the one described here, you cannot make a reasonable estimate of customer longevity, which is needed to calculate the future profits from each customer.

ESTIMATING THE PRESENT VALUE
OF FUTURE PROFITS

Now that we can measure how many customers we are keeping and for how long, we must make one more estimate before completing our sample calculation.

We must estimate the present value of the future profits from each customer.

To do this we *discount* future income into a present value. That is, we individually discount each anticipated sale at an appropriate discount rate.

■ *KEY POINT:* **Estimate present worth by "discounting" future profit.**

For example, if you invested $1000 today in a savings account at 5¾% interest, next year you would have an extra $57.50, making a total of $1057.50. Five years from now you would have accumulated $1322.52.

The original $1000, then, earns you money. You expect a return when you invest money over a period of time. Whether at the end of next year or at the end of five years, you want more than your $1000 back.

Now what happens if you were promised $1000 in five years? That's great, but is it the same as having the $1000 now? No. Because if you had the $1000 now and invested it for the five years in a 5¾% savings account, you would get back at least $1322.52.

So the $1000 you will get in the future must be discounted to today's value.

With the same 5¾% interest rate, the $1000 promised to us in five years would be discounted to today's value of only $756.13. (Compounded back at 5¾% per year.)

PICKING THE RIGHT "DISCOUNT" RATE

Naturally we are hoping to make more than 50% from our mailings. In fact, many businesses aim for profits of 10% to 20% on their invested capital.

Much of business investing is based on risk. The higher the risk, the higher potential profit. When risk is less and the investment is more secure, the anticipated return need not be as high.

■ *CAUTION NOTE:* **Higher risks require higher profits.**

As a guide to picking the rate at which you would like to have invested funds accumulate, you should look at comparable investments made by your company that share approximately the same degree of risk as does your current direct mail venture.

■ *KEY POINT: Seek the same risk as comparable investments.*

For our example we will use the common business investment rate of 15%. If we invest our $1000 at this rate, in five years we expect a whopping $2011.36 back! (Compounded forward each year at 15% for five years.) More important, if we were promised the $1000 in five years, its worth today would be only $497.18. (Compounded back each year at 15% for five years.)

Discounting thus is based on the principle that the earning power of money that we acquire in the future is lost to us until we actually receive the money. Therefore this future income must be "discounted" to determine its value today.

■ *CAUTION NOTE: The earning power of money received in the future is lost in the intervening time.*

■ *KEY POINT: Monies received in the future can be discounted to their present value.*

DISCOUNTING THE VALUE OF FUTURE CUSTOMERS

Now we can learn how to use our retention figures to determine the discounted value of future customer profits.

■ *KEY POINT: Retention figures are used to determine the value of future customers.*

Let's take a retention rate of 75%, meaning that we retain 75% of our original group of 1000 customers each year. The following chart shows that at the end of 10 years, few of the original customers will be left.

					Years					
	1	2	3	4	5	6	7	8	9	10	Total

	1	2	3	4	5	6	7	8	9	10	Total
Number of customers remaining	750	653	422	316	237	178	133	100	75	56	2,830
Reversion factor	0.870	0.756	0.658	0.572	0.497	0.432	0.376	0.327	0.284	0.247	
Present value of customers (no.of cust. × rev. factor)	653	426	278	181	118	77	50	33	21	14	1,851

Total customers for 10 years: 2,830

Present value of future customers: 1,851

In the above chart, we need to make the following calculation to discount the value of customer profits received in the future. To do this, we multiply the present value of 1, to be gained at any given year, when discounted at a specific interest rate for the number of years being considered. This is called the *reversion factor*. These numbers can be found in many investment tables, or by using your calculator:

$$V = \frac{1}{\text{base }^{(\text{exponent})}}$$

Where

V = Present value reversion of 1
Base = 1 plus annual interest rate
Exponent = Number of years required

Note that in this formula the reciprocal is gained by the division into 1. For example, the eighth-year present value of 1 discounted at 15% is:

$$V = \frac{1}{1.15^{\,8}}$$

$$V = \frac{1}{3.059023}$$

$$V = 0.326902$$

Any annual interest rate or time period can be used in this simple formula.

Multiplying the reversion factors computed at 15% by the actual numbers of customers for each of the 10 years gives us the discounted value—the present worth of those future customers for each year.

■ *KEY POINT: Reversion factors convert the value of future customers into their worth today.*

We now add each year's present value and end up with 1851 customers. We have discounted at 15% per year the future value of 2830 actual customers, as accumulated each year, into a one-lump figure of 1851 that represents their present worth.

We now take these 1851 discounted customers and divide the number by the total number of original customers, 1000.

$$\frac{1851 \text{ discounted customers}}{1000 \text{ initial customers}} = 1.851$$

The answer, 1.851, represents the present value of all future customers discounted at 15% for each of 10 years. It is the value of what 2830 customers declines to when discounted annually at 15%.

This example does not account for the small number of customers who remain after 10 years. Therefore the test should be lengthened until there is only a residual number of customers.

FORECASTING MUST BE TEMPERED WITH EXPERIENCE AND JUDGMENT

At this point a preliminary caution is in order. Although this simple system is one of the best ways to forecast future growth and profits, it is still only a tool.

As we found in the last chapter, testing tools cannot always give exact answers. But they can point us in a direction.

The same caveat should apply here. We must not ignore these calculations; they are crucial to our success in direct mail. But whenever we use accounting tools to look into the future, we must temper our answers with experience and judgment.

■ *KEY POINT: Accurate forecasting calculations are critical to success in mail order.*

■ *CAUTION NOTE: Use judgment and experience in any forecasting calculations.*

Also this example assumes that all monies are received at the end of each year. A more sophisticated analysis could control this discrepancy. But for our purposes, the technique presented here is adequate to show the basic concept. It will also be accurate for most analyses.

ADVANCED TESTING: 19
PREDICTING LONG-
TERM PROFITS

In this chapter we will demonstrate how a test works when we analyze our relationship with customers over a period of time.

TESTING MEASURES RESULTS AGAINST SCARCITY OF RESOURCES

As we saw in the sample test for nonrelationship marketers in Chapter 16, it is a mistake to assume automatically that we can make intelligent decisions on "percent return" and "cost per response." Both focus on numbers or cost but fail to look at the most important criterion: profit.

■ *CAUTION NOTE:* *"Percent return" and "cost per response" ignore profit.*

Also direct mail users often overlook the income that can accrue from customers over time. They look only at the preliminary answers from the initial acquisition mailing, rather than developing these answers further and measuring results against resources.

■ *CAUTION NOTE:* *Don't overlook long-term customer income.*

■ *KEY POINT:* *Long-term profits can come from wise use of resources.*

To succeed in direct mail in today's competitive market, we need a more in-depth analysis. Understanding what makes profitable relationships with customers is part of the key to beating the competition.

■ *KEY POINT:* *Direct mail success comes from in-depth study of customer relationships.*

355

TESTING MAKES US MORE PROFITABLE THAN OUR COMPETITION

One problem in direct mail is that few marketers know how to test. They measure everything by percentages but don't know the value of other analyses that might show them how to make more profit. Their thinking about how best to use their resources to gain new and profitable customer relationships is limited. By succumbing to the lure of short-term gains, they unknowingly proscribe themselves to relying on test results that predict losing rather than winning.

■ *CAUTION NOTE:* **Uninformed mailers forever condemn themselves to rely on the wrong test results.**

Your guide to success is diligent testing, which will give you a thorough understanding of how you can best gain profit from customers.

■ *KEY POINT:* **Proper testing and interpretation will lead you to profits.**

If you have the right information and have analyzed it properly, you need not rely on guesstimates. Experience and judgment are fine, but they should be used with, not instead of, hard analysis.

■ *CAUTION NOTE:* **Testing keeps you from relying on guesstimates.**

The example that follows shows the proper technique for testing how best to allocate your most available resource—budget funds or prospect names—to gain the most profit. This particular example is for the sale of products from a catalog, but the principles are the same for raising funds or gaining sales leads.

■ *KEY POINT:* **Testing should always seek the best use of resources.**

The example tests two different catalog mailings: catalog A, with photographs in black and white, and catalog B, with photographs in color. All other elements are the same. One thousand of each are mailed at the same time to every other name on the prospect list.

The example determines the long-range profitability of customers.

Many of the testing tools discussed in the last chapter—how many customers we can retain, how long we keep them, and how we estimate the present worth of future profits—are used in this example.

	Catalog A (black and white)	Catalog B (full color)
Cost/1000 pieces		
List rental	$ 46	$ 46
Mailing	12	12
Postage	110	110
Catalog development	22	37
Production	130	285
Total	$320	$490
Responses/1000 pieces	28	35
Response rate	2.8%	3.5%
Cost/response	$11.43	$14.00
Average order size	$25.00	$28.00
Cost of goods as percent of price	37.0%	37.0%
Overhead as percent of price	15.0%	15.0%
Percent remaining for reinvestment and profit (RRP)	48.0%	48.0%
RRP$/order	$12.00	$13.44
Profit/loss order	$0.57	$0.56
Retention curve	75.0%	75.0%
Discount rate	15.0%	15.0%
Discounted future business (present value of future customers)	1.851	1.851
Estimated yearly increase in order size	10.0%	10.0%

(Continued)

	Catalog A (black and white)	Catalog B (full color)
Period average customer held	2.4 years	2.4 years
Estimated future order size	$31.46	$35.24
Estimated number of future orders/ customer/year	1.3	1.3
Average future income/customer/year	$40.90	$45.81
Estimated RRP$/future year	$19.63	$21.99
Estimated solicitation cost/customer/year	$ 4.00	$ 4.00
Adjusted future annual RRP	$15.63	$17.99
Discounted future profit	$28.93	$33.30
Discounted profit period	$29.50	$32.74
Discounted profit/period/1000 customers	$826.00	$1145.90
Discounted profit/ period/$ expended	$2.58	$2.34

As we see, the list rental costs were the same in both mailings. So were the mailing and postage costs; both catalogs weighed the same and had the same number of pages. Development costs were slightly higher for the color catalog. The cost of production was much higher because of the cost of printing full-color photographs.

The cost per thousand was $320 for the black-and-white and $490 for the color catalog. The number of responses to A was 28 compared with

35 for the full-color catalog. The respective response rates, then, were 2.8% and 3.5%.

The cost of each response was $11.43 ($320/28) for mailing A and $14.00 ($490/35) for mailing B.

Although there were more responses from mailing B, each one cost more than from mailing A. It is here that cursory evaluations of percent return and cost per response can lead uninformed marketers to pick losers as winners.

The average order size was $25 for mailing A and $28 for mailing B. The company's cost for the goods sold averages 37% of the retail price. Overhead (salaries, rent, and so on) are another 15%. In each mailing, then, 52% went for costs and 48% remained for reinvestment and profit.

As we saw in Chapter 16, this amount is used for marketing costs and profit. When we take 48% of the average order size in each mailing, we get $12.00 (48% × $25) and $13.44 (48% × $28). The amount in dollars remaining for reinvestment and profit (RRP), then, is the average order amount multiplied by the RRP in percent (48%).

What remains after the cost of getting each order is subtracted is the immediate profit or loss. In mailing A, the per-response cost of $11.43 subtracted from the $12.00 RRP $ per order leaves a $0.57 profit. When the $14.00 per-response cost of mailing B is subtracted from the $13.44 RRP, we see a loss of $0.56.

Many mailers use profit or loss per response to tell them which mailing they should use to solicit their full prospect universe.

However, this test does not take into account the continuing income from repeat customers. Nor, as we will see later, does it use the most available resources to advantage.

PRESENT WORTH OF FUTURE YEARS OF CUSTOMER BUSINESS

Next we want to compute the present worth of the future income we can expect from our customers over time.

First we select a retention curve of 75% as best typifying the experience we will have with our newly acquired customers. The 75% retention curve means we keep 75% of our customers each year and lose 25% per year.

Second, we select 15% as the discount rate at which we want our money to grow. Again, as we saw in the last chapter, when we apply this 15% rate to the customers retained through our retention curve calculations for a 10-year period, we find our future business is "discounted" to 1.851. This figure represents future business with any one customer discounted to its present-day worth of 1.851 customers. Or, today, the future business of one customer is worth 1.851 customers.

SEEKING THE AVERAGE ORDER SIZE AND INCOME FROM EACH FUTURE CUSTOMER

Next we must estimate which of each of our future orders will grow. If we use a nominal 10% as a guide and apply it to the present average order size for the period of time we hold the average customer, 2.4 years—as determined by our 75% retention curve, we get $31.46 ($25 × 10% for 2.4 years) in mailing A and $35.24 ($28 × 10% for 2.4 years) in mailing B.

Now we estimate the number of future orders we get from each customer each year. Again this should be based on experience. If we already have customers for our products, we know how often they order. If not, make a conservative estimate. The estimate in this example is 1.3, that is, customers order 1.3 times, on the average, per year.

We now relate this 1.3 number of orders per year to our estimate of future order size and find that the future average order size for each customer is $40.90 ($31.46 × 1.3) in mailing A and $45.81 ($35.24 × 1.3) in mailing B.

DETERMINING FUTURE ANNUAL PROFIT

Next we want to find the amount for reinvestment and profit (RRP) for each future year. We take the average future income per year and multiply it by the percent remaining for RRP already computed. We assume that owing to our business practices, this percent will remain consistent during the period we are analyzing. Calculations show that our average RRP in dollars for each future year is $19.63 ($40.90 × 48%) for mailing A and $21.99 ($45.81 × 48%) for mailing B.

Next we estimate how much it costs us to resolicit each customer each year. Through a process of adding up the costs of renewal mailings, list maintenance, record keeping, and staff time, the proposed 10 mailings we will make to each customer will cost us 40¢ per contact, or $4.00 per year.

We now subtract this $4.00 yearly solicitation cost from the average future dollars remaining for reinvestment and profit and get the adjusted future annual RRP of $15.63 ($19.63 − $4.00) for mailing A and $17.99 ($21.99 − $4.00) for mailing B.

DISCOUNTING FUTURE PROFITS

The next step is to determine what the future annual income is in terms of profit. To do this we now use the 1.851 figure we found from the 75% retention curve discounted at 15%, which represents the discounted future years of business we will do with each customer. We multiply it times the future annual income and arrive at $28.93 ($15.63 × 1.851) for mailing A and $33.30 ($17.99 × 1.851) for mailing B. This gives us the discounted profits we will receive per customer.

Our task now is to add or subtract the amount of initial profit or loss. This amount is for the initial acquisition of the customer. In mailing A the initial profit was 57¢ and in mailing B the initial loss was 56¢. Adding and subtracting these we arrive at profit for mailing A of $29.50 ($28.93 + $0.57) and for mailing B of $32.94 ($33.50 − $0.56). Each represents the discounted profit for the period we are examining.

Our next step is to take the discounted profit for the period and multiply it by the number of customers that came from our test mailing. In mailing A the answer is $826.00 ($29.50 × 28) and in mailing B it is $1145.90 ($32.74 × 35). These figures represent the discounted profit per period for each 1000 prospect names solicited.

These discounted profits per period for 1000 prospects let us begin making decisions. As we will confirm in the next stage of our test, if prospect names are the scarcest resource, the higher profit per thousand we gain from mailing B makes the procedure for this test the one we would use for mailing to our whole prospect universe.

When we relate the discounted profit per period per thousand in each mailing to the mailing cost per thousand we see what the discounted profit is for budget dollars spent. The discounted profit per period compared with each budget dollar spent is $2.58 ($826.00/$320) in mailing A and $2.34 ($1145.90/$490) in mailing B.

In contrast to the decision made when prospect names are scarce, the higher discounted profits per budget dollar expended in mailing A shows it to be the better choice if budget dollars are limited.

ANALYZING TEST RESULTS WHEN BUDGET DOLLARS ARE SCARCE

Our task in direct mail testing is to show where we can make the most profit considering that a resource—budget dollars or prospect names—is ultimately limited. In the next section we will see which test mailing would be best for us to use on the full prospect universe if either budget dollars or prospect names is our most limited resource.

This test is similar to the sample nonrelationship marketing test in Chapter 16. Because any mailing campaign has finite limits, in the first scenario we assume budget dollars are scarce.

Scenario 1: Budget Dollars Are Least Available Resource

	Mailing A	Mailing B
Mailing funds available	$20,000	$20,000
Prospect names available	65,000	65,000
Maximum mailing	$21,000/$320 × 1,000 = 62,500 (62,000)	$20,000/$490 × 1,000 = 40,816 (41,000)
Total discounted profit/period	62,000 × $826/ 1,000 = $51,212	41,000 × $1,145.90/ 1,000 = $46,982

Because our budget funds are limited, we cannot mail to our entire prospect universe of 65,000 names. Since we have a budget of $20,000 for each mailing and the cost is $320 for every 1000 prospects in mailing

A, we can mail to 62,000 prospects. This is just short of the full universe of 65,000. In mailing B, however, the cost is $490 for each 1000. Therefore we can mail to only 41,000 prospects, far short of the full universe.

Mailing then to the customers in mailing A at a discounted profit of $826 per 1000 customers, we gain an overall profit for the total mailing of $51,212. In mailing B, although our discounted profit per 1000 is higher at $1,145.90, the number of names we can solicit is less and our profit is also less, $46,982.

In this example, then, if the funds we have available to solicit prospects are limited, we would choose mailing A because its lower mailing cost per 1000 permits us to reach more prospects. Mailing A gives us the most profit if budget dollars is our most limited resource.

ANALYZING TEST RESULTS WHEN PROSPECT NAMES ARE LIMITED

Now we will test which mailing would be best for us to use on the full prospect universe if prospect names is our most limited resource.

Scenario 2: Prospect Names Are Least Available Resource

	Mailing A	Mailing B
Mailing funds available	$35,000	$35,000
Prospect names available	65,000	65,000
Maximum mailing	$35,000/$320 × 1,000 = 109,375 (65,000)	$35,000/$490 × 1,000 = 71,428 (65,000)
Total discounted profit/period	65,000 × $826/ 1,000 = $53,690	65,000 × $1,145.90/ 1,000 = $74,484

In this example we have more budget dollars and can mail to our entire prospect universe of 65,000 names in each mailing. In fact, the names themselves are the finite resource.

In mailing A, our $35,000 budget, at a cost of $320 per 1000 customers, would let us mail to more than 100,000 prospects, substantially more than our available 65,000 names. In mailing B, at a cost of $490 per 1000, we could reach more than 71,000 prospects, also over the 65,000 limit.

Since our $35,000 budget will easily solicit the full universe of 65,000 names, we are constrained only by the fact that we do not have more names to reach. In mailing A, when we relate our discounted profit per 1000 of $826 to the 65,000 prospect names, we get an overall discounted profit on the mailing of $53,690. In mailing B, when we relate the profit per 1000 of $1145.90 to the 65,000 prospect universe, we gain a higher profit, $74,484.

Thus, if prospect names are limited, we would choose mailing B, because its higher profit per thousand allows us to make the most money.

CONCLUSION

As you can see by these last four chapters you must test to see how well you're doing in your mail campaigns. Some things don't always work and others justify themselves. If you look at a simple response rate or cost per order, you won't learn if you're succeeding or failing. The key is knowing how to measure what you get back.

■ *KEY POINT: Success in direct mail is knowing how to measure what you get back.*

EXTRACTING 20
MAXIMUM PROFIT
FROM MAILINGS

In the last few chapters we have focused on the mathematics of direct mail. In this final chapter we will discuss various techniques for keeping customers.

A major theme in this book has been the difference between acquiring customers and keeping them over a period of time, to maximize profits.

■ *CAUTION NOTE:* *There's a big difference between acquiring customers and keeping them.*

As we have seen, we must spend so much initially to acquire customers that it is only common sense for us to try to sell these customers additional products and services. Testing proves that a continued relationship with a customer can bring us far more profit than a one-time sale, primarily because we don't have to repeat the high cost of acquisition.

■ *KEY POINT:* *Profits come from continuing customer relationships.*

A MAJOR GOAL IN DIRECT MAIL IS RETAINING CUSTOMERS

As we saw in Chapter 18, one of our biggest problems is retaining customers. Not everyone who signs up with us for a product, service, subscription, or donation will stay with us. Many drop off, especially, as we saw, in the first year.

■ *CAUTION NOTE:*   *A major problem in direct mail is retaining customers.*

In direct mail, our customers' first purchases are in part a test. They are checking us out to see if we're on the level. After all, they don't know who we are. They are gambling by making a transaction through the mail. They are taking a risk. They want to believe the best about us and what we offer, but they can't be sure. If we pass the test, they will be happy.

■ *KEY POINT:*   *You have to prove yourself to customers.*

SOME CUSTOMERS DROP OUT BECAUSE THEY DIDN'T KNOW WHAT THEY WERE BUYING

People usually drop out of mailing programs for one of two reasons, no matter what the product or service. First, they were not knowledgeable about what they were buying. This is called *ignorance in acquisition.*

■ *CAUTION NOTE:*   *Some customers are unaware of what they are buying.*

It means our customers thought the product would do something it doesn't actually do. Either we didn't explain it well enough in our sales literature or they didn't read our literature carefully or simply misunderstood what the product's limitations and capabilities are.

For example, you might gain subscribers to a magazine who think it will help them buy something or save them money. It it doesn't do what they hoped it would, they will drop their subscription.

Newsletters often have this problem. To be effective and meet the interests of many people, newsletters must change their contents frequently. If new subscribers sign up for your newsletter because they are interested in cutting employee costs, and you keep writing about saving taxes, they will soon lose interest and drop off.

SOME CUSTOMERS DROP OUT BECAUSE THEY FAIL TO USE THE PRODUCT

The second major reason we lose customers is that they fail to use what we sell them. This *failure to use* is more important to us than ignorance in acquisition.

■ *CAUTION NOTE:* **Some customers fail to use the product.**

Customers may order the *Handy-Home Encyclopedia* to help them fix up everyday problems around the house, put it on a shelf, and never read it. Magazines are often bought as status symbols for the coffee table. Subscribers want to be thought of as readers of *The New Yorker*, but may only scan it for the cartoons.

Companies that sell leather-bound editions of literary classics appeal directly to the snobbery of customers who want to own good literature but don't read it.

Failure to use a product is the most serious problem we face as relationship marketers. If a customer does not use our product or service, they will lose interest in continuing a business relationship with us.

It is not surprising that people buy products and fail to use them. As we saw earlier, in direct mail as well as in other selling methods, we point out how our product or service benefits prospects. We position our product so that it appears to have emotional payoffs for buyers. This is fine because it makes sales.

But this is also the approach used by all marketers. That is, we are using many of the same emotional reasons to gain buyers for our products as other marketers use to gain buyers for their products. We try to protect ourselves by making our product unique (one reason why making a product distinctive is crucial). But if our buyers fail to understand our uniqueness, they also fail to use our product to its full advantage or for the partly emotional reasons that motivated their purchase in the first place.

■ *CAUTION NOTE:* **Products sold by direct mail must appear unique but also appeal to universal happiness.**

So if we are to sell to buyers over a period of time, we must address this problem of failure to use.

INDOCTRINATION MAILINGS HOLD CUSTOMER INTEREST

One of the most important strategies for holding customers is the *indoctrination* mailing, a mailing sent after a purchase that ostensibly tells customers how to use the product. The mailing tells them why their decision to buy the product or service in the first place was a smart one. The mailing also tells customers how to get the most out of what they've bought and often describes how to put it together or maintain it. The principle here is to draw customers' attention back into the product, to reinforce their original interest in it.

■ *KEY POINT: "Indoctrination" mailings involve the customer.*

Indoctrination mailings are designed to get people into the habit of using what we sell them. These mailings resell customers on what it was that got them to buy the product in the first place.

For example, we can cut the chances that the *VITACRUSH 4200* will sit on the shelf with a special mailing to new owners telling them of your contest for the best new *VITACRUSH* recipe. Or new needlepoint craft kit owners could be asked to vie for prizes by sending photographs of their completed work.

New magazine subscribers can be sent surveys asking for responses to questions on issues raised in the magazine. *U.S. News & World Report* has used this questionnaire technique. Do they care if they get the questionnaire back? No. The purpose is to get subscribers to read the publication—to draw them back into it.

When this subscription technique was tested, it was found that subscribers who received the questionnaire renewed at a higher rate than those who did not receive it.

Indoctrination, though crucial, is an often-overlooked strategy for marketers who want to keep their customers.

INDOCTRINATION MAILINGS PERMIT LONGER RELATIONSHIPS

Indoctrination mailings affect a customer's longevity with us. Once a customer has gotten into the habit of using our product, whether it be a home appliance, subscription, or even a donation, he or she is more likely to renew or buy again from us another time.

■ *KEY POINT: Indoctrination mailings tend to gain higher renewals.*

These mailings should be sent out to customers soon after they have received the product. Also they should be continued at intervals for as long as your relationship with the customer lasts. The initial mailing helps cement the relationship, while later indoctrination mailings tend to sustain it.

STEPPING CUSTOMERS UP OR DOWN

Another kind of mailing aimed at retaining customers is the *staircase* mailing, which probes them about additional purchases.

■ *KEY POINT: "Staircase" mailings probe customers on another purchase.*

For example, they can be offered an accessory for what they have already bought. *"Dear Ms. Smith, Now that you have your VITACRUSH 4200, have you thought of making pasta? With these unique blade attachments. . . ."*

Or a newer, larger model. *"Dear Ms. Smith, As one of our enthusiastic users of the VITACRUSH 4200 for the last three years, you may be interested to know about our new 6800 series that will. . . ."*

Or one mailing could offer the more expensive proposition. *"Dear Mr. Wilson, As one of our valued subscribers to the* New York Stock SuperPortfolio *financial newsletter, we would like to offer you in addition the* American Exchange *Edition for a special combined price of $525."*

If that fails, the less expensive accessory could be offered in a later mailing: *"Dear Mr. Wilson, You are one of our valued subscribers, and we would like to offer you a three-times-a-year update of* Over-the-Counter Stocks *for $12.95."*

The idea of staircasing is to find the threshold at which the customer will buy again, and then escalate it back up.

Either way we can entice customers up or down the staircase of revenues.

STAGING OFFERS IN SERIES

We can also break up our products and make large offers in *series* mailings. This encourages additional purchases. For example, we could offer a project that requires different levels of skill to complete, or a larger financial investment: *"As a purchaser of our helicopter plans, you are offered a discount on our basic frame kit, down to a price of $495, or a partially completed model for $1295."*

■ *KEY POINT:*   *Offers can be made in series to accommodate different skills or cost structures.*

Or we might offer a product that could be expanded: *"Now that you have our 10-foot greenhouse in place we want you to know you can expand in special 5-foot modules at any time. Our special price right now. . . ."*

Offers staged in series don't always have to be for physical products. Mail-order training programs can offer beginning, intermediate, and advanced programs one after the other.

Any product or service that lends itself to being sold step by step to accommodate different degrees of experience or expense for customers lends itself to a series mailing.

REMEMBER CUSTOMERS ON THEIR PURCHASE ANNIVERSARY

We never need an excuse to mail to customers, but the first anniversary of a purchase is an excellent time to send a mailing offering accessory items: *"Dear Mr. Roberts, One year ago you purchased our model 8000 business computer. Had you bought our supply and maintenance contract then you would have saved 27% on. . . . Even though a year has gone by, we want to offer you this discount again. Don't let another year go by losing this much money."*

■ *KEY POINT:*   *One year from when the buyer first bought can be used as a reminder.*

Anniversary mailings work—they play on the loyalty that has developed over the year the customer has been using the product.

Note that none of these techniques is what is called bait and switch. You are not enticing customers with an offer of something cheap and then switching them to a more expensive product. These people are already your customers: You are simply calling their attention to similar and accessory products that could benefit them.

RETENTION MAILINGS BUILD CREDIBILITY FOR COMPANY AND PRODUCT

Often we send customers *retention* mailings, designed to inform them about subjects we know interest them. For this reason, customers often keep these mailings.

■ *KEY POINT: Retention mailings give information on the product and therefore are held on to.*

One example is catalogs containing a large amount of editorial content. These are called *catazines*, because they are a cross between a magazine and a catalog. They usually contain articles on the general subject area as well as items for sale. A catalog of camping equipment might include articles on hiking in the Rockies and on the Appalachian Trail.

Catazines add credibility for what you sell because they make people feel you know about your products.

You want customers to hold on to retention mailings. These should position you as being the best in your industry, because you tell customers things they never knew about the product. You have become a resource.

ASK CUSTOMERS FOR REFERRAL NAMES

Customers should also be sent *referral* mailings, which ask them for names and addresses of people they know who might also be interested in what you offer.

■ *KEY POINT: "Referral" mailings ask customers for prospect names.*

Give customers enough room to list 8 to 10 names. Often when they start writing names, others come to mind. A self-addressed stamped card or envelope will make it easy for them to send their list back to you.

Referral mailings are one of the least expensive ways to gain names of prospects who are likely to turn into customers.

VALIDATION MAILINGS CONFIRM CUSTOMER INTEREST

A final technique we can use to retain customers is a *validation* mailing, usually sent if we fail to get a response from customers. *"Dear Ms. Johnson, We have been mailing to you for the last 12 months regarding our home health-care system about which you inquired. We want to know if you are still interested. Please let us know, by checking the appropriate box on the enclosed self-addressed stamped postcard and returning it today. If you do not, we will have to take you off our mailing list. Please let us know."*

■ *KEY POINT: Validation mailings establish the level of customer interest.*

Often the response to this type of message is simply no response. Many who do send back the card will tell us they have already bought the product or are still interested. Some even signal their annoyance at our mailings by telling us they have died.

Validation mailings work because they create an extra bit of pressure on the customer. The possibility of losing further contact often rejuvenates interest. Validations should always be used with customers before you drop them—you'll be surprised how many customers you will retain.

Validation mailings serve another purpose in mailings to businessmen. They can confirm job status. For example, if you send validations to a business in which people change jobs frequently, they can help you correct your business listings. You may learn that persons have changed jobs or left the company. And you may also learn the names of their replacements.

■ *KEY POINT: Validation mailings can confirm job status in businesses.*

REMAINING IN CONTACT IS THE KEY TO GROWTH OF CUSTOMER RELATIONSHIPS

The important point to be made here is that we use all of these types of mailings because of the great cost involved in getting new customers. It doesn't make sense to lose customers once we have them, no matter how tenuous the contact may become. It always makes sense to try to keep them.

■ *CAUTION NOTE: It is too expensive to keep looking for new customers.*

■ *KEY POINT: Always work to keep old customers.*

Our customers' interest in us can be highly cyclical. The season of the year, money available, and many other factors can affect the relationship with us. Even losing a customer doesn't mean that he or she won't come back another time ready to do business.

Contact is another key to success in direct mail. We said earlier that we don't use the mail to build an image. We don't wait until we can send out a fancy mailing. It is far more important that we remain in contact with our customers than that we promote ourselves with a gorgeous brochure.

SHOW CONCERN BY FREQUENT CONTACT

It's not your image that you must convince customers of, it's your concern. Mail is a personal medium. You've got to personalize it. And you must mail frequently, as you do to people you love. Show your love and concern, and do it often.

■ *KEY POINT: Show concern for customers by frequent contact.*

We can assume our customers care for us because they are our customers. If this is not true, we had better find out why and what we're doing wrong. If all our mailings fail to rekindle their interest, we should get on the telephone and ask them why they're not interested. Losing them is too expensive.

■ *KEY POINT: Call lapsed customers.*

SUMMARY OF THE KEY POINTS
COVERED IN THIS BOOK

Copy and design of the mailing piece are important, but not as important as sending the piece to prospects with potential interest and the money to buy.

Prospects must be receptive to the offer. They must have a preexisting interest. This is what allows them to act.

Prospects must also be able to afford what is offered. This gives them the ability to act.

When we craft a sales message, we are translating a live selling experience to paper. The copy should be conversational, intimate, specific, and direct. The direct mail piece is a personal, one-on-one communication, from one person to another.

People have relationships with people, not companies. We must keep our messages as personal as possible. We try to capture what happens when two friends sit down across the kitchen table and one is enthusiastically trying to convince the other.

People are not dying to hear from us. They're not waiting for us to bring them a miracle. They resist what we offer, even if it's something they want. We must sell them by having them buy a small piece of readership at a time.

We can never assume that everybody will read our mail.

By diligent testing we can determine, to a reasonable degree, what we will get back from a mailing. Testing shows us how to balance our expectations against our resources.

Testing shows us how much money we must spend to solicit our prospect universe fully. It can point us to the last, hardest-to-get customer who will still give us a profit.

The most important transaction in direct mail is not the first, but the second.

Getting customers is important, but the lifeblood of direct mail is maintaining the existing base of customers. We must never lose sight of our ongoing relationships with customers, subscribers, members, donors. We keep them by frequent mailings, especially "indoctrination" mailings at the start of their relationship with us.

Our mailings should be planned to take place throughout the year.

We should know exactly when to mail the indoctrination mailing, when to send a "referral" request, and when to send a "validation" mailing.

We must retain customers if we want long-term profits, and thus we must try to learn what causes customers to drop off. We should understand our particular prospect universe so we can keep our customers.

INDEX